Richard Whately

A General View of the Rise, Progress and Corruptions of Christianity

With a Sketch of the Life of the Author and a Catalogue of his Writings

Richard Whately

A General View of the Rise, Progress and Corruptions of Christianity
With a Sketch of the Life of the Author and a Catalogue of his Writings

ISBN/EAN: 9783337026769

Printed in Europe, USA, Canada, Australia, Japan

Cover: Foto ©Lupo / pixelio.de

More available books at **www.hansebooks.com**

A

GENERAL VIEW

OF THE

RISE, PROGRESS, AND CORRUPTIONS

OF

CHRISTIANITY.

BY

THE MOST REV. RICHARD WHATELY,

ARCHBISHOP OF DUBLIN.

WITH A SKETCH OF THE LIFE OF THE AUTHOR,

AND A

CATALOGUE OF HIS WRITINGS.

NEW YORK:

WILLIAM GOWANS.

1860.

R. CRAIGHEAD,
Printer, Stereotyper, and Electrotyper
Carton Building,
81, 83, and 85 Centre Street.

ADVERTISEMENT.

THE following pages, by Archbishop Whately, make one
of the six celebrated Introductory Essays which precede
and form a pendent to the new edition of the *Encyclopædia
Britannica*, now in course of publication, the other five
having been produced by Professor Dugald Stewart, Sir
James Mackintosh, with additions by William Whewell,
D.D., Professors John Playfair, Sir John Leslie, and James
Duncan Forbes.

The reputation and popularity of all these Authors are as
universal in the Western as on the Eastern Continent, as
that of Baron Macaulay, Lord Brougham, Dr. Chalmers,
or Sydney Smith. Hence it requires nothing to be said in
commendation of anything that any of these authors may
have written, in presenting them to the public.

This Treatise has never before appeared in book form,
either in Europe or America. In consequence, it was
deemed advisable to present it in this shape, thereby
rendering it accessible to all who had a desire to consult
the subject treated of; namely—" The Rise, Progress, and
Corruptions of Christianity," a subject full of interest to
every intelligent mind.

I have collected the titles of all the Treatises of this
gifted and voluminous author, and presented them in chro-
nological order, with a scanty biographical sketch.

I have the pleasure to announce that I have the approbation, as well as the sanction, of the author, through his bookseller, to print and publish any or all of his books in America, providing that is done in an unmutilated or uninterpolated form, which, I understand, has not been the case with certain of his works which have been reprinted in this country.

With respect to the present Treatise, the reader may rest assured that it is a faithful reprint of the original.

PUBLISHER.

New York, *Feb.* 16*th*, 1860.

BIOGRAPHICAL SKETCH.

Richard Whately, D.D., Archbishop of Dublin, an eminent theologian and writer on political economy, was born in 1789, and is the son of the Rev. Dr. Whately, of Nonsuch Park, Surrey. He was educated at Oxford, in Oriel College, of which, in 1819, he was elected a Fellow. The college of Oriel is famous for having sent out some of the greatest thinkers of which churchmen of the present generation may boast, such as Arnold, Coplestone, Newman (until his apostasy), and the subject of this sketch. He was appointed to read the Bampton Lectures in 1822, in which year he received the rectory of Halesworth, in value £450 per annum. In the contest which took place in the University when Sir R. Peel appealed to his learned constituents upon the Catholic question, Whately voted for the right honorable baronet. In the year 1830, he was appointed President of St. Alban's Hall, and Professor of Political Economy; and in 1831, he was consecrated Archbishop of Dublin, and Bishop of Glendalagh. The diocese of Kildare has since been added to his charge. His lordship has published a considerable number of theological writings, consisting of sermons, charges, miscellaneous essays, and dissertations, all marked by a desire to place religion upon a simple scriptural basis, and in harmony with man's intellectual nature. His style is remarkably luminous, and his reasoning most severe. In the administration of his office, he has displayed a uniform liberality, and has been a constant promoter of the national system of education in Ireland. He is the author of a treatise on political economy, and the best manual of logic extant. In ridicule of Strauss and German rationalism, he wrote a curious treatise to disprove the existence of Napoleon.

He has been a contributor to several Encyclopedias, and lately to that of the new edition of the Encyclopedia Britannica, now in course of publication.

In 1844 he had a controversy with the contributors to and the editors of the New York Churchman, the organ of the high church party in the western world, respecting the ordination of a young man to the ministry named Carey, who was alleged to hold views more in keeping with the church of Rome than that of the church he professed to be a member of. Since that time he has produced several new books and annotated others, a list of which here follows.

A CATALOGUE

OF THE WRITINGS OF

RICHARD WHATELY, D. D.,

ARCHBISHOP OF DUBLIN.

Right Method of Interpreting Scripture.

The Right Method of Interpreting Scripture, in what relates to the Nature of the Deity, and his Dealings with Mankind. Illustrated in a Discourse on Predestination, by Dr. King, late Lord Archbishop of Dublin. Preached at Christ Church, Dublin, before the House of Lords, May 15, 1709, with Notes by the Rev. Richard Whately, M.A. 8vo., pp. 140. London, 1821.

Elements of Rhetoric.

Elements of Rhetoric, comprising the substance of the article in the *Encyclopædia Metropolitana;* with additions, &c. 3d Edition. 8vo., pp. 463. Oxford, 1830.

An Essay on Omissions of Creeds, &c.

An Essay on the Omission of Creeds, Liturgies, and Codes of Ecclesiastical Canons, in the New Testament. 8vo., pp. 56. London, 1831.

Lecture on Political Economy.

Introductory Lectures on Political Economy; delivered in Easter Term—1831. 2d Edition, including Lecture IX. and other additions. 8vo., pp. 205. London, 1832.

Thoughts on Secondary Punishments.

Thoughts on Secondary Punishments, in a Letter to Earl Grey; to which are appended two Articles on Transportation to New South Wales, and on Secondary Punishments, and some observations on Colonization.   8vo., pp. 204.   London, 1832.

Evidence before the House of Lords.

The Evidence as taken before the Select Committee of the House of Lords, appointed to inquire into the collection and payment of Tithes in Ireland, and the state of the laws relating thereto, in the year 1832.   8vo., pp. 55.   London, 1832.

Replies to the Clergy.

Replies (Three) to the Dean and Chapter, and to the Clergy of the Diocese of Dublin, relative to the system of National Education in Ireland.   8vo., pp. 71.   London, 1832.

Address to the Clergy.

Address to the Clergy of Dublin on Confirmation, in August, 1832.   8vo., pp. 38.   London, 1832.

Observations on a Petition.

Observations made on presenting a Petition to the House of Lords from the Clergy of the Diocese of Kildare, relative to Church Reform, August 7, 1833.   8vo. pp. 20   London, 1833.

Essays on St. Paul.

Essays on some of the difficulties in the Writings of St. Paul, and in other parts of the New Testament.   8vo., pp. 408.

London, 1833.

Speech in the House of Lords.

A Speech in the House of Lords, August 1, 1833, on a Bill for the removal of certain disabilities from His Majesty's subjects of the Jewish Persuasion, with additional remarks on some of the objections urged against that measure. 8vo, pp. 81.   London, 1833

Remarks on Transportation.

Remarks on Transportation, and on a Recent Defence of the System; in a second Letter to Earl Grey. 8vo., pp. 174.

London, 1834.

Address to the Clergy.

Address to the Clergy of Dublin on Confirmation in 1834. 8vo., pp. 26.   London, 1834.

A Charge to the Clergy.

A Charge delivered to the Clergy of Dublin in June, 1834, with Notes. 8vo., pp. 31.   London, 1834.

A Charge to the Clergy.

A Charge delivered to the Clergy of Dublin in July, 1835. 8vo., pp. 30.   London, 1835.

Sermons.

Sermons on Various Subjects; delivered in several churches in the city of Dublin, and in other parts of the Diocese. 8vo., pp. 438.   London, 1835.

An Appeal.

An Appeal on behalf of the Association incorporated for discountenancing Vice, &c., with a Sermon in behalf of the Association. 8vo., pp. 30.   London, 1835.

Elements of Logic.

Elements of Logic, comprising the substance of the article in the *Encyclopædia Metropolitana*, with additions, &c. Sixth Edition, revised. 8vo., pp. 478.   London, 1836.

Two Discourses.

Two Discourses, preached in St. John's Church, Dublin, in Vindication of the right of the Beneficed Clergy of the Church of Ireland over their own Pulpits; the first delivered on occasion of the inhibition issued against the Rev. L. I. Nolan, late a Roman Catholic priest, but now a clergyman of the Established Church, by his Grace the Archbishop of Dublin; the second—An Inquiry into the Truth of Transubstantiation, by the Rev. Robert Trail, A.M., with an Appendix, containing the Correspondence which arose out of the Inhibition, and which has excited so deep an interest in the public mind, with the Remonstrance of the Clergy of the Diocese. 12mo., pp. 310.   London, 1837.

The Kingdom of Christ.

The Kingdom of Christ Delineated, in Two Essays on our Lord's own Account of his Person, and of the Nature of his Kingdom, and of the Constitution, Powers, and Ministry of a Christian Church, as appointed by himself. 8vo., pp. 312.   London, 1843.

A Lecture on Instinct.

On Instinct.   A Lecture delivered before the Dublin Natural History Society, 11th November, 1842.   18mo., pp. 32.
Dublin, 1847.

English Synonyms.

A Selection of English Synonyms.   12mo., pp. 179.
London, 1851.

Historic Certainties respecting America.

Historic Certainties respecting the Early History of America developed in a Critical Examination of the Book of the Chronicles of the Land of Ecnarf, by Rev. Aristarchus Newlight. 8vo., pp. 62.   London, 1851.

Cautions for the Times.

Cautions for the Times.   Addressed to the Parishioners of a Parish in England by their former Rector.   In Three Parts. 8vo., pp. about 390.   London, 1852.

Historic Doubts relating to Napoleon.

Historic Doubts relative to Napoleon Buonaparte. 8vo., pp. 70.
London, 1852.

Claims of Truth and Unity.

The Claims of the Truth and of Unity considered in a Charge to the Clergy of Dublin. 8vo.   London, 1852.

Easy Lessons on Reasoning.

Easy Lessons on Reasoning. 12mo., pp. 180.   London, 1856.

Thoughts and Apothegms.

Thoughts and Apothegms from the Writings of Archbishop Whately. 12mo., pp. 442.   London, 1855.

Address at Manchester.

Address delivered to the Members of the Manchester Athenæum, at the Public Breakfast, October 21, 1846. 12mo., pp. 31. See Literary Addresses delivered before the various Popular Institutions. 12mo.   London and Glasgow, Griffin, 1855.

Future State.

A View of the Scripture Revelations concerning A Future State. 12mo., pp. 308.   London, 1855.

Angels Good and Evil.

A View of the Scripture Revelations respecting Good and Evil Angels. 12mo., pp. 171.   London, 1855.

Mental Culture.

Mental Culture required for Christian Ministers. A Sermon delivered in St. Patrick's Cathedral, Dublin, on occasion of the Consecration of William Fitzgerald, D.D., Bishop of Cork, March 8th, 1857 8vo., pp. 31.   London, 1857.

Lord Bacon's Essays.

Bacon's Essays; with Annotations by Richard Whately, D.D., Archbishop of Dublin. 8vo, pp. 536.   London, 1857.

Paley's Evidences of Christianity.

A View of the Evidences of Christianity. In Three Parts. By William Paley, M.A , Archdeacon of Carlisle. With Annotations by *Richard Whately, D.D.*, Archbishop of Dublin. 8vo., pp. 407.
London, 1859.

Lessons on Mind.

Introductory Lessons on Mind. 12mo., pp. 240.   London, 1859.

Remarks on an Address to the King.

Remarks on an Address to the King, proposed for the Signatures of the Archbishops, the Bishops, and Clergy. 8vo., pp. 11.
London, N. D.

Address to Dublin Inhabitants.

Address to the Inhabitants of Dublin and its Vicinity respecting the Lord's Day. 8vo. pp. 20.   London, N. D.

History of the Corruptions of Christianity.

A Dissertation exhibiting a General View of the Rise, Progress, and Corruptions of Christianity. 4to. London, 1853 ; and 12mo.,
New York, 1860.

Paley's Works.

Paley's Works; a Lecture on. 8vo.   London, 1860.

Paley.

Paley's Moral and Political Philosophy ; with Annotations by Richard Whately, D.D., Archbishop of Dublin. 8vo.
London, 1859.

CONTENTS.

A

GENERAL VIEW

OF THE

RISE, PROGRESS, AND CORRUPTIONS

OF CHRISTIANITY.

INTRODUCTION.

A SKETCH, like the present, of the rise, progress, and corruptions of Christianity, would be altogether defective without some notice of those religious systems which it was designed to supplant or to complete.

Not only will much light be thrown upon its genuine character and excellence by a contrast with their errors or deficiencies, but moreover, a knowledge of these will often disclose to us the sources of some of those corruptions which have disfigured the simplicity of the Gospel.

The earliest history of mankind, by far, that we possess, is that contained in the Book of Genesis. It is extremely brief and scanty; especially the earliest portion of it. But it plainly represents the first of the human race, when in the Garden of Eden, as receiving direct communications from God. We have no detailed account, however, of the instruction they received; and even part of what the history does record is but obscurely intimated. For example, it is rather hinted than expressly stated, that the use of language was imparted to them by revelation. This, however, is generally understood to be the meaning of the passage (Gen. ii. 20), in which it is said that God brought unto Adam the beasts and birds, to see what he would call them, and that Adam gave them names.

But our first parents, or their children, must have received direct from God a great deal of instruction of which no particulars are related. For besides being taught something of religious and moral duty (Gen. ii. 16; iv. 7), it is evident that they must have learned something of the arts of life. The first generations of mankind were certainly not left at all in the condition of mere *savages*, subsisting on such wild fruits and animals as they might chance to meet with. We read concerning the first two sons of Adam, that the one was occupied in tilling the ground, and the other in keeping cattle.

And even independently of the Bible history, we might draw the same conclusion from what is matter of actual experience, and as it were before our eyes at this day. For it appears that mere savages, if left to themselves without any instruction, never did, and never can, civilise themselves. And, consequently, the *first* of the human race that did acquire any degree of civilisation, since they could not have had instruction from other *men*, must have had a superhuman instructor. But for such an instructor, all mankind would have been savages at this day. The mere fact that civilised men do exist, is enough to prove, even to a person who had never heard of the Bible, that, at some time or other, men must have been taught something by a superior Being : in other words, that there must have been a *revelation*.

It has been indeed not unfrequently maintained that savages can, and sometimes do, invent for themselves, one by one, all the useful arts, and thus raise themselves to a civilised state, without any assistance from men already civilised. One may meet with fine descriptions—though altogether fanciful—of this supposed progress of men towards civilisation. One man, it has been conceived, wishing to save himself the trouble of roaming through the woods in search of wild fruits and roots, would bethink himself of collecting the seeds of these, and cultivating them in a spot of ground cleared and broken up for the purpose. And finding that he could thus raise more than enough for himself, he might agree with some of his neighbours to let them have a part of the produce in exchange for some of the game and fish they might have taken. Another again, it has been imagined, would endeavour to save himself the labour and uncertainty of hunting, by catching some kind of wild animals alive, and keeping them in an inclosure to breed, that he might have a supply always at hand.

And again, another, it is supposed, might devote himself to the occupation of dressing skins for clothing, or of building huts or canoes, or making various kinds of tools; and might subsist by exchanging these with his neighbours for food. And by thus devoting his chief attention to some one kind of manufacture, he would acquire increased skill in that, and would strike out useful and new inventions.

Thus these supposed savages having gradually come to be divided into husbandmen, shepherds, and artisans of various kinds, would begin to enjoy the various advantages of a *division of labour*, and would advance, step by step, in all the arts of civilised life.

Now, all this description is likely to appear plausible, at the first glance, to those who do not inquire carefully, and reflect attentively. But, on examination, it will be found to be contradicted by all history, and to be quite inconsistent with the real character of such beings as savages actually are. In reality, such a process of inventions and improvements as that just described, is what never did, and never possibly can, take place in any savage tribe left wholly to themselves.

All the nations of which we know anything, that have risen from a savage to a civilised state, appear to have had the advantage of the instruction and example of civilised men living among them. Every nation that has ever had any tradition of a time when their ancestors were savages, and of the first introduction of civilisation among them, always represents some foreigner or some Being from heaven as having first taught them the arts of life.

Thus the ancient Greeks, we know, attributed to Prometheus the introduction of the use of fire. And agriculture and other arts were popularly supposed to have been first introduced into Greece by Triptolemus and Cadmus, and others, strangers from a distant country.

And the Peruvians have a like tradition concerning a person they call Manco Capac, whom they represent as the offspring of the sun, and as having taught useful arts to their ancestors.

On the other hand, there are a great number of savage tribes, in various parts of the world, who have had no regular intercourse with civilised men, but who have been visited by several voyagers, at different times, and in some instances at very distant periods. And it appears from comparing together the accounts of those voyagers, that these tribes remain perfectly stationary ; not making the smallest advance towards civilisation.

For example, the people of the vast continent of New Holland, and of the large island of Papua (or New Guinea), who are among the rudest of savages, appear to remain (in those parts not settled by Europeans), in exactly the same brutish condition as when they were first discovered. They roam about the forests in search of wild animals, and of some few eatable roots, which they laboriously dig up with sharpened sticks. But though they are often half-starved, and though they have to expend as much toil for three or four scanty meals as would suffice for breaking up and planting a piece of ground that would supply them for a year, it has never occurred to them to attempt cultivating these roots.

The inhabitants, again, of the islands of Andaman, in the eastern ocean, appear to be in a more degraded and wretched state than even the New Hollanders.

And to add but one instance more, the New Zealanders, in the interval of above one hundred and twenty-five years between the first discovery of their islands by Tasman, and the second discovery by Captain Cook, seem to have made no advances whatever, but to have remained just in the same condition. And yet they were in a far less savage state than that of the New Hollanders, being accustomed rudely to cultivate the ground, and raise crops of sweet potatoes.

And such appears to be, from all accounts, the condition of all savage, or nearly savage tribes. They seem never to *invent* anything, or to make any effort to improve; so that what few arts they do possess (and which, in general, are only such as to enable them just to support life), must be the remnant that they have retained from a more civilised state, from which their ancestors had degenerated.

When, indeed, men have arrived at a certain stage in the advance towards civilisation (far short of what exists in Europe), it is then possible for them, if nothing occurs to keep them back, to advance further and further towards a more civilised state.

And this it is that misleads some persons in their notions respecting savages. For finding that there is no *one* art which might not have been invented by unassisted man, *supposing him to have a certain degree of civilisation to start from,* they hence conclude that unassisted man might have invented *all* the arts, sup-posing him *left originally in a completely savage state.* But this is contradicted by all experience; which shews that men, in the condition of the lowest sa-vages, never have made the first step towards civili-sation, without some assistance from without.

Human society may be compared to some com-bustible substances which will not take fire sponta-neously, but when once set on fire will burn with continually increasing force. A community of men requires, as it were, to be kindled, and requires no more.

What, perhaps, contributes most to the erroneous views referred to above, is, that when one tries to fancy himself in the situation of a savage, it occurs to him that he would set his mind to work to contrive means for bettering his condition, and that he might perhaps hit upon such and such useful inventions; and hence he may be led to think it natural that savages should do so, and that some tribes of them may have advanced themselves, in the way above described, without any external help. But nothing of the kind appears to have ever really occurred; and what leads some persons to fancy it, is, that they themselves are *not* savages, but have some degree of mental cultivation, and some of the habits of thought of civilised men; and, therefore, they form to them-selves an incorrect notion of what a savage really is —just as a person who possesses eyesight cannot understand correctly the condition of one born blind.

But those who have seen a good deal of real savages, have observed that they are not only feeble in mental powers, but also sluggish in the use of such powers as they have, except when urged by pressing want. When not thus urged, they pass their time either in perfect inactivity, or else in dancing, or decorating their bodies with paint, or with feathers and shells, or in various childish sports. They are not only brutishly stupid, but still more remarkable for childish thoughtlessness and improvidence. So that it never occurs to them to consider how they may put themselves in a better condition a year or two hence.

Now, such must have been the condition of all mankind down to this day, if they had all been, from the first, left without any instruction, and in what is called a *state of nature*—that is, with the faculties man is born with, not at all unfolded or exercised by education. For from such a state, unassisted Man cannot, as all experience shews, ever raise himself. And consequently, in that case, the whole world would have been peopled with mere savages in the very lowest state of degradation. The very existence, therefore, at this day, of civilised men, proves that there must have been, at some time or other, some instruction given to Man in the arts of life, by some Being superior to Man. For, since the *first beginnings* of civilisation could not have come from any *human* instructor, they must have come from one *super*-human.

It has been shewn, then, that the whole world would now have been peopled with the very lowest savages, if men had never received any instruction, and yet had been able to subsist at all. But it is doubtful whether even this bare subsistence would have been possible. It is more likely that the first generation would all have perished for want of those few arts which even savages possess, and which (as has been above remarked) were probably not *invented* by savages, but are remnants which they have retained from a more civilised state. The knowledge, for instance, of wholesome and of poisonous roots and fruits, the arts of making fish-hooks and nets, bows and arrows, or darts, and snares for wild animals, and of constructing rude huts and canoes, and some other such simple arts, are possessed, more or less, by all savages, and are necessary to enable them to support their lives. And it is doubtful whether men left completely in a state of nature—that is wholly untaught—would not all perish before they could invent them for themselves.

For we should remember that Man, when left in a state of nature, untaught, and with his rational powers not unfolded, is far less fitted for supporting and taking care of himself than the brutes. *They* are much better provided both with *instincts*, and with bodily *organs* for supplying their own wants. For example, those animals that have occasion to dig, either for food or to make burrows for shelter—such as the swine, the hedgehog, the mole, and the rabbit, have both an *instinct* for digging, and snouts or paws far better adapted for that purpose than man's hands. Yet man is enabled to turn up the ground much better than any brute; but then this is by means of *tools* which man can be taught to make and use, though brutes cannot. Again, birds and bees have an instinct for building such nests and habitations as answer their purpose as well as the most commodious beds and houses made by men; but Man has no instinct that teaches him how to construct these. Brutes, again, know by instinct their proper food, and avoid what is unwholesome; but man has no instinct for distinguishing the nightshade-berry (with which children have been so often poisoned) from wholesome fruits. And quadrupeds swim by nature, because their swimming is the same motion by which they advance when on land; but a man, falling into deep water, is drowned, unless he has *learnt* to swim.

It appears, then, very doubtful whether men left wholly untaught, would be able to subsist at all, even in the state of the lowest savages. But, at any rate, it is plain they could never have risen *above* that state. And, consequently, the existence of civilisation at this day is a kind of *monument* attesting the fact that some instruction from above must, at some time or other, have been supplied to mankind. And the most probable conclusion is, that Man, when first created, or very shortly afterwards, was advanced by the Creator Himself, to a state above that of a mere savage.

Now this is exactly what is related in Scripture. But it must be remembered that the proof which has been just given of an original revelation to Man, is quite independent of the Bible history; and, therefore, tends to confirm that history. That Man could not have *made* himself, is appealed to, as a proof of a divine *Creator*. And that mankind could not, in the first instance, have *civilised* themselves, is a proof exactly of the same kind, and equally strong, of a superhuman *Instructor*.

And here the inquiry may perhaps be raised, how it ever came about that various tribes of men, from time to time, degenerated into the savage state. We have no distinct records of the progress of this dege-neracy; nor, from the nature of the case, is it possible that we should. But, no doubt, *wars* have always been the principal cause of it. When men were continually harassed by a superior force of ferocious enemies, who hunted them down like wild beasts, and burnt their dwellings, and laid waste the country, they would be driven to shelter themselves in forests, and deserts, and mountains; and would have no opportunity of practising, or of teaching to their children, most of the arts they might be acquainted with. Agriculture, for instance, would necessarily be abandoned. And being entirely occupied in a struggle for bare subsistence, and in providing for defence against their enemies, or for escape, they would have neither leisure, nor means, nor inclination, for keeping up the various arts of civilised life. These, therefore, would, in two or three generations, be forgotten and irrecoverably lost among them; and the whole character of the people would have degenerated.

We have said, that from the very nature of the case, it is impossible we should have any distinct accounts of the progress of this degradation, since men so situated would not compose histories. But it is remarkable that in several savage tribes, there are some faint traditions of their ancestors having formerly come from some distant and better country; doubtless driven out by war.

It is likely that the instruction in the arts of life that was originally bestowed on the human race was merely sufficient to give them a *beginning;* to advance them just so far towards civilisation as to enable them, thenceforward, to advance themselves, and to invent, one by one, by the exercise of their own faculties, various arts, according to their wants and opportunities.

The Bible history informs us of hardly any particulars, either of what was originally taught to mankind, or of their own inventions. We have only a very brief and slight hint of the invention of the art of working metals, and of musical instruments, and perhaps, also of tents. (Gen. iv. 20.) But, doubtless, many other arts were invented before the Flood.

Several of the most important arts, and of those most generally known throughout the world, must have been very ancient; and as their first introduction is not mentioned in the Bible, there is no record or tradition of it. And we are so familiar with these that we are apt to regard them as more simple and obvious than they are; though, on reflection, it will appear that some of them were most likely invented gradually, and by successive steps taken at long intervals.

And here it is worth observing how important an advantage, in reference to the invention of arts, would have been afforded to men in a very early and rude state of society, by their possessing (as Scripture informs us the earliest of them did) a very long continuance of life. In the present day, an ingenious and observant man *writes* down, and generally prints and publishes the experiments and observations he has made; and thus those who come after him are enabled to follow up his inquiries and attempts, so that each generation improves upon the last. But before the use of printing and writing, the chief part of each man's experience would be lost to those who came after him. In those early days, therefore, it was of vast importance, with a view to the invention of arts, that each man should be enabled, by great length of life, to apply his own experience, and to follow up himself the discoveries he might have made.

We have no direct information as to the immediate cause of the great longevity of the earliest generations of men. But it seems likely that it may have been produced by the influence of " *the Tree of Life.*"*

That the produce of this tree (whether its fruits or its leaves) was endued by the Creator with some property of warding off death, we are plainly taught, both by its name and by the exclusion of Adam from

---

* It appears to be a vestige of an early tradition respecting the use of the Tree of Life, that Homer represents his gods as supporting perpetual life and vigour by drinking nectar and *eating Ambrosia,* i. e. (immortality)

the Garden of Eden, "lest he should eat of the tree of life, and live for ever."

It is likely that it had the medicinal virtue, when applied from time to time, of preventing or curing the decays of old age; just as our ordinary food preserves men from dying of exhaustion by famine; and as several well-known medicines prevent or cure certain diseases. We know, indeed, that there does not exist now any medicine that has the virtue of keeping up or renewing youthful health or vigour. But such a medicine would not be in itself at all more strange than many things which we are familiar with, but whose effects we cannot explain, and could never have conjectured.

For example, that opium and some other drugs should produce sleep, and strong liquors a kind of temporary madness, is what no one would ever have thought of, if he had never heard of it, nor seen the experiment tried, of swallowing those substances. Nor, even if he were a skilful chemist, would he be able, by analysing them, to conjecture what their effects would be. If, then, the Tree of Life were such a medicine as we have supposed, a person who always continued the use of it from time to time, would continue exempt from decay and death.

But supposing some persons who had been in the habit of using it (as our first parents doubtless had, since there was nothing to prevent them) should afterwards *cease* to use it, their constitution would probably have been so far fortified, that though they would at length die, yet they would live much *longer* than man's natural term. And they would even be likely to transmit to their descendants such a constitution as would confer on those also a great degree of longevity, which would only wear out gradually in many successive generations.

Now, it is remarkable that this exactly agrees with what we do find recorded. If we look into those parts of the Bible history which relate to this subject, we shall find Man's life in the earliest generations extending to eight or nine centuries, and upwards. And we shall find longevity gradually diminishing in each generation, down to the times of Abraham, Isaac, and Jacob, who lived rather less than two hundred years; and again down to the time of Moses, who began his mission, apparently in the full vigour of life, at fourscore, and lived to one hundred and twenty. Joshua, who succeeded him, lived one hundred and ten years. And from thenceforward human life appears to have been brought down to about its present limit.

The above seems to be the most clear, easy, and natural interpretation of those parts of Scripture we have been examining. There is not, however, any such distinct revelation on the subject as to authorise our pronouncing confidently that such must be the right interpretation, and making this an article of faith.

With respect to religious instruction, although, as has been said, the Maker and Governor of all things did certainly make Himself known to the earliest generations of mankind, and accepted worship from them; we are told very few particulars of the revelations that were made. We find, indeed, a prophecy made to Adam and Eve, just before their expulsion from Paradise: that the seed of the woman should bruise the serpent's head. But whether any explanation was given them, of the reference this had to our Saviour's triumph over Satan and Death, we are not told. And it is even a matter of doubt among the learned, whether the sacrifices (Gen. iv. viii.) that were offered up in the earliest times, and afterwards by Noah, were of express divine appointment, or were merely a mode of worship which men devised of themselves, and which God thought fit to approve and accept. And there is nothing so distinctly said in Scripture on the subject, as to authorise any one to decide confidently, one way or the other. If it had been necessary that we should have any certainty as to this point, doubtless we should have had some plain declarations upon it.

Of Enoch we find it recorded, that he "walked with God," that is, led a life of eminent holiness, and was so far favoured, as to be withdrawn from the earth without tasting of death. And he is referred to, in the Epistle to the Hebrews, as an example of *faith*, inasmuch as "without faith it is impossible to please God." But as to the *subjects* of his faith, the Apostle himself seems to have had no distinct and particular knowledge, except that he must have believed in the existence and in the goodness of God,—"For he that cometh to God must believe that He is; and that He is a rewarder of them that diligently seek Him."

Of course what is meant in this passage by the word "God," is—what we also understand by it—the Creator of the world. We cannot doubt that He must have made Himself known to the earliest of mankind, as the Maker of themselves, and of all things around them. And the account given in Genesis, of the creation, and of some other of the earliest events, is probably a tradition of this most ancient revelation, and was very likely committed to writing, long before the time of Moses.

Some persons have imagined that we are bound to take our notions of Astronomy, and of all other Physical Sciences, from the Bible. And accordingly, when astronomers discovered and proved that the earth turns round on its axis, and that the sun does not move round the earth, some cried out against this as profane, because Scripture speaks of the sun's rising and setting. And this probably led some astronomers to reject the Bible, because they were taught that if they received *that* as a divine revelation, they must disbelieve truths which they had demonstrated.

So also, some have thought themselves bound to believe, if they receive Scripture at all, that the earth, and all the plants and animals that ever existed on it, must have been created within six days, of exactly the same length as our present days. And this, even before the sun, by which we measure our days, is recorded to have been created. Hence, the discoveries made by geologists, which seem to prove that the earth and various races of animals must have existed a very long time before Man existed, have been represented as completely inconsistent with any belief in Scripture.

We may not stop to discuss the various objections (some of them more or less plausible, and others very weak), that have been brought—on grounds of science, or supposed science—against the Mosaic accounts of the state of the early world, and of the flood, and to bring forward the several answers that have been given to those objections. But it is important to lay down the PRINCIPLE on which either the Bible or any other writing or speech ought to be studied and understood, viz., with a reference to *the object proposed* by the writer or speaker.

For example, if we bid any one proceed in a straight line from one place to another, and to take care to arrive before the sun goes down, he will rightly and fully understand us, in reference to the practical object which alone we had in view. Now, we know that there cannot really be *a straight line* on the surface of the earth ; and that the sun does not really *go down*, only our portion of the earth is turned away from it. But whether the other party knows all this or not, matters nothing to our present object ; which was not to teach him mathematics or astronomy, but to make him conform to our directions, which are equally intelligible to the learned and the unlearned.

Now, the object of the Scripture revelation is to teach men, not astronomy or geology, or any other physical science, but *Religion*. Its design was to inform men, not *in what manner* the world was made, but WHO made it; and to lead them to worship Him, the Creator of the heavens and the earth, instead of worshipping his creatures, the heavens and earth themselves, as gods; which is what the ancient heathen actually did.

Although, therefore, Scripture gives very scanty and imperfect information respecting the earth and the heavenly bodies, and speaks of them in the language and according to the notions of the people of a rude age, still it fully effects the object for which it was given, when it teaches that the heavens and the earth are not gods to be worshipped, but that " *God created the heavens and the earth*," and that it is He who made the various tribes of animals, and also Man.

But as for astronomy and geology and other sciences, men were left, when once sufficiently civilised to be capable of improving themselves, to make discoveries in them by the exercise of their own faculties.

But whatever may have been the religious instruction originally afforded to mankind, most of them appear not to have made the proper use of their advantages; but to have fallen, in very early times, into idolatry and superstitions of various kinds.

Whether false religion was introduced before the flood, we are not expressly told; but there is every reason to think it must have been. For we read that mankind had become excessively wicked, and that this brought on them that terrible judgment. And all experience shews that great moral depravity and gross religious corruption accompany each other. Moral corruption favours the introduction of corrupted and false religious notions; and a false religion, in turn, favours immorality.

Moreover, there is a passage in Genesis (chap. iv. 26), which, though it be but an obscure hint, seems to relate to the first introduction of false gods, in the times of Enos, grandson of Adam, and apparently about three or four centuries after the creation. The passage is translated in the text of our version, "Then began men to call upon the name of the Lord: אָז הוּחַל לִקְרֹא בְּשֵׁם יְהֹוָה. (Gen. iv. 26.) But the translation in the margin is, "Then began men to call themselves by the name of the Lord." And some learned men translate it, "Then began men to call the Lord by name."

The sense of the passage certainly cannot be that divine worship was then introduced for the first time; which, we know, from the preceding history (ch. iv. 3), was not the case. But it probably means that, then, those who worshipped the true God, began to apply to Him some distinct name or title, such as *Adonai* or *Jehovah*, to distinguish Him from the pretended gods worshipped by others, and that they called themselves "by his name," that is, described themselves as his worshippers, to distinguish themselves from those who served other gods. As long as one God only was acknowledged in the world, there was no need to apply to Him any distinguishing title. But when the worship of other Beings was introduced, it would be necessary for the true worshippers to mark the distinction. It is probable, therefore, that this was the time when such false worship first became prevalent.

In later times, we know, false religions did prevail very extensively, as indeed they still do, among a large portion of mankind.

We shall next consider what was the real character of the Pagan religions, and in what way it is likely they were introduced.

THE PAGAN RELIGIONS.

THE worshippers of false gods, such as the greater part of mankind formerly were, are usually called *Heathens* or *Pagans*. The word *Heathen* as well as the word *Gentiles*, which had the same meaning, signified originally *Nations*. But since all, or nearly all, nations except the Jews (who called themselves the Lord's *People*) were worshippers of false gods, hence the word " Heathen"* came to be used as it is now. And the word " Pagan" also, which originally signified a *Villager*, came to be used in the same sense; because, in the early times of Christianity, many of the inhabitants of retired country villages retained their old superstitions, after the inhabitants of the *towns* had been converted to the Gospel.

There are some persons, who though possessing a considerable knowledge of things connected with Mythology, yet mistake altogether the real character of the Pagan religions. They sometimes imagine that all men, in every age and country, had always

* This is the commonly received etymology, though some think it is derived from the German "Heiden," inhabitant of a "heath" or wilderness.

designed to worship one Supreme God, the maker of all things;* and that the error of the Pagans consisted merely in the false accounts they gave of Him, and in their worshipping other inferior gods besides.

But this is altogether a mistake. Few, if any, of the ancient Pagans ever thought of worshipping a Supreme Creator at all. Those who believed, or sus-pected, that the world had been created, never pretended that it was the work of any of the gods they worshipped.† Many held that the world was not created, but eternal; and others maintained that though it had a beginning, it was the production of what they called chance; that is, they fancied that the particles of matter of which the world consists, moved about at random, and accidentally fell into the shape it now bears.

These persons were what we should call *Atheists*. For by the word GOD, we understand an Eternal Being, who made and who governs all things. And if any one should deny that there *is* any such Being, we should say that he was an Atheist; even though he might believe that there do exist Beings *superior*

---

* *See* POPE's *Universal Prayer*.

> "Father of all, in every age,
> In every clime adored;
> By saint, by savage, and by sage,
> Jehovah, Jove, or Lord."

† Sic ubi dispositam *quisquis fuit ille Deorum* Congeriem secuit, sectamque in membra redegit, &c. &c — *Ovid. Metam.* 1.

*to man ;** such as the Fairies and Genii in whom the uneducated in many parts of Europe still believe.

Accordingly, the Apostle Paul (Eph. ii. 12) expressly calls the ancient Pagans Atheists (ἄθεοι), though he well knew that they worshipped certain supposed superior Beings which they called gods. But he says in the Epistle to the Romans, that they " worshipped the creature more than† (*i.e.* instead of) the Creator." And at Lystra (Acts xiv. 15), when the people were going to do sacrifice to him and Barnabas, mistaking them for two of their gods, he told them to " turn from these vanities to serve the *living* God, *who made heaven and earth.*"

This is what is declared in the first sentence of the Book of Genesis. And so far were the ancient Pagans from believing that " in the beginning God made

---

* " Now, suppose that any one in those ages had denied the existence of God and his angels, would not his impiety justly have deserved the appellation of Atheism, even though he had still allowed, by some odd capricious reasoning, that the popular stories of elves and fairies were just and well-grounded? The difference, on the one hand, between such a person and a genuine *Theist*, is infinitely greater than that on the other between him and one who absolutely excludes all invisible intelligent power. And it is a fallacy merely from the casual resemblance of names, without any conformity of meaning, to rank such opposite opinions under the same denomination. To any one who considers justly of the matter, it will appear that the gods of all *Polytheists* are no better than the elves or fairies of our ancestors, and merit as little any pious worship or veneration. These pretended religionists are really a kind of superstitious Atheists, and acknowledge no Being that corresponds to our idea of a deity."—HUME'S *Natural History of Religion*, sec. 4.

† παρὰ τὸν κτίσαντα.

the heavens and the earth," that, on the contrary, the heavens, and the earth, and the sea, and many other natural objects, were among the *very gods they adored.*

The heavens—that is the sky, the atmosphere around us—they worshipped under the titles of Zeus or Dis—of Jupiter or Jove—and (among the Canaanites and Babylonians) of Baal, Bel, or Belus.* They worshipped the earth also under the names of Demeter and Cybele; called by our Anglo-Saxon ancestors Hertha (whence our words "earth" and "hearth"), and by them most especially venerated.

The Pagans also worshipped the sea, under the title of Neptune; the sun, under that of Phœbus or Apollo; and the moon under that of Diana. These last they called the son and daughter of Jove; meaning that the sun and moon were produced by the heavens.

The Egyptians also worshipped the same kind of gods, and, among others, the great river Nile, on which the fertility of their country depends. The plagues which the Lord sent on Egypt (Exod. xii. 12) when he delivered the Israelites, seem to have been partly designed to prove his superiority and dominion over these pretended gods, by making them the very instruments of his judgments. Their *river* was turned into blood; the *earth* brought forth a plague of frogs; the *sky*, or atmosphere which they worshipped, sent forth destructive hail and lightning; and the *sun* was darkened. This was a useful lesson, both to the

* Æl. B;... Herodotus.

Israelites and to the Egyptians themselves, as many as would learn from it.

The ancient Pagans seem to have supposed that certain living spirits resided in, and ruled over, the air, the sun, moon, earth, and sea. And besides these, they also worshipped a number of other supposed Beings who presided over the several passions, and faculties, and actions of man. Thus Minerva was the goddess of wisdom; and Mars the god of war: and they often used the word Minerva to signify *intelligence*, and Mars to signify *valor*. So Hermes (or Mercury) was supposed to preside over *traffic*, and also over *eloquence*. And thence it was that the Lystrans "called Paul 'Mercurius,' because he was the chief speaker." (Acts xiv. 12.)

None of the ancient Pagans considered any of their gods as *eternal*. They generally supposed them *immortal*—that is, exempt from *death*; but, for the most part, they had some tradition about the *birth* of each of them. Indeed, several of them were confessedly dead men, whom they imagined to have been raised to the ranks of the gods by their great deeds on earth. Thus Romulus, the founder of Rome, was worshipped by the Romans under the title of Quirinus. And Hercules, and many others, worshipped by the ancient Pagans, were deified men, supposed to have gained immortality, by their eminent virtues, and especially by their feats of war.

The Northern nations, however, thought that the gods they worshipped were not immortal, but doomed finally to perish, after a very long life.* These gods, nevertheless, are supposed, most of them, to have answered to the Greek and Roman gods, though with different names. Of these names we have still a kind of record in the names of the days of the week, which were dedicated by our Pagan forefathers, each to one of their gods.† Many of the Jews, and of the early Christians, seem not to have disbelieved the *existence* of the heathen gods, but to have considered them as evil demons whom it was impious to worship. They did, indeed, often deride the Heathen for worshipping images, "the work of men's hands, wood and stone." (Isa. xliv.) But it is plain that any one who so worships, must believe that there is some living spirit residing in the image, or somehow connected with it. For no one *could* pay adoration to a mere stone, believing it himself to be nothing more than a mere stone. And it appears that many of the Jews and early Christians believed the Beings that were represented by the heathen idols to be demons. Thus we find the Jews calling Beelzebub the prince of the demons, and blasphemously attributing to him the

* "Till Lok has burst his tenfold chain,
    . . . . till substantial night
Has reassumed her ancient right."—GRAY.

† The first day of the week was dedicated, as its name shews, to the sun, and the second to the moon; Tuesday was sacred to Tuisco, the same as the Roman Mars; Wednesday to Woden, who is supposed to be the same with Mercury; Thursday to Thor, that is Jupiter; Friday to Friga, who was the Venus of the Romans; and Saturday to Saturn.

miracles of our Lord. Now Beelzebub was the Philistine god of Ekron. (2 Kings i.)

And certainly the character which the Pagans attributed to their gods, was very much that of evil demons. The very best of these gods were represented by them as capricious and profligate tyrants, whom they worshipped more from fear than love. One, in particular, who was especially dreaded, was Pan, the god of shepherds. In particular, they attributed to him all sudden and unaccountable terrors, such as sometimes seize armies or other large bodies of men, and which have thence received the name of Panic. Their images represent him as partly in the human form, and partly in that of a goat, with horns and cloven hoofs. And hence it is, that by a kind of tradition, we often see, even at this day, representations of Satan in this form. For, the early Christians seem to have thought that it was *he* whom the Pagans adored under the name of Pan.

This is certain, that several savage tribes at this day profess to believe in a *good* god, and an evil one; and address all their worship, and offer their sacrifices to the *evil* one. They suppose that the Good Being will, of his own accord, without being asked, do all the good in his power; and all their prayers and offerings are to the Evil one—or to several evil Beings—whose malice they hope to soften.*

---

* We have an amusing instance of this tendency of the human mind in the anecdote (a true one), of the schoolboy who was observed to bow in church whenever the name of Satan was mentioned; and being asked the reason, replied, "I was afraid he might do me some harm."

The images and pictures of the gods of the ancient Egyptians, and of the Hindoos at this day, are usually strange monstrous figures, half man and half brute. And such was the Philistine image of Dagon, which was half man and half fish.* The Greeks and Romans, on the contrary, represented the greater part of their deities as handsome men and women ; but the image of Pan and some others were exceptions. And the emblem† of Diana at Ephesus, which they worshipped as having " fallen down from Jupiter," is said to have been a rude, shapeless stone. It was most likely an aerolite—one of those stones which do really sometimes fall from the sky. So probably, is also the black mass of stone at Mecca, in the Caaba, venerated by the Mahometans. For though Mahomet was opposed to idolatry, he found the veneration of the Arabians for this stone to be so great, that he did not venture to oppose it.

As for the kind of worship which the Pagans paid to their gods, it was very much what might have been expected, considering what kind of Beings these gods were, according to their own accounts of them. When Moses is cautioning the Israelites against being led away by the example of their idolatrous neighbours, he says, " Every abomination unto the Lord, which he hateth, have these nations done unto their gods ; for

* The name does actually signify a fish.

† In our version (Acts xix.), it is called "the *image* which fell down from Jupiter," but the word "image," is supplied by the translators ; the original merely speaks of their being worshippers, τ.ῦ Διοπετοῦς, of ' that which fell down from Jupiter."

even their sons and their daughters, have they burned in the fire unto their gods." And the inhabitants of the South Sea Islands, at this day, offer human victims to their gods; as did also the people of Mexico. The grossest profligacy, and the most atrocious cruelties, were not only not *forbidden* by the Pagan religions, but were even a *part* of their religious worship; especially at the festivals of Bacchus.

And even the best of their gods were supposed to be more gratified by costly offerings and splendid temples, than by a pure and virtuous life in their worshippers. This, indeed, was quite natural; since these gods were described as not only themselves committing the most abominable actions, but as patrons of such actions. Mercury, for instance, was reckoned the god, not only of traffic, but of cheating; and the Romans had a goddess of thieves, called Laverna,* who was regularly worshipped, as well as the rest. Mars and Bellona are described as delighting in human carnage. And, indeed, there are in modern languages, words still in use, derived from the Pagan religions, and generally signifying something *evil.* For instance, the words Martial, Panic, Bacchanalian, Jovial, and many others that might be added.

As for the notions of the ancient Pagans respecting a future state, the Popular Mythology of the Greeks and Romans did certainly contain ample descriptions of a life after this, and of the places prepared for the

---

*　.　.　.　.　.　.　.　.　.　." Pulchra Laverna,
Da mihi fallere, da justo sanctoque videri;
Noctem peccatis, et fraudibus objice nubem."—HORACE.

reward and punishment respectively of the virtuous and the wicked. It might indeed be urged with truth, that this Mythology, resting as it did on no other evidence than that of vague, and incoherent, and contradictory traditions, could not afford any *rational assurance* of a future state. And such, of course, must be the case with the notions of Pagans of the present day on the subject, as well as with those of the barbarian nations of antiquity, of whose Mythology we have no distinct and authentic accounts. How far the doctrine of a future state did or does prevail as a matter of *serious belief*, in those nations, it is by no means easy to determine on sufficient evidence. In those of modern times it is also difficult, if not impossible, to decide whether, and to what degree, some parts of their religion may have been derived, through a remote and corrupt tradition, from the Gospel. The fairest mode of trying the question, therefore, seems to be, by examining the opinions that prevailed before the promulgation of the Gospel. And these afford, as we have said, no well-founded assurance. Nor again, did the Pagan Mythology inculcate the doctrine of a resurrection; and it was in many other points greatly at variance with what Christians receive as the authentic and true accounts. Still it must be admitted that a system so far correct in its outline, as to contain the notion of a just judgment and a state of retribution hereafter, to be influenced by our conduct during the present life, would in some degree supply the want of the Gospel revelation on these points, provided it were (on whatever evidence) fully and firmly and generally *established* among the mass of the community. But that this was not the case with respect to the accounts of a future state current among the ancients, is the conclusion which will present itself to any one who examines the question fully and candidly. We say fully and candidly, because one whose researches are very limited, will not be unlikely to have met with such passages only in ancient writers as would, of themselves, lead to a contrary conclusion; and one who is strongly prepossessed in favour of that conclusion, will confine his attention to those passages, seeking only to explain away all that militates against it.

The truth is, there *are* many passages to be found (and that frequently in the same authors) of each description; some that seem to imply the general belief, and others the disbelief, of the accounts of a future life. And some have dwelt on the *numerical* superiority of those passages that favour the doctrine; as if a book were to be regarded in the same light as a legislative assembly, in which we have only to *count* the votes on each side, and consider the decision of the majority as that of the whole. But it should be remembered that, in such a case, the expressions which negative the belief, are entitled to far the greater weight. For there can be no doubt that the fables of Elysium and Tartarus were a part of the popular religion, which it was usually thought decorous to speak of with respect: and the doctrine of a future state was regarded as especially expedient to be inculcated on the vulgar, in order to restrain them in cases beyond the control of human laws; so that a good reason can be assigned for a philosopher's appearing to consider the doctrine as indubitable, though he neither believed it himself, nor could flatter himself that it was so generally believed as he might think desirable: whereas, on the other hand, no reason whatever can be assigned for any one's treating it as a fable, if he really did believe it.

When, then, we find Socrates and his disciples represented by Plato as fully admitting, in their discussion of the subject, that "Men in general were highly incredulous as to the soul's future existence," and as expecting that it would at the moment of our natural "death, be dispersed (as he expresses it) like air or smoke, and cease altogether to exist. So that it would require no little persuasion and argument to convince them that the soul can exist after death, and can retain anything of its powers and intelligence." When we find this asserted, or rather alluded to, as notoriously the state of popular opinion, we can surely entertain but little doubt that the accounts of Elysium and Tartarus were regarded as mere poetical fables, calculated to amuse the imagination, but unworthy of serious belief.

Again, the testimony of Thucydides, not as to the *professed* belief, but as to the conduct, of the Athenians, under those trying circumstances in which the near approach of death impresses the most forcibly the thought of a future state on the minds of those who expect it—his testimony, we say, as to their conduct on such an occasion, must alone prove almost decisive of the question. For it will hardly be denied, that those who firmly believe in a future state, or even regard it as a thing highly probable, however the pursuits and occupations of this world may have drawn off their attention from it, will be likely, when death evidently draws near,—death, not in the tumultuous ardour of battle, but in the calm yet resistless progress of disease,—to think with lively and anxious interest of the life of another world. If they have any apprehensions at all of judgment to come, they will usually wish to " die the death of the righteous," even though they may not have been willing to lead the life of the righteous. Even those who have been in some doubt respecting this truth, or who have studied to keep it out of sight, are often found to believe in it the most firmly at that awful moment, when they would be most glad to disbelieve it, and then to think most of it, when the thought is most intolerable.

It is not necessary for the present purpose to contend that what has been just said constitutes a rule without exception; let it be admitted only as applying to the generality, or even to a considerable portion merely, of mankind (and thus far, at least, we are surely borne out, both by reason and experience); and let any one, with these principles before him, contemplate the picture drawn of the pestilence which ravaged Athens during the Peloponnesian war, by that judicious historian who was an eye-witness, and a partaker of the calamity. Whether the ancient poets or philosophers be regarded as the better instructors in the doctrine of a future state, Athens had no deficiency in either; and a plague so wide-spreading, so irresistible, and which brought with it to those whom it seized (as we are expressly told), such an utter despair of recovery, may be fairly expected to have had the effect, in some minds at least, of awakening whatever belief, or even suspicion, they might have entertained respecting Tartarus and Elysium, and of calling into action their fears and hopes on the subject. We might expect to find *some* of them, at least, bewailing their sins, making reparation to those they had injured, and in every way striving to prepare for the judgment that seemed impending.

The very reverse took place. The historian tells us, that "seeing death so near them, they resolved to make the most of life while it lasted, by setting at nought all laws, divine and human, and eagerly plunging into every species of profligacy." Nor was this conduct by any means confined to the most vile and worthless of the community; for he complains of a general and permanent *depravation* of morals, which dated its origin from this calamity. Nor again, does the description apply to such only as had been, either openly or secretly, contemners of the whole system of the national religion; for we are told, that "at first, many had recourse to the offices of their religion, with a view to appease the gods; but that when they found their sacrifices and ceremonies *availed nothing against the disease*, and that the pious and the impious alike fell victims to it, they at once concluded that piety and impiety were altogether indifferent, and cast off all religious and moral obligations." Is it not evident from this, that those who did reverence the gods, had been accustomed to look for none but *temporal* rewards and punishments from them? Can we conceive that men who expected that virtue should be rewarded and vice punished, in the other world, would, just at their entrance into that world, *begin* to regard virtue and vice as indifferent? It is but too true, indeed, that men have been found in countries where Christianity is professed, so hardened, as to manifest, even at the approach of death, no regard to the judgment which Christianity teaches is to succeed it; who have availed themselves of present impunity for the commission of crimes, or have endeavoured to drown thought in sensual excess; but instances of this kind rather go to prove that such men do *not*, than that the heathen *did*, believe in a future retribution; if by belief is to be understood, not a mere unthinking assent, or a mere *non-denial* of the doctrine, but a deliberate, firm, and habitual conviction.

Those who have been long hardened in habits of extreme profligacy, may ultimately become as blind to all ideas of a future state, as if they had never heard of it; but experience, as well as reason, forbids us to believe that, where the Gospel is assiduously preached and accepted, such a degree of ignorance, or of depravity, can ever be general, much less universal.

And accordingly, it appears that the great plague which desolated London, produced, on the whole, an effect exactly opposite to that at Athens. Some abandoned wretches, no doubt, took the same advantage as the Athenians did, of the calamity; but the generality seem plainly to have shewn that their belief of a future state, however it might have lain dormant during a time of apparent security, and however easily it might be thrown off on a return to such a state, was real and deep-rooted. No instances are recorded *there* of pious men *renouncing* their piety when they saw death approaching: on the contrary, serious devotion seems, for the most part, to have prevailed; and if not reformation, at least alarm and contrition, to have been generally produced among sinners. Many are said, when attacked by the plague, to have even rushed into the public streets, confessing aloud and bewailing crimes long ago committed, and never before imputed to them, and earnestly seeking to make reparation.

Can we, then, on comparing two such cases together, come to the conclusion, that in each the notions respecting a future state were the same, or at all similar? Is not the inference obvious, that, at least, the Athenians of that age considered the accounts of a future life as no more than amusing fictions, of whose utter falsity there was no reason even to doubt? And accordingly, when Pericles is represented by the same historian, as exhausting every topic of consolation, in his address to the friends of those who had fallen in battle,* he speaks of their glorious memory, and of the hope of other sons to be born, who may fill their place, and emulate their worth, but adds not one word of their future life and immortality.

And that the prevailing belief, at other times, and in other states, Greek or Italian, was the same as at

* THUCYD., lib. ii., c. 35, *et seq.*

Athens at the period just spoken of, there is at least a strong presumption till evidence of the contrary is produced. The Athenians were noted for their religious devotion; the popular mythology which prevailed among the other Grecian states, and, we may add, at Rome, was the same, or nearly the same, with theirs; and therefore may be presumed, in the absence of all proof to the contrary, to have had the same results in respect of the belief of a future life. Indeed, we find the younger Pliny,* in his account of the eruption of Vesuvius, in which his uncle perished, recording, among the striking events of that scene, the excitement of a feeling not unlike that of the Athenians in the plague—viz., a general distrust of divine aid, arising from the notion that the gods themselves were possibly involved in the impending ruin.

The belief, then, of a life to come, though nominally professed, cannot be considered as practically forming any part of the creed of those ancient nations with whom we are best acquainted. Cicero acknowledges that the epistle of Sulpicius to him on the death of Tullia, comprehended *every* argument for comfort which the case admitted; yet we find in it no allusion to the one topic which would have been uppermost in the mind of a believer. It is no wonder, therefore, that when at Athens, Paul came to speak of the resurrection of the dead, some of his hearers mocked; and that when Festus heard him declaring the same doctrine, he exclaimed, "Paul, thou art beside thyself."

* Epist., lib. ii., ep. 20.

So far, indeed, were the promulgators of Christianity from finding the belief of a future state already well established, that they appear to have had no small difficulty in convincing of this truth even some of their converts. Some of those who denied a *resurrection*, may, indeed, with good reason, be supposed to have looked for some other kind of future existence ; but when Paul finds it necessary to urge "*if in this life only we have hope* in Christ, we are of all men most miserable—let us eat and drink, for to-morrow we die,"* it is plain he must have been opposing such as expected *nothing* beyond the grave. And when he exhorts the Thessalonians not to sorrow for the deceased, "even as *the rest*† (of mankind), who have *no hope*," we have the testimony, if we will receive it, of one who knew better than we can, the real sentiments of the heathen on this point.

It may be said, however (and this, perhaps, is the most prevailing notion), that little as the vulgar believed in the doctrine of a future state, it was received and inculcated by many eminent philosophers. But, in reality, the doctrine never was either generally admitted among the ancient philosophers, or satisfactorily proved by any of them, even in the opinion of those who argued in favour of it. On the one hand,

---

* Thus Catullus:—

> Soles occidere et redire possunt :
> *Nobis* cum semel occidit brevis lux,
> *Nox est perpetua una dormienda.*

† ol λοιποί, not as in our version, *others.*

not only the Epicurean school openly contended against it, but one of much greater weight than any of them, and the founder of a far more illustrious sect, Aristotle, without expressly combating the notion of a future state, does much more—he passes it by as not worth considering, and takes for granted the contrary supposition, as not needing proof. He remarks incidentally in his treatise on courage, that "death is formidable beyond most other evils, on account of its excluding hope; since it is a complete termination, and there does not appear to be *anything either of good or evil beyond it.*"   And in the same work, in discussing the question whether a man can justly be pronounced happy before the end of his life, he proceeds all along (as indeed is the case throughout), on the supposition, that after death a man ceases altogether to exist.   And it should be observed, that his incidental and oblique allusion to this latter opinion, implies (as we have said) much more than if he had expressly asserted and maintained it.   In *that* case he would have borne testimony only to his *own* belief; but as it is, we may collect from his mode of speaking, that such was the *prevailing* and generally uncontradicted belief of the rest of the world.

Of those philosophers, again, who contended for a future state, it is to be observed, not only that, as Dr. Paley remarks, they did not, properly speaking, effect a *discovery;* "it was only one guess among many: he only discovers who proves;" but also, that (as has been said above) their arguments did not fully succeed in convincing even themselves.   Those which at one time they bring forward as decisive proof, they seem, at another time, to regard as hardly possessing that degree of probability, which, now that the doctrine is established, most are ready to allow them. Cicero, especially, who is frequently appealed to on this question, we find distinctly acknowledging, at least in the person of one of his disputants, that though, while he is reading the Phaedo, he feels disposed to assent to the reasons urged in favour of a future state, his conviction vanishes as soon as he lays down the book, and revolves the matter in his own thoughts; which was the feeling probably with which the author himself had written it. Many, indeed, of the deistical writers of modern times have come to much more decisive conclusions on this, and also on many other points, than the ancients did, and, indeed, than are fairly warranted by any arguments which unassisted reason can supply; but this only affords a presumption of the powerful, though unacknowledged and perhaps unperceived influence which the Gospel revelation has exercised even on the minds of those who reject it. They have drunk at that stream of knowledge, which they cannot or will not trace to the real source from which it flows.

As, however, even the faintest conjecture of a future existence, though it must not be confounded with a full assurance of it, is, as far as it goes, an approximation towards the knowledge of truth; so also, notions considerably incorrect respecting that existence, if they are but such as to involve the idea of enjoyment or suffering, corresponding with men's conduct in this life, have so far something of a just foundation, and of a tendency to practical utility. This, however, appears by no means to have been the case with the systems of any, as far as we can learn, of those ancient philosophers who contended the most strenuously for the immortality of the soul. For not only do they seem to have agreed, that no suffering could be expected by the wicked in another life, on the ground that the gods were incapable of anger, and therefore could not punish; but the very notion of the soul's immortality, as explained by them, involved the complete destruction of distinct *personal* existence. Their notion was, that is, when they spoke their real sentiments (for in their *exoteric* or popular works, they often inculcate, for the benefit of the vulgar, the doctrine of future retribution, which they elsewhere laugh at), that the soul of each man is a portion of that spirit which pervades the universe, to which it is reunited at death, and becomes again an undistinguishable part of the great Whole, just as the body is resolved into the general mass of matter. So that their immortality, or rather eternity, of the soul, was anterior as well as posterior; as it was to have no end, so it had no beginning; and the boasted continuance of existence, which, according to this system, we are to expect after death, consists in returning to the *state in which we were before birth;* which every one must perceive is the same thing virtually with annihilation.

Such, then, were the views which prevailed among the most enlightened nations of antiquity on this subject. On the other hand, the Hindoos of the present day do seem to believe in a future state of existence. They hold the doctrine of transmigration, *i. e.*, that the souls of all men (except those of extraordinary holiness) are doomed to migrate into the bodies of various brutes, and at length, if found worthy, are admitted into heaven.* And the kind of holiness which they expect will entitle men to future happiness, consists not in virtuous conduct, but in rich offerings, and the performance of various ceremonies, many of them excessively cruel; such as hanging themselves up by iron hooks plunged into their flesh, and other self-inflicted tortures. And a woman who burns herself alive along with her husband's corpse, and any one who drowns himself in the sacred river Ganges, or gives himself to be devoured by certain sacred alligators, or to be crushed under the wheels of the sacred car of the idol Juggernauth, is supposed to gain the special favour of their gods.

The real character, then, of the Pagan religions, being such as we have described, we are naturally led to wonder that the Israelites should so often have fallen into idolatry, after having had the true God revealed to them. Although He had so earnestly warned them not to worship any other gods, we find them continually joining the worship of Baal and other heathen gods with that of Jehovah. This appears to some persons so strange as to be hardly

* The heaven of the Buddhists, however, is manifestly annihilation circuitously described.

credible; and yet the very same thing is going on, almost before our eyes, in christian countries at this very day. For in all parts of Europe the most uneducated portion of the people in remote districts are found to believe in, and fear various superhuman Beings, which are in reality no other than the gods of their Pagan forefathers. And though they do not give them the title of *gods*, they often pay them great reverence, and make some kind of offerings to them.

In some parts of the British Islands, Fairies are believed in and venerated. In Scotland, besides these, we hear of Bogles, Brownies, and Kelpies, as names of certain superhuman Beings dreaded by the superstitious. In Denmark and Iceland, we hear of Trolls; in Germany of Nixes, and many other such Beings, who are supposed to have power in human affairs. In Norway, the country people are said to make an offering of a cake once a year to a demon which they dread; and also of the first cheese that is made each spring. In some parts of our own country, a cottier's wife will not venture to bake bread or churn butter, without offering a portion to the fairies. And several other such acts of superstitious devotion are practised in various parts of Europe.

Now, there is every reason to believe that all these Beings who are thus reverenced, are, as we have already said, the very heathen gods which were formerly worshipped in each country. And the persons who shew them this reverence, and who seek their help, and dread to displease them, and aim at obtaining their good-will, are doing exactly the same as the Israelites of old, when they worshipped Baal, and Astaroth, and other gods of the heathen.

But what misleads people in their notions on this subject, is, that the *words* we use are not the same as the ancient Pagans used. What were formerly called by some name answering to "gods," are now called fairies, or "kelpies," or genii, &c., and the reverence shewn them is not called *worship;* and the offerings made to them are no longer called *sacrifices.* And thus it is that professed Christians deceive themselves by means of words, and fancy that they are not paying worship to any gods besides the Lord, though they are doing the same thing under other names.

With respect to the way in which false religions were first introduced, there can be no doubt that they must have crept in gradually. For men would not all at once forsake the worship of the Great Creator, and forget his very existence, and serve other gods *instead* of Him. But it is likely that, when they had come to imagine certain inferior spirits to reside in the sun and moon, the sea, rivers, groves, &c., they would next be led to call upon these Beings, in the hope that, *perhaps*, such prayers might be heard. And when once the practice has arisen of men's *adding on* to the worship of the Most High, some invocations of other inferior Beings, this latter kind of worship always tends to prevail over and drive out the other. Men seem to think that an inferior Being who approaches more nearly to their own nature, is more likely to feel sympathy with them, and perhaps is also more likely to be gratified by their adoration and their offerings, than the Supreme God. And even at this day there are some Pagan nations who are said to acknowledge the existence of a Great Being, who is the Supreme Ruler of all things, but whom they think it would be presumptuous for them to address; so that all their worship is reserved for some supposed gods of a lower order.

This at least is certain, that the Apostle Paul expressly informs us (Romans i.) that false worship did not first originate among men from their knowing nothing, and having no means of knowing anything, of the true God, and being left entirely to their own conjectures. For he distinctly declares, that some at least, "when they knew God, glorified him not as God," and "did not like to retain God in their knowledge, but changed the truth of God into a lie, and worshipped the creature more than the Creator."

It is very probable (and this seems to have been the apostle's notion) that many of the more intelligent portion of mankind, in the days when false worship first arose, did not themselves partake of the superstitions of the weaker and more ignorant, but encouraged those superstitions for the sake of gratifying the vulgar, or keeping them in subjection to themselves, by means of a religion suited, as they thought, to unenlightened and feeble minds. Certain it is, that some dishonesty of this kind has often been practised in various ages and countries, and under various religious systems. Men of education and intelligence have often thought themselves justified in disguising, or concealing, or altering some portion of what they believed to be religious truth, and teaching or encouraging the vulgar to believe something different from what they themselves believed. And this dishonest system has always led, in the end, to the grossest corruptions, both of doctrine and of morals.

One great cause, probably, of the multiplication of gods among the Pagans, was the use of images or pictures. When men had introduced the practice of making some kind of emblem, intended to represent either the Supreme God, or any other Being they worshipped, they would easily be led to pay more and more veneration to the emblem itself, so as to become what is properly called " idolaters," that is, worshippers of an image or picture. And it would often happen that one set of men would venerate one image, and others another somewhat different, though originally designed to represent the same being. And there would also be some difference in the kind of worship paid to each of these images, and in the tales related concerning it; so that by degrees some of them would come to be considered as so many distinct gods.

Thus it seems to have been a matter of doubt whether there were not two Jupiters; whether there were one, or two, or three Mercuries; whether the Moon, and Diana, and Hecate, were three goddesses or one; and the like in many other instances. And, probably, this was one reason why the Israelites were so strictly charged, in the law of Moses, to worship, all of them at one place, " which the Lord should chuse to set his name there," lest, from having seve-ral different temples, that barbarian and gross-minded people should come to imagine there were several gods.

It often happened that different tribes of men wor-shipped either different gods, or the same under some different emblem, and with different ceremonies. And there is reason to believe that the confusion which is recorded as having occurred at Babel—after-wards called Babylon—and which caused the disper-sion of mankind into various countries, was in reality a dispute among them as to their worship of some god or gods. This, at least, is certain, that the scheme mentioned in Gen. xi. was something displeas-ing to God, and therefore could not have been *merely* the building of a tower. And it is plain, also, from the Bible history, that some ages after the Flood mankind had very generally fallen into gross idolatry, though we are not told expressly when and how it was introduced.

As for the Tower of Babel, it is said indeed in our version that a number of persons joined together to build " a tower whose top should reach to heaven " (our translators meant an exceeding high tower), in order that they might not be "scattered over the face of the whole earth ;" and that God sent on them a confusion of language, which caused them to "cease building the tower, and scattered them." But it is to be observed that the word " reach " is supplied by our translators, there being nothing answering to it in the Original, which merely says, " whose top to the hea-vens."

And the meaning doubtless is, that the top of the tower should be *dedicated* to the Heavens—that is, that a temple should be built on it to Bel, Belus, Zeus, or Jupiter; under which titles the ancient Pagans worshipped the heavens. For we find the historian Herodotus,[*] who many ages after visited Babylon, expressly declaring that there was there, in his time, a very high tower, on the top of which was a temple to Belus; who, he says, was the same with the Zeus of the Greeks.

The ancient Pagans, it is well known, were accustomed to erect altars to the Heavens, or to the Sun, on "high places" (Numb. xxxiii. 52), on the loftiest *mountains.* And as the land of Shinar is a very fertile *plain* of vast extent, and quite level, it seems to have been designed to make a sort of artificial mountain on it—that is, a very high tower—and to build a temple, on the top of this, to their god Belus, and so establish a great empire consisting of people worshipping at this temple.

The "confusion" which God sent among them, and which caused the tower to be less lofty than originally designed, and dispersed many of the people into other lands, was most likely not a confusion of *language,* but a dissension about *religious worship.* .The word in the original literally signifies *lip.*[†]   And it is more

---

[*] Διὸς Βήλυ ἱρὸν χαλκόπυλον, καὶ ἐς ἐμὲ τῦτο ἔτι ἐὸν, δύο σταδίων, πάντη, ἐὸν τετράγωνον· ἐν μέσῳ δὲ τῷ ἱρῷ πύργος στερεὸς οἰκοδόμηται, σταδίυ καὶ τὸ μῆκος καὶ τὸ εὖρος· καὶ ἐπὶ τύτῳ τῷ πύργῳ ἄλλος πύργος ἐπιβέβηκε, καὶ ἕτερος μάλα ἐπὶ τούτῳ, μέχρι οὗ ὀκτώ πύργων· * * Ἐν δὲ τῷ τελευταίῳ πύργῳ νηὸς ἔπεστι μέγας. —HERODOTUS, *Book* i. clxxxi.

[†] שָׂפָה χείλη (Septuagint).

likely that it was used to signify *worship* than *language*. A dissension as to *that* which was the very object of the building, would much more effectually defeat the scheme than a confusion of languages. For, labourers engaged in any work, and speaking different languages, would in a few days, learn, by the help of signs, to understand one another sufficiently to enable them to go on with their work. But if they disagreed as to the very object proposed, this would effectually break up the community.

As for the different languages now spoken in the world, there is no need of explaining that by any miraculous interference. For, tribes who have not the use of letters, and have but little mutual intercourse, vary so much from each other in their language, after even a few generations, as not to be able at all to understand each other.

But while, as was remarked before, we have no express accounts of the first origin of the Pagan religions, this at least is certain, that it was not even pretended that these religions rested on any evidence worth listening to. A Pagan's reason for holding his religion is, and always was, that it had been handed down from his ancestors. They did indeed relate many miracles, said to have been wrought through their gods; but almost all of these they spoke of as having been wrought among people who were already worshippers of those gods, not as having been the means of originally bringing in the religion. And all the Pagan miracles were believed merely because these were a part of the religion which they had learned from their fathers. In a word, the religion did not rest on the miracles, but the miracles rested on the religion.

The christian religion was distinguished from these by its resting on evidence—by its offering a reason, and requiring Christians to be able to give a reason for believing it.

THE MOSAIC DISPENSATION.

It is plain from Scripture history, that both before the Flood and afterwards, God did, from time to time, hold communication in some way or other, with mankind—that is, with such as continued faithful worshippers of Him.

To Noah, in particular, we find Him giving commandments both before the Flood and immediately after it, and accepting sacrifice from him. In a later age we read of divine commands issued to Abraham, and promises made to him of peculiar blessings to a nation which should descend from him through Isaac; and also of an extension of blessings to all mankind through them—that "in his seed should all the nations of the earth be blessed." (Gen. xii., xxii.)

And although idolatry and gross wickedness seem, in Abraham's time, and afterwards, to have overspread most parts of the world, still there were some besides him and his family, who retained the worship of the true God. For, in the history of Abraham we find mention of Melchizedek, a king, who held also the office of "a priest of the Most High God." (Gen. xiv.)

Jethro, again, the father-in-law of Moses, appears to have been a worshipper of the true God; and the prophet Balaam, though a wicked man, is spoken of as a real prophet of the Lord.

It is probable, also, that some of the Egyptians were worshippers of the Lord, though so many of that nation had fallen into idolatry. For we read of Joseph's marrying the daughter of an Egyptian priest (Gen. xli.), and though possible, it does not seem likely, that so eminently pious a man would have married the daughter of an idolatrous priest. This, at least, is certain, that the historian Plutarch speaks of a certain portion of the land of Egypt which was exempted from the tax levied on the rest for the support of idolatrous worship. And this, he says, was on account of their being worshippers only of ONE, whom they called Cneph, "the unbegotten God."* And the plagues inflicted on Egypt by the Lord God of Israel,† the complete dominion He displayed over the Beings the idolaters worshipped, must, no doubt, have brought some of the Egyptians to acknowledge and worship Him. (Exod. ix.) But we are told very

---

* 'Αγέννητον ὄντα καὶ ἀθάνατον. They were the inhabitants of Thebais.—PLUTARCH, *De Iside et Osiride.*

† "On all the gods of Egypt will I execute judgment."—(Exod. xii. 12.)

few particulars of the faith or the worship* of the servants of the true God, till we come to the time when Moses, by divine command, delivered to the " chosen" (elect) " people of Israel" that system of religion which is called " The LAW."

Of this—the Mosaic law—we find a full account in the last four Books of Moses. And these should be carefully studied by any one who would gain as accurate an understanding as possible of the system under which that most remarkable nation, the Israelites, were placed.

For our present purpose, it will be sufficient to mark out the most important points which *distinguished* the Mosaic Dispensation—the religion of the Israelites— from what came before it, and from what followed it; on the one hand, from the religion of those worshippers of the true God who lived *before* the time of Moses, and on the other hand, from the Gospel-Dispensation —the religious system under which *we* are placed.

The Law was designed to prepare the way for Christianity—a religion intended for all mankind— according to the promise made to Abraham, that some

---

* It is the opinion of many learned men that it was the practice of the servants of the true God, in the earliest times, to keep holy the last day of the week [Saturday] in memory of the close of the work of creation. And this seems probable, though no such practice is expressly recorded. But their *mode* of observing the day could hardly have been altogether the same with what was enjoined to the Israelites. To these the Sabbath seems to have been, in the *particulars* of the observance, a *new* and a *peculiar* institution. And accordingly we find, in the Prophecy of Ezekiel, the Lord saying, " I *gave them* [the Israelites] my Sabbaths, to be a *sign* between me and them."

person or persons descended from him should prove a blessing to all nations. Yet the Law itself was given to *one* people alone. And accordingly, when the Apostles of Jesus Christ, who were themselves Jews, converted vast multitudes of Gentiles to Christianity, teaching them, among other things, to acknowledge the divine origin of the Mosaic Law, they yet taught them that the ordinances of that law did not extend to Gentiles.* (Gal. v.)

It is to be remembered, however, that before the Gospel revelation, a Gentile was allowed, if he wished it, to become a proselyte; and thenceforth he was not regarded as "unclean" (Acts x.), and an "alien" (Eph. ii. 11, 12), but only as ranking next below the Israelites by birth.

And, moreover, Gentiles who, though they had renounced idolatry, yet did not conform to the whole Law, but only to a certain small number of regulations, were admitted to worship in the outer court of the Temple ("the court of the Gentiles," 1 Kings viii. 41), and to attend divine service in the synagogues. These Gentiles are often alluded to in the Book of Acts (Acts x. 2; xiii. 16, 26, 43; xvi. 14; xvii. 4, 17), under the title of "the devout,"† or "they who feared God "‡ (that is, the Lord Jehovah), such as was Cornelius the centurion. And after the time of the Cap-

---

* "Let no man judge you" (says the Apostle Paul, when writing to the Gentiles), "in meat or in drink, or in respect of an holyday, or of the new moon, or of the sabbath-days, which are a shadow of things to come; but the body is of Christ."—(Col. ii. 16.)

† οἱ σεβόμενοι.   ‡ οἱ φοβούμενοι τὸν Θεόν.

tivity, there were, in various countries, many Jews residing dispersed among the Gentiles;* and these Gentiles had thus an opportunity of learning (as a considerable number of them did learn) to know and to serve the true god. But those Gentiles who had no Jews resident among them had no such opportunity.

Why it was that the Most High thought fit to make a revelation to this one people, and not at once to all the world, we cannot explain, and must not presume to decide. Indeed, we cannot explain why the Gospel was not preached to the very first generation of mankind; and why Jesus Christ came into the world just when He did; nor yet why many nations, in various parts of the world, have been left, even to this day, in the darkness of idolatrous superstition; or indeed, why any such thing as EVIL should exist at all.

All this, we must conclude, would have been explained to us in Scripture, if it had been necessary for us to understand it. As it is, any attempt to explain these things is fruitless and presumptuous. It is *our* business to inquire, not what *we* should have done, had the regulation of things been left to us, but what God has actually done, and what He requires us to do.

We have the most satisfactory reasons for believing that the Law of Moses was given by divine command;

* These are called "the Jews of the Dispersion" (see the beginning of the Epistle of James); or simply "the Dispersion."

and also that it was given to the one nation of Israel, and not designed for the rest of mankind.

One of the many marks one may perceive of this design is, that it was a *local* religion. The Israelites were directed to offer sacrifices, and to worship three times a-year, at the one "place which the Lord should chuse to set his name there" (that is, to place there the manifestation of his presence and power); and they were strictly forbidden to sacrifice anywhere else. (Deut. xii. 13.) And accordingly, when the Temple at Jerusalem had been finally fixed on as the chosen place, the destruction of that Temple made it thenceforth impossible for an Israelite to keep up the chief ordinances of his religion.

Hence the final destruction of that Temple abolished, manifestly and totally, the Mosaic system of religion.

And it is very remarkable that that religion is almost the only one that *could* have been abolished *against the will* of the people themselves, and while they resolved firmly to maintain it. *Their* religion, and theirs only, could be, and has been, thus abolished in spite of their firm attachment to it, on account of its being dependent on a particular *place*. The christian religion, or again, any of the Pagan religions, could not be abolished by any force of enemies, if the persons professing the religion were sincere and resolute in keeping to it. To destroy a christian place of worship, or to turn it into a Mohammedan mosque (as was done in many instances by the Turks), would not prevent the exercise of the christian religion. And even if Christianity were forbidden by law, and Christians persecuted (as has in times past been so frequently done), still they might assemble secretly in woods or caves, or they might fly to foreign countries to worship God, according to their own faith; and Christianity, though it might be driven out of one country, would still exist in others.

·· l the same may be said of the Pagan religions. If it happened that any temple of Jupiter, or Diana, or Woden, were destroyed, this would not hinder the worshippers of those gods from continuing to worship them as before, and from offering sacrifices to them elsewhere.

But it was not so with the Jews. Their religion was so framed as to make the observance of its ordinances impossible, when their Temple was finally destroyed. It seems to have been designed and contrived by divine providence, that as their law was to be brought to an end by the Gospel (for which it was a preparation), so, all men were to perceive that it did come to an end, notwithstanding the obstinate rejection of the Gospel by the greater part of the Jews. It was not left to be a question and a matter of *opinion*, whether the sacrifices instituted by Moses were to be continued or not; but things were so ordered as to put it out of man's power to continue them.

But, moreover, this local character of the religion shewed, from the very first, that it could not be designed for all mankind.

And the same thing is indicated by the way in which all the laws are expressed. For it is remarkable that even those duties which, from their very nature, must be duties for all men, such as to worship the one true God only, and to honour one's parents, —even these are enjoined to the Israelites in commandments which expressly refer to that one peculiar people. "I am the Lord thy God, who *brought thee out of the land of Egypt;* thou shalt have none other gods but Me;" and "Honour thy father and thy mother; that thy days may be long in *the land which the Lord thy God giveth thee,*"—that is, the land of Canaan.

Of course Christians are bound to practise these and all other moral duties. But that is because they are in themselves *moral* duties; not because they are enjoined in the Law of Moses; which was designed for the one people of Israel.

Other commandments there were, relating to matters originally indifferent, but respecting which God laid down certain rules; and required the Israelites to comply with those rules in submission to his will.

Some of these commandments related to religious ceremonies or observances, such as the keeping of the Feast of the Passover—coming up to the temple at Jerusalem three times a-year—abstaining from certain meats, and wearing certain peculiar garments; with other things of that kind. These are commonly called *ceremonial* laws.

And, again, there were other commandments called *civil* laws; being such as relate to matters which the civil governors of any country have a right to regulate, from time to time, as they think best; and to

enforce by penalties, such as imprisonment, banish-
ment, or death.

For, the Lord was not only the *God*, but also the
King (or civil governor) of this peculiar people; and
enacted all such laws for their good government as
the rulers of any other nation are authorized to enact
and enforce, and to annul or alter whenever they see
fit.

Of this kind was the law that no man should part
with his landed property finally, but that, if sold, it
should return to him, or his heirs, at the jubilee; and
that which directed that a man should marry his
brother's widow if his brother died childless (Deut.
xxv. 5, and Luke xx. 29), with many other such
laws.

Now, the ceremonial and the civil laws being such
as relate to matters in themselves indifferent, are
what are commonly called "*positive* precepts:" those
relating to points of natural duty being called "moral
precepts." And it is very important to keep in mind
the distinction between these two classes of laws.
Any thing enjoined by a *positive* precept is *right
because it is commanded:* any thing *enjoined* by a
moral precept is *commanded because it is right.*

Thus it was, to the Israelites, a duty to keep the
Passover, as it is to Christians to celebrate the Lord's
Supper; *because* divine commands to do so were
given, and it is a moral duty to obey divine commands. But there was no such duty *before* those
express commands were given.

On the other hand, to honour one's parents is, from

the nature of the case, a duty of all men; and the Israelites were commanded to do so, because it is right in itself.

Again, to abstain from all worship of false gods, or of images, and to reverence the true God, is a *natural duty*, and was enjoined to the Israelites because it is so. But no one would say that it is a natural duty to keep holy one day in seven, rather than one in six, or in eight; or to keep holy the last day of the week, rather than the first, or any other; or to abstain from kindling a fire (Exod. xxxv. 8) on that day. But all this became a duty to the Israelites when they had received a divine command to observe in that particular manner that particular day; and so with other commandments.

Again, the Mosaic Law was distinguished from every other revelation ever bestowed on man, by the great number and minuteness of its regulations, and the multitude of its ceremonial observances. It gives exact directions to the Israelites as to their diet, their dress, and their mode of life in many particulars.

One purpose answered by these numerous ordinances, was to keep them quite distinct from other nations; that they might be the better preserved from falling into the idolatrous worship of their neighbours, and might be marked out, both to them and to themselves, as the Lord's peculiar people.

And moreover, it was needful for a half-barbarian and gross-minded people, such as the ancient Israelites, to keep up in their minds the thought of their religion, by a great number of outward ceremonies and observances. These served to remind an Israelite continually of the God whose servant he was, by his being required from day to day to observe certain rules, and to perform certain acts, as a sign of his obedience to the Lord, and as a part of his religious duty.

And a great part of the ceremonies of this law had also a *typical* meaning. In particular, the Passover, and all the other sacrifices of animals, were types representing the sacrifice of Christ on the cross for man's redemption. And, accordingly, we find the Apostle Paul expressly calling Him "our passover, who is sacrificed for us." (1 Cor. v. 7.) For as the blood of the first paschal-lamb sprinkled on the door-posts of the Israelites in Egypt (Exod. xii. 7) was to preserve their first-born from the destroying angel which slew the Egyptians, so the sacrifice of Jesus Christ brings eternal deliverance and salvation to those who will be truly his disciples. And He is thence called in Scripture, "The Lamb of God, who taketh away the sin of the world."

And throughout the New Testament, there are numerous references to the sacrifices and other ceremonial ordinances of the law, as types representing the redemption by Christ, and foreshewing the Gospel dispensation.

But all this was not understood, nor designed to be understood, by the Israelites to whom Moses delivered the Law. They were only required to observe strictly and carefully the directions given, without understanding the full meaning of all that was ordained.   The Law of Moses, therefore, was like some important document written in *cypher*, or in an unknown language; which a man is directed to preserve very carefully till such time as he shall be furnished with a key to the cypher, or a translation.   Just so, the Gospel, when it was revealed, furnished an interpretation of many things in the Mosaic Law, which had been before unintelligible as to their inward meaning.

And this is what the Apostles mean when they speak of "*making known* the *mystery* of the Gospel." For "mystery" signifies, in *their* use of the word, something that *has* been concealed, and is afterwards *revealed* and explained.   (Eph. vi. 19.)

Another distinguishing character of the Mosaic Law was, that it was enforced by a system of *temporal rewards and judgments*, administered according to an *extraordinary providence*.

The Israelites were promised, as the reward of obedience, long life, and health, and plentiful harvests, and victory over their enemies.   And the punishments threatened for disobedience, were pestilence, famine, defeat, and all kinds of temporal calamity.   (Deut. xxviii.)

And the history of this most remarkable people is full of examples of the fulfilment of these promises and threats.

In the Books of Moses himself, and the historical books that follow, we find abundant instances of both kinds recorded.   The Lord (Jehovah) was, as has been remarked above, not only the God, but also the *King* (or civil governor) of this peculiar people. And hence the word "Theocracy" is often applied to the system under which the Israelites lived. Hence, too, it was, that among them the worship of other gods was made a *capital crime;* because, under such a system, it amounted, in fact, to *high treason.* (Deut. xvii. 2.) For, it is to be remembered, that the Pagans regarded *their* gods as their temporal rulers: looking to them for victory and success of all kinds, consulting them, and acting on their supposed directions. The ideas of *tutelar* god, and *king,* were so blended in the minds both of the Pagans and the Israelites, that an Israelite could not worship Baal or Moloch, without so far withdrawing his allegiance from Jehovah his king. And even when they were ruled by judges, or by kings, they were under this theocracy; these rulers being considered as merely agents or deputies of the Lord their King, and appointed or removed by Him. He issued direct commands, from time to time, to the nation, or their governors, as to various temporal concerns, such as are regulated by the supreme rulers of each state. (1 Sam. xv.)

And as all rulers enforce their commands by temporal penalties on the disobedient, such as forfeiture of goods, bodily chastisement, or death, so the Lord enforced on the Israelites obedience to his commands by temporal rewards and punishments, distributed according to an extraordinary providence.

It appears to have been designed in that dispensation

to exhibit to mankind a sensible specimen, or rather *representation*, by way of proof, of that moral government of God, the system of which is but imperfectly displayed in the world at large; and which is to be completed, and fully realised, only in a future state.

It would be inconsistent with the present occasion to enter into a full explanation and defence of this hypothesis: let it be allowed, however, to adopt for the present, the supposition, merely *as a supposition*, that the Mosaic dispensation was, in part, designed for the purpose just mentioned; that we may examine how far the peculiar circumstances of that dispensation correspond with and are explained by it. It would manifestly be necessary, then, with a view to the object in question, that the Israelites should be exhibited as *uniformly and regularly* rewarded or punished, according to their obedience or disobedience to the divine commands. And moreover, in order that the correspondence of their situation with their conduct might be more *conspicuously* displayed, it was necessary that they should be *nationally* as well as individually, prosperous or unfortunate, in consequence of their good or ill conduct; since the fate of individuals would have been too *obscure* to engage general attention. It was requisite, for the same reason, that the obedience required of them should not consist in *moral rectitude* alone; because in that case the correspondence of their circumstances to their behaviour would not have been sufficiently *manifest*. For moral virtue consists, chiefly, in purity of motives, and propriety of inward feelings; concerning which other men cannot with any certainty form a judgment. It was requisite, therefore, that their obedience should be tried in the practice of *external* rites, and in a conformity to certain *positive ordinances.* For these observances, though originally matters of indifference, yet, as we have before observed, assume a moral character, and become duties, when enjoined by divine authority; and the obedience or disobedience of a people on such points, is a matter open to general observation, and on which no one would be liable to mistake.

Lastly, with the same view, it was no less requisite that the *rewards and punishments* also, which should be the sanction of such a law, should be of a nature no less palpable and open to general observation; and should therefore not consist in anything inward and invisible, as in peace of mind, and in horrors of conscience; nor in the hopes and fears of a future state; but in the immediate and conspicuous distribution of outward worldly prosperity and adversity.

The close correspondence, in all points, of the dispensation actually given, with the foregoing description, is no slight presumption that the object of that dispensation was, in part at least, such as we have supposed,—viz., to exhibit to mankind (that is, to those who should be in early times neighbours to the Israelites, or have any intercourse with them, and subsequently to us, and to all others who should read their history, and view their present fate); to exhibit, we say, a striking picture of God's moral government, —to convince all men of his superintending providence,—and to instruct them in the principles of justice, by which his dealings with them will be regulated.

We must, however, carefully keep in mind the distinction between an extraordinary providence, such as that under which the Israelites were placed, and the ordinary divine providence by which the world generally is governed, and which is sometimes called the " course of Nature."

God has appointed that, as a general rule, though not an invariable one, good conduct shall lead, on the whole, to temporal success and welfare, and ill conduct to misfortunes of various kinds. Thus, the *general* tendency of industry and frugality is to lead to prosperity; and of idleness, improvidence, and extravagance, to poverty and distress. Temperance conduces, on the whole, to health, and intemperance usually brings on disease and death. The quarrelsome, the hard-hearted, and the unjust, are likely to be hated or despised; while gentleness and kindness tend, in general, to procure a man the good-will of his neighbours; and (according to the proverb) in the long run, " honesty is the best policy."

Accordingly, in the ordinary course of events, we are generally able to *trace* men's good or ill success in life, to their good or ill conduct. For instance, when a man who has lived a life of sensuality and extravagance is ruined in health and in fortune, we can perceive the connection between his misery and the vice and folly that have *naturally* caused it. Or again, if an honest, industrious, and prudent man becomes rich, we say that this is according to the *natural* course of things. And so in other such cases. We do not mean, when we speak thus, that the " natural course of things " is *not* regulated by divine providence, but merely that such is the *ordinary*, established, and regular course of God's government of the universe.

On the other hand, when any occurrence is spoken of as " supernatural " (or " miraculous "), although the word " providential " is sometimes applied in the same sense, any one who believes that God is the supreme disposer of *all* events, cannot mean that such an occurrence is *more providential* than others, but merely that it belongs to God's *extraordinary* providence.

And in any such case we can trace no connection between the sin and the punishment, or between the good conduct and the reward, except so far as we learn it from *express revelation*. For instance, when Korah (Numb. xvi.) and his company were swallowed up by an earthquake, as a punishment for having " provoked the Lord," we know that this was a judgment on them for that sin, solely because Moses, by divine command, expressly declared the sin, and *foretold* the punishment.

And again, when the Israelites were defeated before Ai, as a judgment for the transgression of one of them (Josh. vii.), and when the land of the ten tribes was burnt up with drought, in the days of Ahab, as a punishment for their idolatry (1 Kings xvii.), we can trace no *natural* connection between the sin and the consequences of it ; and we know this connection only because we are expressly told it in Holy Scripture.

Would it not, then, be in the highest degree presumptuous for any one of us, uninspired men, to pronounce judgment on those who are cut off by sudden death, or who are visited by such calamities as an earthquake, a famine, or a pestilence? Shall we take upon ourselves to declare the counsels of the Most High, when He has *not* revealed them? and, in defiance of our Master's express warning, proclaim that these men *were* sinners above those who have escaped such a fate?

And yet some persons do occasionally presume, without any commission from Heaven, to pass judgment on their neighbours, and to declare that such and such a calamity is a mark of divine displeasure, and a punishment for such and such a sin.

Such men are like the false prophets of old—their language is, "Thus saith the Lord, when the Lord hath not spoken." Whatever high pretensions they may make, it is not piety, but daring *im*piety, thus to mimic the voice of God's inspired messengers, and to come forward, without any divine commission, setting forth their own fancies as revelations from Heaven. It is not wisdom from above, but gross ignorance of *both* the volumes which the same divine Author has opened for our instruction—the volume of *Nature*, and the volume of *Revelation*,—that leads men thus to confound the ordinary and the extraordinary dispensations of his Providence. *Some* design, no doubt, the Allwise Governor of the world must have, in all his dispensations, whether of sorrow or of joy. He sends want, and He sends abundance,—He allots affliction, and temporal deliverance and prosperity, not at random, but according to some fitness which He perceives in the respective parties, to be the recipients of these dispensations.

The hardships undergone by the Apostles, they were exposed to, we may be assured, for some good reason ; and so also, health, plenty, and every kind of temporal success, are doubtless bestowed with some wise design on those who obtain such advantages. But when He has not thought fit to reveal *what* his designs are, it is not for us, shortsighted mortals, to pronounce upon them, and presumptuously to usurp the office of his prophets. "Wherefore judge nothing," says the Apostle, "before the time, until the Lord come, who will bring to light the hidden things of darkness, and will make manifest the counsels of the hearts! and *then* shall every man have [his] praise* of God."

The notion, however, that calamity is *necessarily* a token of the divine displeasure, was one which the Jews very much clung to—and very naturally; inasmuch as that particular nation *had* been originally placed under such a system of temporal rewards and punishments. They found it hard to believe, therefore, in the change of that system, when the Gospel was preached. And accordingly, the sufferings and death undergone by Jesus and many of his disciples, formed the chief stumbling-block to the Jews (1 Cor. i. 23), most of whom would not believe that He could

---

* ὁ ἔπαινος: viz., whatever he is justly entitled to. The Greek article has the force of our pronoun.

4*

be the true Christ, or a favoured servant of God; because they regarded His *sufferings* as a proof of the divine *dis*favour.

And their objection to Him, on this very ground, was accordingly foretold by the Prophet Isaiah (Isa. liii.): "a man of sorrows and acquainted with grief; and we hid, as it were, our faces from Him:" "we did esteem Him stricken, *smitten of God* and afflicted," &c. &c.

It seems strange to us that so many of the Jews should refuse to be convinced by such prophecies as this. But it is much more strange that there should be some Christians, who, though professed followers of a Master who was crucified, still persist in regarding temporal calamities as a proof of the divine displeasure against those who are so visited; and that there should be Christians who presume, against their great Master's express prohibition, to declare what the sins are that have called down on their neighbours such calamities.

Some persons, however, there are, who carelessly use the words "providential" and "miraculous," merely to denote any thing *unusual* and strange. They talk of a "miraculous" escape from some danger, meaning merely a *wonderful* escape; and of a man's being delivered "providentially," when they mean only that the deliverance was striking and *remarkable.** But it is best to abstain from this loose

---

* The reason some give for *distinguishing* some particular events as "providential," is in truth a reason on the opposite side. An unexpected recovery from a disease which seemed hopeless, or a wonderful escape from a shipwreck, &c, is, they say, more *striking* to their minds,

kind of language, lest we should be understood to mean either that other events are *not* providential, and that God's government does not extend to the ordinary course of things; or else, that we—uninspired men—are permitted to decide (in cases where there is no evident miracle) what are the designs of the Most High, and what are the occurrences that do, and that do not, belong to his extraordinary dispensations.

The nation of Israel was, as we have said, placed under an extraordinary providence, which allotted to them victory or defeat,—plenty or famine,—and other temporal blessings and punishments, according to their conduct. And these were the rewards and punishments that formed the sanction of the Mosaic Law. As for a future state of retribution in another world, Moses said nothing to the Israelites about that. Whatever may at any time have been revealed to himself, and to some other highly favoured individuals, on that subject, it does not appear that he was commissioned to deliver to the people any revelation at all concerning a future state. This was reserved for a GREATER than Moses, and for a more glorious dispen-

and impresses them more with a sense of the goodness of Providence than ordinary occurrences.

Now, for this very reason, they should labour the more carefully to bring themselves to reflect on the *daily* benefits they receive from " Him in whom we live and move and have our being." The more prone we are to pass by with careless indifference our being preserved from *falling into* a dangerous sickness, or from *being* shipwrecked at all, the more we should study to bring our minds to dwell on such preservation; which is, in truth, *no less "providential"* than a man's being delivered *out of* a sickness or a shipwreck.

sation than his Law. For as we read in the Epistle to the Hebrews "the law *made nothing perfect;* but the *bringing in of a better hope* did" (Heb. x.)—namely, the promises given through "Jesus Christ, who brought life and immortality to light, *through the Gospel.*"

Why Moses was not instructed to reveal this momentous truth, is a question which will naturally occur to every one. It is a question which we are not competent completely to answer; because, as has been elsewhere observed, we cannot presume to explain why the Gospel was reserved for that precise period at which it was proclaimed. But *that* inquiry,—why a different and more imperfect dispensation was needful to prepare the way for the Gospel,—being waived, as one surpassing man's knowledge and powers, it is easy to perceive that the revelation of the doctrine in the Mosaic Law would have been neither necessary nor proper. It was not necessary for the purpose of affording a sanction to the Law of Moses, because the Israelites alone, of all the nations of the world, were, as we have seen, under an extraordinary providence.

The necessary foundation, therefore, of all religion, "that God is a *rewarder* of them that diligently seek him," did not require, as it must in all other nations, the belief in a future retribution, to remedy all the irregularities of God's ordinary providence, which among this peculiar people did not exist, at least in the same degree and form as among all others. Nor, again, would it have been proper for Moses, commissioned as he was to promulgate, not the Gospel, but the Law, to proclaim *that* life and immortality which the Gospel was destined to "bring to light;" much less, to represent eternal happiness as attainable *otherwise* than through the redemption by Christ, which the Gospel holds out as the only efficacious means of procuring it.

And accordingly it is observable that the slight hints of this doctrine which the books of the prophets contain—the faint dawnings, as it were, of a scheme which was to bring "life and immortality to light," and which appear more and more bright as they approached the period of that more perfect revelation, are in perfect consistency with the rule we have supposed Moses to have observed; since it is in proportion as they give more and more clear notices of the Redeemer to come, and in almost constant conjunction with their descriptions of his mission, that the immortal life, to which He was to open the road and lead the way, is alluded to by the prophets; and also in proportion as the *extraordinary* and regular administration of divine government in this world, by which the Law had been originally sanctioned, and under which the Jews had hitherto lived, was gradually withdrawn. That it was in these writings, and not in those of Moses, that the Jews must have sought for indications of a future state is strongly confirmed by the opinion of that celebrated and learned divine, Joseph Mede, who declares that he cannot tell on what Scripture authority the Jewish Church could have founded their belief in a future state, except the well-known passage in Daniel; and even of that, it may be observed, that it does not necessarily imply a resurrection of *all* men.   Doubtless it did not escape Mede that there are in the other prophets many allusions to a future state, which were so understood by the inspired authors themselves, as they are by us *Christian* readers; but it does not follow that the great mass of the people—any besides the studious and discerning few—would be able clearly to perceive such meaning, especially when a different interpretation of those very passages applicable to temporal deliverances, might, without destroying their sense, be adopted. Nothing appears to us more evident than the description in Isaiah, for instance, of a *suffering* Messiah; yet we well know that a prosperous and triumphant temporal prince was generally expected by the Jews, and that the frustration of this hope was the grand stumbling-block of the unbelieving among them.

So also many passages of the prophets, which convey to Christians, who have enjoyed the Gospel revelation, the intimation of a future state (at least in their secondary sense), might very easily be otherwise understood; or, at least, might appear not decisive, to those who lived before Jesus Christ had "*abolished death*, and brought life and immortality to light through the Gospel."

We are told, indeed, that even at a time long antecedent to that of Moses, Abraham "eagerly desired * to see the day of the Lord Jesus; and he saw it, and was glad."   In these words our Saviour is doubtless

* This is the exact sense of the original, ἠγαλλιάσατο, John viii. 56: though our version renders it "rejoiced;" but Abraham's *joy* is what is mentioned afterwards.

alluding to the sacrifice of Isaac, and to Abraham's being instructed on that occasion, that the transaction was a "*figure*" (Heb. xi. 19); representing the death and resurrection of Christ. But our Lord could not have meant that the revelation then made to Abraham was imparted by Moses to the whole nation of Israel.

It is highly probable, that both Moses himself, and Abraham, and other eminent and highly favoured servants of God in those days, received, more or less, revelations of several things which they were not commissioned to impart to all the people.* And among other things, it is likely they were taught something concerning the resurrection, and concerning Him who was to procure it. And accordingly we find the very same Apostle who speaks of the Gospel as "bringing in a better hope" than was in the *Law*, speaking also of some of the Patriarchs as "looking for a better country, that is, a heavenly." (Heb. xi. 16.)

But when we look to what Moses wrote, by divine command, for *the instruction and guidance of the Israelites*, and as belonging to the Law—the dispensation committed to him—we find him dwelling very fully, and minutely, and earnestly, on the temporal rewards and temporal punishments they were to look for; saying nothing at all about a resurrection and a day of judgment in the next world.

Many persons however are accustomed, in speaking of the present subject, to confound together two very

* The eminently pious king, Hezekiah, however, seems to have had no idea, at least at the time when he composed his hymn (2 Kings xx.), of any future state.

different questions: (1.) What was the actual belief of the Jews—or of some particular Jews—on this or that point? and, (2.) What was *revealed* to them in the LAW? No unprejudiced reader of that, can think that Moses designed to teach, therein, the doctrine of a future state of rewards and punishments as the sanction of his Law.

On the actual belief, indeed, of the great mass of the Israelites, we have no means of deciding positively; but if any one should suppose most of them to have thought little or nothing, one way or the other, about what should become of them after death, nor, consequently, to have either believed or disbelieved, properly speaking, the doctrine in question, his conjecture certainly would not be at variance with the representations Moses gives of the grossness of ideas, and puerile shortsightedness of the nation; who, while fed by a daily miracle, and promised the especial favour of the Maker of the universe, had their minds set on "the flesh-pots of Egypt, and the fish, and the cucumbers, and the leeks." Christians of these days are not surely *more* gross-minded and unthinking than those Israelites; yet a large proportion of *them* require to be incessantly reminded that this life is not the whole of their existence; though the doctrine be one which is expressly declared in their religion; and silence on that subject is quite sufficient, if not to eradicate from their minds all *belief*, at least to put an end to all *thought*, about the matter.

There is no doubt, however, that some considerable time before our Lord's advent, the belief in a future state did become prevalent (though, as the case of the Sadducees proves, not *universal*) among the Jews. In the Second Book of Maccabees, a work of small authority, indeed, as a history, but affording sufficient evidence of the opinions of the writer and his contemporaries, we find not only unequivocal mention of the doctrine (though by the way not as an *undisputed* point), but persons represented as *actuated by the motives* which such a doctrine naturally suggests; which doubtless we should, sometimes at least, have met with also in the historical books of the Old Testament, had the same belief prevailed all along.

And our Lord himself alludes to the prevailing opinion of the generality of those whom he addresses: "Search" (or Ye search*) " the Scriptures, for in them *ye think* ye have eternal life, and they are they that testify of me;" as much as to say, the very prophets who allude to the doctrine of eternal life, do likewise foretell the coming and describe the character of me, the Bestower of it; these two parts of their inspired word hang together; he who is blind to the one, can found no *rational* hope on the other; since " I am the way, and the truth, and the life;" and " he that hath the Son hath life, and he that hath not the Son, hath not life." This passage, indeed, as well as the others to the same purpose in the New Testament, though they imply the prevalence of this tenet among the Jews, and the general *sincerity* and *strength* of their conviction, do not at all imply either that this, their

---

* The word in the original, ἐρευνᾶτε, may bear either an imperative or an indicative sense.

confident expectation, was *well-founded* on Scriptural evidence, or that their notions respecting a future life were *correct.*   Had these last two circumstances been superadded (which is evidently impossible) to the general sincere reception of the doctrine, it could not have been said with any propriety, that "Christ *brought life and immortality to light* through the Gospel."

The truth probably is, that as the indications of a future state which are to be found in the prophets, are mostly such as will admit of an interpretation referring them to a promise of temporal deliverance, those persons would most naturally so understand them, in the first instance at least, who were so "slow of heart" as to the prophecies respecting the Messiah, as to expect in Him a glorious *temporal* prince only; while those who were more intelligent, and took in the spiritual sense of the prophecies relating to *Him,* would be led to put the spiritual interpretation on the other also. We say in the *first instance;* because when the belief of a future state had been introduced, from whatever quarter, and did prevail, all who held it would naturally interpret in that sense whatever passages in their Scriptures seemed to confirm it.   But it does not follow that such a belief was correct, even when supported by an appeal to passages of Scripture which really do relate to the doctrine in question; for if one part of a scheme be understood literally and carnally, and another part spiritually, the result will be a most erroneous compound; if eternal life be understood to be promised, but the character and kingdom of Christ, who was to bring it to light and procure it, be misunderstood, the faith thus formed will be essentially incorrect.

So far, then, as any of the Jews disjoined the prophetic annunciations of immortality from those relating to the spiritual kingdom of Christ, and looked for eternal rewards as earned by obedience to the Mosaic Law, so far their expectations were groundless, their faith erroneous; even though resting on the authority of such parts of Scripture as, in a different sense, do relate to the doctrine in question.

It is highly probable, however, that the belief of a future state, as it prevailed among the Jews in our Lord's time, and for a considerable period after, was not, properly speaking, *drawn* from their Scriptures, in the first instance; was not *founded* on the few faint hints to be met with in their prophets, though these were afterwards called in to *support* it; but was the gradual result of a combination of other causes with these imperfect revelations. For otherwise, one would expect that there would have been some notice in the Books of Ezra and Nehemiah (written after all the most important prophecies had been delivered) of so mighty a revolution having taken place in the minds of the Jews of their time, as a change from ignorance to a full conviction, on so momentous a point, by a supposed decisive revelation.

Respecting the details of the rise and prevalence of the doctrine of a future state among the great majority of the Jews, the scantiness of historical authority leaves us chiefly to our own conjectures. Without entering at large into a disquisition which must, after all, be obscured by much uncertainty, it may be allowable to suggest, that the Jews were likely to be much influenced by the *probable* arguments which their own reason partly supplied, and which they partly learned from the neighbouring nations, with whom (and with some of the more intelligent and enlightened of them) they had much more, and much more extensive, intercourse after the captivity than before. Nor does such a supposition militate, as might at first sight be suspected, against what has been elsewhere advanced respecting the prevailing disbelief, among the heathen, of the popular fables of Elysium and Tartarus, and respecting the emptiness of the pretended immortality of the soul, held by philosophers. For whatever their belief might be, they would be likely, in any discussion with their Jewish neighbours, to set forth either such arguments as occurred to them in favour of a future retribution, which undoubtedly was a part of the religion they professed, or such pretended proofs of the natural and necessary immortality of the soul, as their schools supplied. And such discussions we cannot but suppose must have been frequent; since the intercourse of the dispersed Jews with the Gentiles was such as to lead to the disuse of their own language, and the consequent necessity of a translation of their Scriptures into Greek. Now the Jews, who claimed to be favoured with an authentic revelation of God's will, and to be his peculiar People, could not have been satisfied to rest their pretensions to such superiority, and their boast of its advantages, on the extraordinary providence under which their *ancestors* had lived, but which seems to have been nearly, if not entirely, withdrawn from themselves; but would be likely to set up a rival claim to that of the Pagan religions, and to produce from their Scriptures every thing that might seem to favour the hope of a future reward. And this, not insincerely; for the very circumstance of the withdrawing of that miraculous providence under which their nation had formerly lived, would lead them to the expectation of something beyond the grave to compensate the loss. God's moral government of *their* nation, at least, they were assured of from their own past history; and if He had formerly been "a rewarder of them that diligently seek Him," they would perceive an improbability of his ceasing to be so; though in *this* world the "just recompense of reward" was evidently no longer to be looked for. It was to be expected, therefore, that they should be more inclined to believe sincerely in a future retribution than the Pagans, who had not the same experimental assurance that the Deity is indeed the moral Governor and Judge of mankind.

Some, however, make a careless use of those common words "know" and "believe." When discussing questions as to what was "believed" by such and such persons, they sometimes speak as if there were but these two states of mind,—to believe a certain doctrine, or to disbelieve it; forgetting, apparently, that belief admits of many different *degrees*, from a mere presumption, up to the most perfect confidence. Yet every one's own experience might teach him this.

For we commonly say, "I *believe* so and so is the case, but I am not *quite sure.*" Some again, when they speak of what was "known" to the Pagans, or to the Jews, seem to forget that the word "knowledge" implics three things;—(1.) *Confident belief;* (2.) of what is *true;* (3.) on sufficient *evidence.* For no one could be said to *know* any thing that was not true. And again, if any one had before him one of Euclid's demonstrations, he would not be said to *know* the conclusion (though a truth in reality fully proved) if he himself felt at all *doubtful* about it. And lastly, suppose two persons were quite positive, the one that the moon is inhabited, and the other that it is uninhabited, neither would be said to know the truth of his opinion; because, though one or the other must be, in fact, true, there is no sufficient *proof* of either.

It would be unsuitable to our present purpose—even if space admitted—to examine all the passages in the Books of Moses which have been interpreted as relating to a future state; it may be needful, however, to say a few words respecting that one which is cited by our Lord himself against the Sadducees, in proof of the doctrine: "Now, that the dead are raised," says He, "even Moses shewed at the bush, when he saith, 'I am the God of Abraham, and the God of Isaac, and the God of Jacob; He is not the God of the dead, but of the living; for all live unto Him.'" (Luke xx. 37.)

Now this passage is sometimes misunderstood, though the meaning of Jesus is sufficiently plain to an attentive reader of common intelligence. There was a dispute between two parties, whether there were or were not to be a resurrection. They had both of them heard of the doctrine, and had been accustomed to debate the question. And He refers them to a passage which, *to men so circumstanced*, would afford an argument in favour of the doctrine. But Jesus does not say that Moses designed in this passage to *reveal* the doctrine to the unreflecting and gross-minded people he was instructing; or that for *that* purpose those words were sufficient. No man of common sense—much less an inspired lawgiver, such as Moses—would have entrusted so important a revelation to one, slight, obscure, and incidental hint—so slight that the passage seems to have quite escaped the notice of the Pharisees when disputing with the Sadducees on this very point.

Had Moses been commissioned to teach the Israelites that they were all to rise from the dead, and to stand before God's judgment-seat, and be rewarded or punished in another world, according as they had obeyed or disobeyed the Law he was delivering, he would not, we may be sure, have thought it sufficient for this purpose, to record the words, "I am the God of Abraham, Isaac, and Jacob." He would, doubtless, have dwelt on the rewards and punishments of a future state even *more* copiously and more strongly than he does on the temporal rewards and punishments which he does set before them.

For, let it be considered, that as the condition of the departed is *unseen*, and as the rewards and punishments of a future life are not only comparatively *remote*, but also must be considered as of a nature very *different* from any thing we can have experienced; from all these causes, it is found necessary that the most repeated assurances and admonitions should be employed, even towards those who have received the doctrine on the most satisfactory authority. A Christian minister, accordingly, in these days, finds that his hearers require to be perpetually reminded of this truth, to which they have long since given their assent; and that even, with all the pains he takes to inculcate it, in every different mode, he is still but very partially successful in drawing off men's attention from the things of this world, and fixing it on the "*unseen* things that are eternal." Much more must this have been the case with the Israelites whom Moses was addressing, who were so dull and gross-minded, so childishly shortsighted and sensual, that even the immediate miraculous presence of God among them, of whose judgments and deliverances they had been eye-witnesses, was insufficient to keep them steady in their allegiance to Him. Even the temporal sanctions of the Law,—the plenty and famine—the victory and defeat, and all the other points of that alternative of worldly prosperity and adversity which was set before them—things in their nature so much more easily comprehended by an unthinking and barbarous people, and so much more suited to their tastes—it was found necessary to detail with the utmost minuteness, and to repeat and remind them of in the most impressive manner, in a vast number of different passages. (See Exod. xv. 26; xx. 12; xxiii. 20;—Lev. xxv. 17;

xxvi. 3;—Numb. xiv. 20; xxxii. 10; xxxiii. 55;—
Deut. i. 35; iv. 1; v. 29; vi. 2; vii. 12; viii. 1; xi. 8;
xv. 4; xvi. 20; xvii. 19; xxviii. 1; xxix. 22;
xxx. 1; xxxi. 16; xxxii. 23–43.)

Is not, then, the conclusion inevitable, that if to
such a people the doctrine of future retribution had
been to be revealed, or any traditional knowledge of
it confirmed, we should have found it still more
explicitly stated, and still more frequently repeated?
And when, instead of anything like this, we have set
before us a few scattered texts, which, it is contended,
allude to or imply this doctrine, can it be necessary
even to examine whether they are rightly so interpreted? Surely it is a sufficient reply to say, that if
Moses had intended to inculcate such a doctrine, he
would have clearly stated and dwelt on it in almost
every page. Nor is it easy to conceive, how any man
of even ordinary intelligence, and not blinded by
devoted attachment to an hypothesis, can attentively
peruse the Books of the Law, abounding as they do
with such copious descriptions of the temporal rewards
and punishments (in their own nature so palpable),
which sanctioned that Law, and with such earnest
admonitions grounded on that sanction, and yet can
bring himself seriously to believe, that the doctrine
of a state of retribution after death (which, it cannot
be contended, is even mentioned, however slightly, in
more than a very few passages) formed a part of the
Mosaic revelation.

It deserves to be remarked here how strong an
internal evidence of the truth of what Moses wrote, is

afforded by the fact, that he thus represented the sanction of his Law as consisting of temporal rewards and punishments only.

For had he been a false pretender, he would have known that he could not secure the constant *fulfilment* of his promises and threats. And his imposture would have been detected, when men found that they were not regularly rewarded and punished according as they obeyed or disobeyed his law. We may be sure, therefore, that a crafty impostor would not have trusted entirely to promises and threats of temporal goods and evils alone. He would, doubtless, have taught the Israelites to look for a state of future retribution also ; which was done by the ancient heathen law-givers. Most of these, probably, did not themselves believe in what they taught about Elysium and Tartarus; but they judged it wise to try to make their people believe it, for the sake of keeping them in awe. And they knew that the falsity of their promises and threats respecting *another world* could not be detected by *experience.*

And Moses, no doubt, would have proceeded in the same manner, had he been a pretender. But he was fully convinced that the Israelites really did live under that miraculous Providence which he described. And their own experience taught them that what he said was true. (Deut. iv. 3, 4.)

As for the particulars of all the various instructions given to the Israelites, both by Moses and by the other writers of what is called the Old Testament, these are to be learned only from a careful study of the se books themselves. Our present design was merely to give a sketch of the general character of what is called the Mosaic Dispensation, especially as to the points wherein it differs from other religious systems.

It is to be borne in mind, then—1*st*, That it was designed for one People alone, though it was preparatory to a religion intended for all the world; and its ordinances accordingly are not at all binding on us; 2*dly*, It was full of very minute directions and regulations, designed, partly to keep the Israelites separate from the Gentiles, and faithful to the true God, but partly, by their hidden typical meaning, to foreshew and prepare the way for the Gospel revelation; 3*dly*, It was a theocracy; a system of direct, special, temporal government by God's extraordinary providence. And accordingly, the sanction of the Mosaic Law was not the rewards and punishments of a future state, but temporal blessings and judgments.

These are the points which it is the most important to keep clearly and constantly before the mind; for this reason among others: That mistaken notions on some of these points may endanger a man's christian faith, by giving rise to difficulties and objections much greater, than our religion—such as it really is—can ever be exposed to.

Objections there are, indeed, to which no complete answer can be given, except by shewing that there are much *stronger* objections on the opposite side. But none of the objections to the christian revelation, *such as it was really given*, are so strong as those brought against what it is sometimes *erroneously represented* to be.

Suppose, for instance, any one is taught to believe, as a part of his religion, that some portion of the Mosaic Law is binding on Christians; although the persons who teach this are far from being all of them agreed as to which precepts are binding, and which not; and although the Apostle Paul speaks most clearly of the Gentiles as not being at all "under the Law" (Rom. vi. 14), he would find in this a difficulty which is caused entirely by a misapprehension of Scripture.

Again, suppose a man to have taken up the notion that temporal blessings and calamities are now a sign of the Divine favour or displeasure towards individuals or nations, and that whenever some great calamity occurs, we are at liberty to declare that such and such a sin has called down the divine vengeance, this leaves an opening for objections which can never be got over; for he sees that bad men often escape such temporal calamities, while much better men are exposed to them; and he knows also that Jesus Christ and his apostles endured great affliction in this world, and were rejected by the Jews on that very ground. So that this doctrine would make Scripture contradictory both to itself and to daily experience.

And again, if he is taught that Moses was commissioned to reveal to the Israelites the doctrine of a resurrection, he will not be able to answer an infidel who may point out to him how very imperfectly (at best) the Books of Moses accomplish this purpose;

and also, how completely at variance this is with the declaration that "Jesus Christ brought life and immortality to light." So that here, again, Scripture will be made to contradict itself.

All these will be great stumbling-blocks to the Christian. But when we look to the plain meaning of the Sacred Books, without attending to the fanciful theories of uninspired men, all these difficulties vanish.

As for the question, what will be the lot, in another world, of those Jews or Pagans who never heard of the Gospel, the only answer is, that the Gospel revelation contains instructions designed for those who *have* heard the Gospel, as to what their duty is, in living according to it themselves, and doing their best to impart it to others.

As for those whom Providence has shut out from the knowledge of it, all inquiries respecting *them* must be answered as our Lord answered Peter's inquiry what was to be the fate of the Apostle John: "What is that to thee? follow thou me." (John xxi. 21, 22.)

INTRODUCTION OF THE GOSPEL.

ALTHOUGH the Jews were in eager expectation at the time when the Lord Jesus appeared, of an ANOINTED Saviour (Messiah or CHRIST),* whom the predictions of their prophets had taught them to expect about that time, they did not expect Him to introduce anything that could be called a *new* religion; but rather to confirm and extend through the world the Mosaic Law. And this, it is well known, is what the unconverted Jews of this day expect.

Yet some of the prophecies relating to the Christ's kingdom, do contain allusions to the introduction of a *new* religion, distinct from that taught by Moses. The most decisive of these prophecies, in relation to this point, is that of Jeremiah,—"Behold the days come [are coming] saith the Lord, that I will make a NEW COVENANT with the House of Israel * * * * not *according to the covenant* that *I made with their fathers*," &c.

Now the system of divine Laws under which the

---

* These words signify in the Hebrew and the Greek "The Anointed," from the ancient practice of anointing a *king*, or a *priest*, or a *prophet*, as a part of the ceremony of appointing him to his office.

Israelites lived, is, in the Books of Moses, always called (in our version) the "Covenant" which the Lord made with them. And in the Gospels and the Apostolic Epistles, the same word (in the Greek) is always applied to the christian system.

This, however, is likely to escape the notice of the mere English reader; because, in our version, the very same word *Diathekè* which, *in reference to the Mosaic Law*, is generally rendered COVENANT, is translated—when it has reference to the *Gospel*—by the word TESTAMENT.* And even in the very

---

* Yet in Gal. iii. 15–19, it is translated Covenant, and what is more remarkable, the very same words in the original are translated, Heb. viii. 6, "Mediator of a *Covenant*," and in Heb. ix. 15, "Mediator of a *Testament*."

It would be unsuitable in a work of this kind, to enter on the discussion of the interpretation of a disputed text, but it may be remarked :—

I. That the passage in Exod. xxiv., which is cited in Heb. ix., ought to have been translated in both by the same English words.

II. That though *we* are accustomed to connect the idea of a covenant [compact] with signing and sealing, and not with any *death* of a sacrificed victim; and again, are familiar with the idea of a man's bequeathing his property by a *will*, which is to take effect after his death,—with the Jews it was the reverse. They (as well as many other ancient nations, as may be seen in many passages of Homer) were accustomed to see every covenant ratified by the blood of a victim. And, on the other hand, *Wills* they had none; since the Mosaic Law disposed of a man's property at his death. Accordingly, no one, in writing to *Hebrews* (even though speaking of the Gospel alone), would have been likely to introduce a reference to Wills. But,—

III. The writer is evidently drawing a parallel between *the Mosaic Law* and the *Gospel.* Now the *Law* was not at all of the nature of

passage of Exodus (xxiv. 8) which is cited in the ninth chapter of the Epistle to the Hebrews, the very words which our translators had before rendered "*Covenant,*" they have changed into "*Testament.*" (Heb. ix. 20.) And yet the word is so far from having different meanings in reference to the *Law* and to the *Gospel,* that, on the contrary, both the Lord Jesus Himself and his Apostles most plainly draw a *parallel* between the two, and point out the circumstances of the former Covenants as types and shadows of the Gospel Dispensation.

In particular, it was anciently the universal practice to ratify and sanction every kind of *Covenant* by the sacrifice of a *victim,* the shedding of whose blood was a necessary ceremony, so this took place in both cases.

Moses, on the occasion of the establishment of the LAW, offered a sacrifice, and sprinkled the blood of the victim on the people; saying, "This is the blood of the Covenant (Exod. xxiv. 8) [Testament] (Heb. ix. 20) which the Lord hath made with you." And

a Will [Testament], not being bequeathed by Moses at his *death*, but fully established forty years before. And accordingly,

IV. We may observe, that, in the passage before us, the parallel drawn is not between Christ and *Moses*, but between Christ and the *victim* slain by Moses as the ratifier of the Covenant.

To speak of the death of a "Testator," therefore, totally destroys the parallel which plainly was in the writer's mind, and makes the whole passage unmeaning. But when the *death* spoken of is understood of the death of the sacrificed victim—even Jesus Christ, who offered Himself to die in our stead, and for our deliverance, the parallel which the writer is dwelling on becomes intelligible and striking.

the Lord Jesus, at the Last Supper, when about to offer up Himself as a sacrifice, says, on giving to the disciples the wine which represented his blood, that is, his life, "This cup is the new Testament [Covenant] in my blood, which is shed for you."

The word Testament, therefore, whenever it occurs in Scripture, is always to be understood in the sense of " *Covenant* " [or " Dispensation"].

The Christian religion, then, though springing out of the Mosaic, of which it was the fulfilment and completion,* yet was in itself a *new* Religion. It was the *fruit*, of which the Mosaic Dispensation was the *blossom*. And it was as distinct from it, and in many respects unlike it, as a fruit compared with the blossom which precedes it and produces it.

The chief points which distinguish the Christian Dispensation from the Mosaic, are these three: 1. *Spirituality ;* 2. *Universality ;* and, 3. *Unity.* The new kingdom of God was to be "not of this world," but *spiritual ;* it was to be open to *all* mankind as its subjects; and it was to admit all of them to *equal* privileges.

The former kingdom of God was a kingdom of this world. The Lord was, as has already been pointed out, not only the God, but the *temporal Ruler* of the Israelites ; prescribing to them not only the religious rites with which He was to be worshipped, but also the civil regulations under which they were to live,

---

* " I am not come," says our Lord, " to destroy the Law and the Prophets, but to fulfil."

and enforcing obedience by temporal rewards and penalties.

Jesus Christ, on the contrary, refused an earthly kingdom, when attempts were made to force it on Him, and declared that "his kingdom was not of this world." He disclaimed all right to interfere in temporal concerns; saying to one who wished Him to decide between him and his brother, "Who made me a judge or a divider over you?" He bid his hearers submit to the civil government of the Romans, saying, " Render to Cæsar the things that are Cæsar's, and to God the things that are God's." And, so far from promising victory, and long life, and worldly prosperity, to his followers, as a reward of their obedience to Him, He prepared them for suffering and death in his cause; even such as He endured Himself; and pronounced them "blessed when men should hate and persecute" them for His sake, saying, " great is your reward in heaven."

For, the rewards and punishments which formed the sanction of this New Dispensation were those of the next world, and those only. Jesus rebuked his disciples for proposing, in their zeal for his honour, to call down fire from heaven on a village which had rejected Him; as the Prophet Elias [Elijah] had been divinely commissioned to do, under the old dispensation. (Luke ix. 54.) Jesus reproved them, as "not knowing what manner of spirit *they* were of," He having " come not to destroy men's lives, but to save."

But this was not from his regarding a rejection of Him as *more pardonable* than the sins of those who

had lived before the days of the Gospel. He taught
the reverse of this. For shortly after, when He sent
out seventy disciples to preach the Gospel, He denounced *heavier* judgments than what had fallen on
sinners of old, against such as should reject that Gospel. "It shall be *more tolerable*," said He, "for Sodom
and Gomorrah" (which did suffer destruction by fire
from heaven) "in the day of judgment, than for that
city." And while He forewarned His disciples that
"in the world they would have tribulation," He promised to the faithful Christian "to raise him up at the
last day," and to "prepare a place" for such, in his
"Father's house."

Thus different was the New Dispensation from the
Old, in respect of the *rewards and punishments* which
formed the sanction of each.

The *Worship* also that was required under the Gospel, was of a more spiritual character than that prescribed by the Law.

It is true, the Israelites were commanded to "love
the Lord their God, with all their heart, and with all
their soul, and with all their strength." But a great
part of their service of Him consisted (as the Apostle
Paul expresses it) "in meats and drinks, and *carnal*
ordinances"—that is, outward bodily acts; most of
which had (as has been before observed) an inward
hidden signification in reference to the Gospel.

Jesus, on the contrary, tells the woman of Samaria,
that the time is at hand "when the true worshippers
shall, neither on Mount Gerizim, nor at Jerusalem,
worship the Father;" but that they "shall worship

Him in spirit and in truth." (John iv. 23.) What He means by worshipping in *truth*, and what the Apostle means by saying that "the law was given by Moses, but grace and *truth* came by Jesus Christ" (John i. 17), is, not that the Mosaic religion was not *true*, but that its ordinances contained the *shadow* of that of which the Gospel contains the substance. The *truth* of the Gospel is not (in reference to the Law) truth as opposed to *falsehood*, but *reality*, as contrasted with *shadows* and figurative representations. Thus, we read in the Epistle to the Hebrews, "If the blood of bulls and goats, &c., sanctify to the *purifying of the flesh*" (that is, remove *ceremonial* impurity, so as to enable a man to attend the assemblies of worshippers), "how much more shall the blood of Christ purify your conscience from dead works."

In the Mosaic religion, the number is very great of what may be not improperly called "Sacraments." For a large portion of the very numerous ordinances of the LAW—the various sacrifices, purifyings, and other ceremonial observances,—were of the nature of what *we* call Sacraments—that is, outward visible signs [figures], divinely appointed, and having an inward meaning connected with religion. The worship, in short, of the Israelites, may be considered as almost made up of Sacraments.

But a great part of the inward signification of these Sacraments was hidden from the worshippers; though they were taught that a divine blessing would accompany their observance of those rites, in pious obedience to the Lord. In the Passover, for instance, all that they understood as signified in that ordinance, was the commemoration of their deliverance from the plague which slew the Egyptians. But the more important part of its signification, the sacrifice of the true "Lamb of God, who taketh away the sin of the world," was not made known till the Gospel revelation appeared.

Under the Gospel, on the contrary, the religious rites instituted by Christ himself were only the Sacraments of Baptism and the Lord's Supper: the one for the admission of members into his Church, and the other to commemorate his death for man's redemption, and to represent our partaking of his Spirit. The one Sacrament denotes the spiritual *Birth* of the Christian; the other, the *continued support* of his Spiritual *Life.**

And the signification of these two ordinances is much more clearly and fully explained to Christians in the New Testament Scriptures, than the signification of the Mosaic ordinances was in the Law. And moreover, the directions given as to the mode of observing these ordinances, are much less minute and particular than those given by Moses. For instance, there is nothing said in Scripture as to the use of *leavened* or unleavened bread at the Lord's Table;— or the posture of the communicants, or the words to be used, &c. These particulars, and also all other forms

---

* John vi. 48–63. See also 1 Cor. xii. 13, where the Apostle gives exactly the above view of the two Sacraments, saying, "By one Spirit ye are all baptized into one Body . . . and have been all *made to drink* into one Spirit."

and ceremonies for religious worship, Jesus left to be regulated in and by each Church from time to time, with merely the general direction from the Apostles, " Let all things be done to edifying."

Under the LAW, in short, the worship prescribed contained a great number of *outward acts*, striking to the senses, and according to forms which were precisely laid down ; while the *inward signification* of those forms was obscure and partially hidden. Under the Gospel, on the contrary, the worship prescribed was more spiritual ; the external acts (as far as enjoined by Christ himself) being very few and simple, and without any precise directions as to the forms of them ; while the inward signification of them is plainly made known.

And in what relates to *moral conduct* also, the precepts given under the New Covenant, are much less numerous and less precise than those of the LAW. Not that Christians were meant to be less scrupulously careful in leading a virtuous life than the Israelites ; but that they are left to regulate their conduct by the PRINCIPLES of the Gospel, according to the best of their own judgment, instead of having a multitude of precise *precepts* laid down for their guidance.

Just as the christian worship was left to be regulated as to its FORMS, from time to time, by each Church, under the *general principle* of all " being done to edifying," even so christian *practice* was left to be regulated by Christians themselves, in conformity with Gospel *principles*, and the examples set before us by Christ and his Apostles.

Thus not only does the Gospel require a morality in many respects higher and more perfect in itself than the Law, but it places morality universally on higher grounds.

Gratitude for the redeeming love of God in Christ, with mingled veneration and affection for the person of our great Master, and an exalted emulation, leading us to tread in his steps,—an ardent longing to behold his glories and to enjoy his presence in the world to come,—with an earnest effort to prepare for that better world,—love towards our brethren for His sake who died for us and them,—and, above all, the thought that the Christian is a part of " the temple of the Holy Ghost " who dwelleth in the Church,—even the Spirit of Christ, " without which we are none of His," a temple which we are bound to keep undefiled; —these, and such as these, are the sublime principles of morality, into a conformity with which the Christian is to fashion his heart and his life; and they are such principles as the Mosaic dispensation could not furnish.

The Israelites, as not only living under a revelation which had but a shadow of the good things of the Gospel, but also as a dull and gross-minded, and imperfectly civilized people, in a condition corresponding to that of childhood, were in few things left to their own moral discretion, but were furnished with precise rules in most points of conduct. These answered to the exact regulations under which children are necessarily placed, and which are gradually relaxed as they advance towards maturity; not by any means on the ground that good conduct is less required of *men* than children; but that they are expected to be more capable of regulating their own conduct by their *own* discretion, and of acting upon principle.

When, then, the Mosaic code was abolished, we find no other *system of rules* substituted in its place. Our Lord and His Apostles enforced such duties as were the most liable to be neglected,—corrected some prevailing errors,—gave some particular directions which particular occasions called for,—but laid down no set of *rules* for the conduct of a Christian: they laid down christian *principles* instead; they sought to implant christian dispositions. And this is the more remarkable, inasmuch as we may be sure, from the nature of man, that precise regulations, even though somewhat tedious to learn, and burdensome to observe, would have been highly acceptable to their converts. Hardly any restraint is so irksome to man (*i.e.* to "the natural man") as to be left to his own discretion, yet still required to regulate his conduct according to certain principles, and to steer his course through the intricate channels of life, with a constant vigilant exercise of his moral judgment. It is much more agreeable to human indolence (though at first sight the contrary might be supposed) to have a complete system of laws laid down, which are to be observed according to the letter, not to the spirit,—and which, as long as a man adheres to them, afford both a consolatory assurance of safety, and an unrestrained liberty as to every point not determined by them,—than to be called upon for incessant watchfulness,—careful and candid self-examination,—and studious cultivation of certain moral dispositions.

Accordingly, most, if not all systems of man's devising (whether corruptions of Christianity, or built on any other foundation) will be found, even in what appear their most rigid enactments, to be accommodated to this tendency of the human heart. When Mahomet, for instance, enjoined on his disciples a strict fast during a certain period, and an entire abstinence from wine and from games of chance, and the devotion of a precise portion of their property to the poor, leaving them at liberty, generally, to follow their own sensual and worldly inclinations, he imposed a far less severe task on them, than if he had required them constantly to control their appetites and passions, to repress covetousness, and to be uniformly temperate, charitable, and heavenly-minded. And had Paul been (as a false teacher always will be) disposed to comply with the expectations and wishes which his disciples would naturally form, he would doubtless have referred them to some part of the Mosaic Law as their standard of morality, or would have substituted some other system of rules in its place. Indeed, there is strong reason to think (especially from what we find in 1st Corinthians), that something of this nature had actually been desired of him. He seems to have been applied to for more precise rules than he was willing to give; particularly as to the lawfulness of going to idol-feasts, and as to several points relative to marriage and celibacy; concerning which and other matters, he gives briefly such directions as the occasion rendered indispensable, but breaks off into exhortations to "use this world as not abusing it;" and speedily recurs to the general description of the christian character, and the inculcation of christian principles. He will not be induced to enter into minute details of things forbidden and permitted,—enjoined and dispensed with; and even when most occupied in repelling the suspicion that Gospel liberty exempts the Christian from moral obligation, instead of retaining or framing anew any system of prohibitions and injunctions, he urges upon his hearers the very consideration of their being exempt from any such childish trammels, as a reason for their aiming at a more perfect holiness of life, on purer and more generous motives: "Sin," he says, "shall not have dominion over you; for *ye are not under the law but under grace:*" and he perpetually incites them to walk worthy of their vocation, on the ground of their being "bought with a price," and bound to "live unto Him who died for them;"—"as risen with Christ" to a new life of holiness,—exhorted to "set their affection on things above, not on things on the earth;"—as "living sacrifices" to God;—as "the temple of the Holy Ghost," called upon to keep God's dwelling-place undefiled, and to abound in all "the fruits of the Spirit," and as "being delivered from the Law, that we should serve in newness of the Spirit, and not in the oldness of the letter."

He who seeks, then (as many are disposed to do), either in the Old Testament, or in the New, for a precise code of laws by which to regulate his conduct, mistakes the character of our religion. It is indeed an error, and a ruinous one, to think that we may "continue in sin, because we are not under the law but under grace;" but it is also an error, and a far commoner one, to inquire of the Scriptures, in each case that may occur, what we are strictly bound to do or to abstain from, and to feel secure as long as we transgress no distinct commandment. But he who seeks with sincerity for christian *principles* will not fail to find them. If we endeavour, with the aid of the Holy Spirit, to trace on our own heart the delineation of the christian character which the Scriptures present, and to conform all our actions, and words, and thoughts, to that character, our heavenly Teacher will enable us to have a right judgment in all things, and we shall be "led by the Spirit" of Christ to follow *his* steps, and to "purify ourselves even as He is pure;" that when He shall appear, we may be made like unto Him, and may behold Him as He is.

Besides Spirituality, another striking feature of the Christian Dispensation, as contrasted with the Mosaic, is its UNIVERSALITY. It was to be *unlimited*, both in *time* and in *place*.* The Mosaic Law being only a preparation for the Gospel, was to come *to an*

---

* Hence the term Catholic (καθολικὴ—universal) is applied to the Christian Church—specially in opposition to the Jewish. It may be remarked, by the way, that the term Roman Catholic does, in strictness of speech, imply a contradiction,—Roman suggesting a necessary connexion with one place, while Catholic denotes having *no* necessary connexion with any one place more than another.

end on the establishment of the new Kingdom of Heaven, which is to *continue* to the end of the world.

And again, the Old Dispensation was designed for *one* nation; the New for *all* nations. The "People of God" was henceforth to comprise, not merely the "seed of Abraham after the flesh," but all mankind, as many as would embrace the Gospel. "As many as received Him" (Jesus Christ), "to them gave He power to become the Sons of God." (John i.) The language of Moses, and of those who came after him under the Law, was, "What nation is there so great, that hath God so nigh unto them, as the Lord our God is, in all things that we call upon Him for?" and "He hath not dealt so with any nation; neither have the heathen knowledge of his laws." The language of Jesus Christ and his Apostles was, "Go ye into all the world, and preach the Gospel to every creature:" "Go and teach (make disciples of) all nations:" "There is neither Jew, nor Greek, barbarian, Scythian, bond, or free." And in writing to Gentile believers, the Apostle calls them (Gal. vi. 16) "the Israel of God;" and says, "if ye are Christ's, then are ye Abraham's seed, and heirs according to the promise." (Gal. iii. 29.)

Hence it was, no doubt, that the Apostles never applied the term "Christians"* to the members of any

* The word Christian (Χριστιανός) occurs but three times in the New Testament, Acts xi. 26, xxvi. 28; 1 Peter iv. 16.—In no one of these places do we find it *applied by Christians themselves to one another*. It is mentioned as a name first given to the disciples at Antioch in Syria, doubtless by the Romans, as the word is of Latin formation. King

church. It was not, of course, that they were ashamed of it: but they seem to have chosen not to adopt any *new* title, but to confine themselves to those which had been applied to God's People of old; in order to point out that He had now admitted Gentiles into the number.

The Israelites had always been called "brethren," being of one race. They are also called a "*holy*" people ("saints"), as being dedicated to the Lord; and his "chosen" ["elect"] People. And hence Christians are called "the brethren," the "elect," and "saints," (ἅγιοι) that is *holy*, as being dedicated at baptism to the Lord Jesus.

One necessary circumstance in such a Dispensation, was, that it should not be, like the Mosaic, a *local* religion. The Jews, indeed, clung (and still cling) to the notion that, even when all the world should be brought to the knowledge of the true God, still their nation should have a preëminence; and that the Temple of Jerusalem should be the great centre of religious worship for all mankind. And we know there are even some Christians who expect that Jesus Christ is to return to this earth in bodily person, and reign at Jerusalem in great worldly splendour for a thousand years. But such notions are quite at variance with the whole character of the Gospel, as described in our Sacred Books.

Agrippa, again, uses the word in speaking to Paul, and the Apostle Peter introduces it as denoting what was accounted a crime by the heathen rulers. "If any man suffer for being a Christian, let him not be ashamed."

The Temple at Jerusalem—"the place which the Lord had chosen to cause his NAME to dwell there,"* that is, to manifest his presence—was to be totally and finally destroyed. And Jesus declared, that "wheresoever even two or three should be gathered together in his name, He would be there in the midst of them." And hence, a christian *congregation*—not a literal building—was to be henceforth a portion of the temple of the MOST HIGH.

"Know ye not," says the Apostle Paul, "that your bodies are a temple of the Holy Ghost, which dwelleth in you?" (1 Cor. vi. 19.)

And as the collective body of worshippers was called a *temple*, so the individual Christians are called "*living stones*" of God's temple. "Ye as living stones, are builded together into an holy temple to the Lord" (1 Peter ii. 6). Hence arose the use of the word "edify," (οἰχοδομεῖν) literally "to build up"—as applied to christian instruction and exhortation.

While Jesus Christ was on earth in bodily person, HE was the temple of the Lord; inasmuch as "in Him dwelleth all the fulness of the Godhead bodily" (Col. ii. 9). And accordingly, He not only speaks

* There are two words in the original which are both translated "Temple," Ἱερόν, that is, the "sacred place," which included the courts of the Temple; and Ναός (from Ναίω, "to dwell"), the "House of God," which was the building in which *sacrifices* were offered. For this was the main purpose of a temple; which was not (like the synagogues, and like our churches and chapels) a place for religious assemblies.

Ναός is the word used by our Lord when he calls his body a temple, and by Paul, when he applies it to Christians.

expressly "of the temple of his body"* (John ii. 21), but makes several allusions† (which are often overlooked) to this character of Himself.

And this, by the way, is a clear proof of his claiming a *divine* character. For the Jews understood (as He well knew) by "the temple of the Lord," not a synagogue,—a place of assembly for worshippers, but "the habitation where his honour (glory) dwelleth."

And it is worth remarking, that they also understood his calling Himself the "Son of God," and saying, "that God was his *own proper‡* Father," as a claim to be a divine person. His words, indeed, might, in themselves, conceivably, bear another meaning. But He must have *known* that *they* so understood Him. And if they had mistaken his meaning, He would not have failed to correct their mistake: else He would have been bearing false witness against Himself.

They *rightly* understood Him, therefore, to be claiming a divine character. And thereupon they pronounced him guilty of blasphemy (Matt. xxvi. 65), and liable to death by their Law (Deut. xviii. 20), as teaching men to worship another besides the true God.

For they did not expect that the Christ was to be a *divine* person; as is plain from their being unable to solve the question which Jesus put to them, about David's calling him LORD (Mark xii. 37). When

---

* Ἔλεγε περὶ τοῦ ναοῦ τοῦ σώματος αὐτοῦ.

† So the Evangelist—"The Word became flesh and tabernacled" (ἐσκήνωσε) not merely *dwelt*, as in our version, "among us."

‡ πατέρα ἴδιον.   John v. 18.

therefore, they understood Him to "make Himself God" (John x. 33), this was so far from favouring their belief in him as the Christ, that it convinced them of his being a false pretender and a blasphemer.

When Jesus departed from the earth, He sent to his disciples the promised "Comforter," to abide with them for ever; even the Holy Spirit, whose temple is the whole body of Christians throughout the world. And every christian congregation, as has been already observed, is a portion of this temple; each individual Christian being called in Scripture a "living stone" of it.

But our Lord takes care to make his disciples understand that it is not a *different Being* they are to look for, and who is to be their new Master; but a different *manifestation* of the same God;—a return of their Master to them under a new character. For He says expressly, "I will not leave you *comfortless, I will come unto you:*"—"*I* will *see you again;* and your heart shall rejoice; and your joy no man *taketh from you;*" "if any man love me, he will keep my saying, and my Father will love him; and We will come unto him, and make *our abode with him.*" And the like, in several other passages.

And the Apostles, accordingly, speak of "the LORD (that is, Jesus Christ) being the *Spirit*" (2 Cor. iii. 17), and assure us that "if any man have not the Spirit of Christ, he is none of his." (Rom. viii. 9.)

The same God, then, who, to the Israelites, was made known only as *Creator and Governor* (God the Father), was afterwards manifested to Christians as being also the *Redeemer* (God the Son), and the *Sanctifier* (God the Holy Ghost): and He is to be acknowledged by them in this threefold manifestation, according to our Saviour's injunction to "baptise in* the Name of the Father, and of the Son, and of the Holy Ghost."

There have been, therefore, in all, three *Temples* of the ONE GOD; first, under the Old Dispensation, the Temple at Jerusalem; secondly, during the abode on earth of the Lord Jesus, "the Temple of his Body;" and, thirdly, (that which is also often called Christ's body,) (Eph. iv. 12, 16), the holy Catholic or Universal Church, comprising all believers throughout the world.

This third and final manifestation of the ONE GOD plainly belongs to a Dispensation characterised (as we have said) by UNIVERSALITY.

Another distinguishing feature of the New Dispensation, was, as has been said, its UNITY (or *Oneness*); by which we mean, that it not only admits all mankind to christian privileges, but all of them to *equal* privileges. "There is," as the Apostle expresses it, "one Lord, one faith, one baptism." "There is neither Greek, nor Jew, barbarian, Scythian, bondman, or freeman." (Eph. iv. 5, and Col. iii. 11.)

This christian unity (ἑνότης) is often alluded to, and earnestly dwelt on, by our Sacred writers. But the passages relating to it are sometimes imperfectly understood, or entirely mistaken.

It does not mean *agreement* in *doctrine*, nor yet *con-*

* More properly *to* or *into* the Name, εἰς τὸ ὄνομα.

cord and mutual good-will; though these are strongly insisted on by the Apostles. But the *unity* which they speak of is something distinct from these.

Nor, again, does it mean that all Christians belong, or ought to belong, to some *one society on earth.* For this is what the Apostles never aimed at, and what never was actually the state of things, from the time that the christian religion extended beyond the city of Jerusalem.

The teaching of Scripture upon this subject, clearly is, that believers on earth are part of a great society (church or congregation), of which the Head is in heaven, and of which many of the members only "live unto God," or exist in his counsels,—some having long since departed, and some being not yet born. Of such a community *the centre* cannot possibly be on earth; and accordingly, the Apostle Paul expressly distinguishes the christian church [assembly or congregation] ἐκκλησία, from that of Israel:—" Ye [that is, ye Christians] are not come to the mount that might be touched; [as the Israelites were collected in a great assembly (those of them that *were alive that day*) round Sinai, as a holy place on earth] . . . . but ye are come to Mount Sion, and unto the city of the living God, *the heavenly Jerusalem,* and to an innumerable company of angels, to the general assembly and church of the first-born, which are written in heaven, and to God the Judge of all, and to the spirits of just men made perfect, and to Jesus the mediator of the new covenant" (Heb. xii. 18–24). So, in the Epistle to the Galatians,—" Mount Sinai answereth to Jerusalem which now is, and is in bondage with her children ; but Jerusalem *which is above* is free, *which is the mother* of us all." (Gal. iv. 25, 26.)

The Universal Church of Christ may therefore be said to be ONE in reference to HIM, its supreme Head in *heaven;* but it is not *one Community* on earth. And even so the *Human race* is *one*, in respect of the *one Creator* and *Governor;* but this does not make it *one Family*, or one *State*.

All men, again, ought to live in *peace*, and to be kindly disposed towards every fellow-creature. And all are bound to *agree* in thinking and doing whatever is right. But they are not at all bound to live under one *single government*, extending over the whole World. Nor, again, are all nations bound to have the *same form* of government, regal or republican, &c. That is a matter left to their discretion. But all are bound to do their best to promote the great *objects* for which all government is instituted;—good order, security of person and property, justice, and public prosperity.

And even so the Apostles founded christian communities, all *based* on the *same principles*, and having the same *object* in view, but quite independent of each other, and having no one common Head on Earth.

The Apostles, indeed, exercised a general government over the various churches which they founded; but it does not appear that they appointed any person to succeed them in that *general* government. We read of their appointing "Elders in every city," but we do not read of their setting, or intending to set, any one *over the whole Church.*

Any one who looks at the account of Paul's taking leave of the Elders of Ephesus and Miletus (Acts xx.), *whom he expected never to see again*, will plainly see that he could not possibly have had any notion of any supreme *central authority*, lodged either in the church of Jerusalem, or of Rome, or in Peter and his successors, or in any *General Council.* For he there directly foretells that false teachers should arise out of their own body [that is, from amongst the clergy], and anxiously impresses on them the best advice he could think of for guarding against such a danger. Yet that advice is only *to watch, and remember what he had taught them.* This seems to imply that each particular church was left sufficient *means* within itself of ascertaining the true doctrine of Christ, continuing, and preserving it; but that the actual preservation of such doctrine depended on the *watchfulness* of the churches themselves. For the occasion was one on which he could not have failed to bid them have recourse, in case of any difficulties or disputes among themselves (such as he actually foresaw), to some central Authority, if any such had existed, or were to be set up.

Nor does the Apostle Peter (though writing his Second Epistle in the near prospect of death (2 Pet. i. 14, 15), and anxious to provide a record of his teaching that might last after his decease), say a word to the disciples of the duty of submitting to his successors ; but refers them back for guidance to the words of the holy prophets, and the commandments of the apostles, and to his own letters, and to those of Paul.

In the beginning of the Revelation of John, too, we

find the Lord addressing *each* of *the seven churches of Asia* as severally independent of any earthly power, and responsible to Him alone for their conduct as christian churches.

It is plain, therefore, that the christian Unity spoken of in Scripture did not consist in the placing of all Christians in one Society under one government on Earth.

It consisted (as we have said) in the admission of all men to equal christian privileges, instead of having two or more different kinds or *degrees* of Christianity, for different classes of persons.

Now, there did exist something of this kind under the Mosaic Dispensation. The "devout Gentiles" (sometimes called "Proselytes* of the Gate"), were admitted to worship in the outer court of the Temple, and to frequent the Synagogues. Those who had embraced the whole Mosaic Law (who were called "Proselytes of righteousness") were accounted as ranking higher than the others, and next in holiness to the Israelites by birth. Then, of the born Israelites, the *Levites* were more especially dedicated to the Lord than those of the other Tribes, and were employed in his immediate Service about the Tabernacle, or the Temple. Of the Levites themselves again, the family of Aaron were alone admissible to the priesthood. And lastly, of the Priests themselves, none except the high priest was permitted to enter the Holy of Holies, —where he offered the yearly sacrifice on the great day of atonement.

* προσήλυτες, one who *comes over to* some religion or religious sect.

And these several gradations, it is to be observed, are something quite different from the various degrees of moral worth and piety, or of intelligence and knowledge, in individuals.

One Israelite (and the like may be said of Christians) might exceed another of the same Tribe and Family, in pious obedience to the Lord; and a third might surpass them both. But these differences would not be distinctions *introduced by the Mosaic Religion;* but merely those of the individual characters of those men. And again, a pious Israelite, of superior understanding, and of a reflecting turn of mind, and of more extensive knowledge than the generality, would have a clearer, and more intelligent, and more comprehensiye view of some parts of the Revelation given him, and of God's Providence generally, than another, equally pious, but of humbler powers and attainments. And the like must be the case with Christians also.

But these differences between one man and another, are such as we find to exist in reference to *all* subjects, and do not particularly pertain to the Mosaic system of Religion; not being introduced and created by it.

Those distinctions, on the contrary, which were noticed just above, are such as did specially belong to the religion of Moses, and formed a part of the Dispensation.

The Gospel, on the other hand, admitted of no such gradations as those established under the Law.

Various Officers, indeed, were appointed in the christian churches; because no Society can subsist without them. But all persons, of whatever Race or

Family, were admissible, if properly qualified, to any Office.

And again, (as was said just above,) men of superior intelligence and mental cultivation, will be able, by piously and humbly employing their powers in the study (among other things) of the christian Scriptures, to take a clearer and more intelligent view of the Gospel revelation, than those of ordinary abilities and education ; provided they are careful not to indulge in rash conjectures respecting things beyond human reason, and which God has not thought fit to reveal.

Such men, if they do use this care, will find that the more they advance in general cultivation of mind, the more will the prospect of divine wisdom and good-ness spread around them; the horizon, as it were, extending itself in proportion to their elevation.

But this (as was observed above) is a kind of distinction between man and man, which was not *intro-duced by the Gospel*, but takes place in *all* subjects.

Nor does such a distinction make one man *more a Christian*, properly speaking, than another. In fact, a learned Philosopher would be a *worse* Christian than pious men of ordinary ability and education, if he were content to remain, in point of religious know-ledge, just *on a level* with these, while in all *other* matters he was intellectually superior to them. He would be like a person offering as the *tithe* of an increased produce, the same *absolute* amount as would be a fair proportion from a smaller or less fertile field.

And in respect of piety of sentiment, also, and

purity of conduct, one man may be a better Christian than another, that is, he may make a *better use* of his christian privileges. But the *Gospel itself* does not exclude any man from any christian privileges to which it admits others.

This is one of the points wherein (as has been said) it differs from the Mosaic Law.

And this feature of the Gospel was one which proved a great stumbling-block to the Jews. They could not easily reconcile themselves to the thought of Gentiles being placed completely on a level with them. And they clung to the idea that the Jews by Race must continue to be in an especial manner God's peculiar People, even when both they and the Gentiles should have become subjects of Christ's kingdom. And even among the Gentile Christians themselves, there seems to have been a tendency to consider the different "spiritual [miraculous] gifts" bestowed on different persons, as dividing Christians into so many distinct Orders. This tendency we find the Apostle Paul earnestly contending against in several parts of his writings; especially in 1 Cor. xii.

The miraculous gifts were bestowed not for the benefit of the possessor, but of the Church. And they did not either *prove* the possessor to be peculiarly acceptable to God, or necessarily *make* him so. For Judas Iscariot, who afterwards betrayed his Master, had been endowed, along with the other Apostles, with miraculous powers. And our Lord declares that He will say, at the Day of Judgment, to some who should boast of having, in his Name, "done many mighty works," "I know you not; depart from me all ye workers of iniquity."

Yet in all ages of the Church, there has been a tendency, more or less, to draw some unwarranted distinctions between ordinary Christians, and those to whom the name of SAINTS has been confined, either from their having been inspired, like the Evangelists and Apostles, or from their being supposed to possess some extraordinary personal holiness, beyond what is expected of Christians generally.

The Apostles, on the contrary, (as was observed above,) call *all* Christians "Saints;" as being all *dedicated* to Christ in Baptism, and all admitted to be equal partakers (as far as relates to their own holiness of character, and power of becoming acceptable to God) of his sanctifying Spirit. There is no hint given that a less degree of personal holiness will suffice for us, than for an Apostle; and Peter or Paul, however superior to us in their miraculous gifts, yet called themselves Saints in reference not to any thing *peculiar* to them, but to what was *common* to them with us.

Nevertheless, one may find persons, even now, who seem to regard Christianity as not, in reality, one religion, but two; one, for persons of pre-eminent holiness, or who are admitted to certain superior christian privileges, beyond the generality; and the other for the multitude; who are to believe implicitly whatever the most eminent Saints think fit to impart, and to do whatever they bid them.

But nothing can be more at variance than such a

notion is with the whole character of the Gospel Dispensation. For this was designed as a revelation to men of all classes, in every tolerably-civilized country. And the endeavour of the Apostles was to "*make known* the *mystery* of the Gospel" to *all*, in proportion as they were *able* and *willing* to receive it. And they laboured, by assiduous instruction and exhortation, to *make* men, more and more, thus able and willing. They urged them "to *grow* in grace and in the knowledge of the Lord Jesus Christ." And they reckoned themselves to be "pure from the blood of all men," only inasmuch as they "had not shunned to declare to them *all* the counsel of God."

When we look back to these distinguishing points in the Gospel Dispensation which have been here noticed—its *Spirituality, Universality,* and *Unity*—as well as to several other remarkable features of it, we cannot but perceive what a strong confirmation they afford of its divine origin.

It was altogether the most unlikely thing to have occurred to the mind of any man, whether dreaming enthusiast or crafty impostor. And of all men, *Jews* were the most unlikely to have imagined anything of the kind. Indeed, the great stumbling-block to the Jews was its being so utterly at variance (as has been remarked above) with all their most deeply-rooted prejudices, and all their long-cherished hopes.

But it was almost equally at variance with many of the notions of the Heathen also. And these latter had nearly as much difficulty in receiving a religion from Jews—a people generally despised by them—as the Jews had, in acknowledging the "Gentiles" as fellow-heirs with themselves. And both parties—Jews and Gentiles—had never conceived an idea of such a thing as a religion without any literal *Temple*, without an *Altar*, without Sacrifices, and without any Sacrificing Priest on earth.

Such a Religion could never have been *invented*, in those days, by any man, Jew or Gentile; and could never have been established throughout the chief part of the civilised World, except by the overpowering force of miraculous proofs.

ESTABLISHMENT OF CHRIST'S KING-DOM.

WHEN the bodily presence of our Divine Master was withdrawn from the earth, his Apostles proceeded, according to his directions, to establish "the kingdom of heaven," over which He had placed them, saying, "I appoint unto you a kingdom, as my Father hath appointed unto me."

For, that Gospel which had been proclaimed by Himself and his disciples, during his personal ministry, was, that "the kingdom of heaven was *at hand*." That kingdom was *then* only in preparation. It was not completely begun, till the Apostles, after the outpouring on them of the Holy Spirit, on the day of Pentecost, founded at Jerusalem the first christian church, and baptised into the Name of the Lord Jesus about three thousand persons, who were thus enrolled as subjects of that kingdom.

The number of these in Jerusalem increased rapidly. Other churches were established in Judea, in Galilee, in Samaria, and elsewhere. And a few years after, the apostles having learnt by an express revelation—quite contrary to their own expectations—that Gentiles were to be admitted on equal terms, as subjects of Christ's kingdom, great numbers of churches, consisting chiefly of these, arose in various parts of the world.

Although, however, mention is made in Scripture of several of these churches, we have only incidental, slight, and scanty accounts of the way in which the Apostles proceeded in founding them. Very few particulars are given of the regulations established,—of the appointment of the several Orders of Ministers, —of the Divine service celebrated,—or, in short, of any of the details of matters pertaining to a christian church.

One reason for this, probably, was, that a Jewish Synagogue, or a collection of Synagogues in the same neighbourhood, *became* at once a *christian Church*, as soon as the worshippers, or a considerable portion of them, had embraced the Gospel, and had separated themselves from unbelievers. They had only to make such additions to their public Service, and such alterations, as were required by their reception of the

Gospel; leaving everything else as it was. For, the Apostles, we know, acted on the rule of "becoming all things to all men;" that is, of complying with men's habits, and avoiding all shock to their feelings, as far as this could be done without any sacrifice of principle, or detriment to the great objects proposed. It is incredible, therefore, especially considering that for several years the only converts were persons frequenting the synagogues,—Jews or devout Gentiles, —that they should have utterly disregarded all the existing and long-reverenced Institutions and Offices, which could so easily be accommodated to the New Dispensation. To have established everything on a perfectly new system, through mere love of novelty, —to have erected, as it were, a fresh building from the very ground, when there was one standing which with small and easy alterations would answer all the same purposes, would have been to raise up, wantonly, difficulties and obstacles to their own success. They did not indeed, no doubt, think themselves bound or authorised, to adhere blindly to existing institutions in any points in which these were at variance with the spirit of the Gospel, or were capable of being changed for the better: and doubtless they introduced from time to time, (and designed that their successors should do the same,) such alterations in the functions of the several officers, and in all regulations respecting other non-essential points, as circumstances of time and place might require. But we cannot suppose that they aimed at originality for its own sake, or altered for the sake of altering. And the correspondence, accordingly, which has been traced by learned men between the Synagogue and the Church, is no more than what we might antecedently have expected.

The attempt to effect this conversion of a Jewish synagogue into a christian church, seems always to have been made, in the first instance, in every place where there was an opening for it. Even after the call of the idolatrous Gentiles, it appears plainly to have been the practice of the Apostles Paul and Barnabas, when they came to any city in which there was a synagogue, to go thither first and deliver their sacred message to the Jews, and "devout (or proselyte) Gentiles;"—according to their own expression (Acts xiii. 16); to the "men of Israel," and those "*that feared God;*"—adding, that "it was necessary that the word of God should first be preached to them."

And when they founded a church in any of those cities in which (and such were probably a very large majority) there was no Jewish Synagogue that received the Gospel, it is likely they would still conform in a great measure to the same model.

Now, Jewish synagogues, and all things pertaining to them, were so familiarly known in the days of our sacred writers, that there was no need to enter into any minute particulars respecting the officers, regulations, and practices of a synagogue.

Nevertheless, it seems probable that we should have found in Scripture something more than we do find, of incidental notices of some of these particulars, if there had not been some especial reason for omitting them.

The same may be said with respect to the Creeds, Catechisms, and Forms of Prayer, and of administering the Sacraments, which were in use in the days of the Apostles. We have no record in Scripture of any of these. And yet the more we reflect on the subject, viewing not merely the abstract probabilities of the case, but also what has actually occurred in respect of other religions, the more strongly we shall feel that the first founders of a religion might naturally have been expected to have transmitted to posterity some, more or less systematic, compositions, such as we have been speaking of.

For if we look, for instance, to the Koran, we find Mahomet, in the midst of much extraneous matter, fitted only to gratify the appetite for the marvellous, inserting, however, also, not only a precise description of the Mahometan Faith, but likewise minute directions concerning Fasts, Prayers, Ablutions,—the amount of Alms,—and all other points of the Mussulman's service of God. The same is represented to be the character of the Hindoo Shaster, and other Pagan books professing to contain a divine revelation of any system of religion.

And that there is nothing in the christian religion, considered in itself, that stands in the way of such a procedure, is plain from the number of works of this description which have appeared from the earliest times, (*after the age of inspiration*,)* down to the pre-

---

* A proof, it should be observed, is thus afforded, that the New Testament Books are no *forgery* of the early Christians, since these

sent;—from the writings entitled the "Apostles' Creed," and the "Apostolical Constitutions," &c. (compositions of uncertain authors, and amidst the variety of opinions respecting them, never regarded as Scripture), down to the modern Formularies and Confessions of Faith.

Nor, again, can it be said that there was anything in the founders of the religion, any more than in the religion itself, which, humanly speaking, should seem likely to preclude them from transmitting to us such compositions. On the contrary, the Apostles were brought up Jews: accustomed, in their earliest notions of religion, to refer to the Books of the Law, as containing precise statements of their belief, and most minute directions as to religious worship and ceremonies. So that, to give complete and regular instructions as to the character and the requisitions of the new religion, as it would have been natural for *any* one, was more especially to be expected of *these* men.

And even supposing that the other avocations of the Apostles would not allow any of *them* leisure for

would have been sure to insert what we do find in their own acknowledged writings, and which is altogether wanting in the Sacred Books.

The same inference may be drawn from a fact which we have already spoken of, the entire absence in the New Testament of the title of *Christians*, as applied by themselves to each other. It seems to have been adopted by Christians very early; probably soon after the destruction of Jerusalem; and if the Books of the New Testament had been forged or interpolated by them, at that, or at any subsequent period, there can be no doubt we should have found it frequently so employed therein such compositions,—though we know that some of them did find time for writing, two of them not a little,—even this supposition does not at all explain the difficulty; for the Acts and two of the Gospels were written by men who were only attendants on the Apostles. Nor would such writings as we are speaking of have required an *inspired* penman; only one who had access to persons thus gifted. We know with what care the Apostolic Epistles were preserved, first by the churches to which they were respectively sent, and afterwards, by the others also, as soon as they received copies. How comes it, then, that no one of the Elders (Presbyters) of any of these Churches should have written down, and afterwards submitted to the revision of an Apostle, that outline of catechetical instruction—that elementary introduction to the christian faith—which they must have received at first from that Apostle's lips, and have afterwards employed in the instruction of their own converts? Why did none of them record any of the prayers, of which they must have heard so many, from an Apostle's mouth, both in the ordinary devotional assemblies, in the administration of the Sacraments, and in the "laying on of hands," by which they themselves had been ordained.

Paul, after having given the most general exhortations to the Corinthians for the preservation of decent regularity in their religious meetings, adds, " the rest will I set in order when I come." And so, doubtless, he did; and so he must have done, by verbal directions, in all the other churches also: is it not strange, then, that these verbal directions should nowhere have been committed to writing?

This would have seemed a most obvious and effectual mode of precluding all future disorders and disputes; as also the drawing up of a compendious statement of christian doctrines, would have seemed a safeguard against the still more important evil of heretical error. Yet if any such statements and formularies *had* been drawn up, with the sanction, and under the revision of an Apostle, we may be sure they would have been preserved and transmitted to posterity, with the most scrupulous and reverential care. The conclusion therefore seems inevitable, that either no one of the numerous Elders and Catechists ever thought of doing this, or else that they were forbidden by the Apostles to execute any such design: and each of these alternatives seems alike inexplicable by natural causes.

For it should be remembered that, when other points are equal, it is much more difficult to explain a *negative* than a *positive* circumstance in our Scriptures. There is something, suppose, in the New Testament, which the first promulgators of Christianity—considered as mere unassisted men—were not likely to write; and there is something else which they were, we will suppose, equally unlikely to omit writing; now, these two difficulties are far from equal. For with respect to the former, if we can make out that *any one* of these men might have been, by nature or by circumstances, qualified and induced to undertake the work, the phenomenon is solved. To point out even a single individual able and likely to write it, would account for its being written. But it is not so with respect to the other case, that of omission. Here we have to *prove a negative;*—to show, not merely that this or that man was likely not to write what we find omitted, but that *no one was* likely to write it. Suppose we could make out the possibility or probability of Paul's having left no Creed, Catechism, or Canons, why have we none from the pen of Luke, or of Mark? Suppose this also explained, why did not John or Peter supply the deficiency? And why, again, did none of the numerous Bishops and Presbyters whom they ordained, undertake the work, under their direction? The difficulty, therefore, in this case exceeds the other, *cæteris paribus,* more than a hundredfold.

Since, then, no one of the first promulgators of Christianity did that which they must—some of them at least—have been *naturally* led to do, it follows that they must have been *supernaturally* withheld from it; how little soever we may be able even to conjecture the object of the prohibition. For in respect of this, and several other (humanly speaking, unaccountable) circumstances in our religion, it is important to observe, that the argument thence derivable in favour of the divine origin of Christianity, does not turn on the supposed *wisdom* of this or that appointment, which we conceive to be worthy of the Deity, and thence infer that the religion must have proceeded from Him; but on the utter improbability of *its having proceeded from Man;* which leaves its divine origin the only alternative. The Christian Scriptures considered in this point of view, present to us a standing Miracle; at least, a Monument of a Miracle; since they are in several points such as we may be sure, according to all natural causes, they would *not* have been. Even though the character which these writings do in fact exhibit, be such as we cannot clearly account for on *any* hypothesis, still, if they are such as we can clearly perceive no false pretenders would have composed, the evidence is complete, though the difficulty may remain unexplained.

Although, however, we cannot pretend, in every case, to perceive the reasons for what God has appointed, it is not in the present case difficult to discern the superhuman wisdom of the course adopted. If the Hymns * and forms of Prayer,—the Catechisms,—the Confessions of faith,—and the Ecclesiastical regulations, which the Apostles employed, had been recorded, these would have all been regarded as parts of *Scripture:* and even had they been accompanied by the most express declarations of the lawfulness of altering or laying aside any of them, we cannot doubt that they would have been in practice most scrupulously retained, even when changes of manners, tastes, and local and temporary circumstances of every kind, rendered them no longer the most suitable. The Jew-

---

* Pliny's account of the early Christians, derived in part from those who had belonged to the Society, mentions that they recited " a hymn to Christ, as to a God." This ancient hymn has not been transmitted to us, so as to be recognised. It is not unlikely, however, that it, or some part of it, formed the basis of that which we call the *Te Deum.*

ish ritual, designed for one Nation and Country, and intended to be of temporary duration, was fixed and accurately described. The same Divine Wisdom from which both dispensations proceeded, having designed Christianity for all Nations and Ages, left Christians at large in respect of those points in which variation might be desirable. But we think no *human* wisdom would have foreseen and provided for this. That a number of *Jews*, accustomed from their infancy to so strict a ritual, should, in introducing Christianity as the second part of the same Dispensation, have abstained not only from accurately prescribing for the use of all Christian Churches for ever, the mode of divine worship, but even from recording what was actually in use under their own directions, does seem utterly incredible, unless we suppose them to have been restrained from doing this by a special admonition of the Divine Spirit.

And we may be sure, as we have said, that if they *had* recorded the particulars of their own worship, the very words they wrote would have been invested in our minds with so much sanctity, that it would have been thought presumptuous to vary or to omit them, however inappropriate they might have become. The Lord's Prayer, the only one of general application that is recorded in the Scriptures, though so framed as to be suitable in all Ages and Countries, has yet been subjected to much superstitious abuse. A superstitious Christian mutters his "paternosters," as a kind of sacred charm, on all occasions, however inappropriate.

In like manner, the Apostles' Creed, from its acknowledged antiquity, together with the title it bears, and the tradition (probably, in part, true*) of its being the composition of the Apostles, is held by many Christians in a kind of veneration which may justly be characterised as superstitious. There are persons of the lower orders, and some above the very lowest, who are accustomed to recite it in their private devotions as a *prayer.*

No doubt there must ever be danger of all prayer degenerating into a superstitious formalism; but this danger must evidently be increased in proportion as the words uttered are the less appropriate to the occasion, and to the circumstances of the petitioner; and this must inevitably have been more likely to take place with a Liturgy transmitted to us from the times of the Apostles, as a part of Scripture.

With respect to Catechisms again,—elementary introductions to the christian faith,—nearly the same reasons will hold good. For though the christian religion is fundamentally "the same yesterday, and to-day, and for ever," it is impossible that any one mode of introducing its truths to the mind of the catechumen, can be the best adapted for children and adults,—the civilized and the barbarian,—and for all the other varieties of station, sex, country, intellectual culture, and natural capacity.

* If, as there seems good reason for thinking, part of this creed was actually in use with the Apostles, this circumstance renders it the more remarkable that it should not have been recorded by them in their writings.—See KING's (afterwards Lord King) *History of the Apostles' Creed.*

Each church, therefore, was left, through the wise foresight of Him who alone "knew what is in Man," to provide for its own wants as they should arise;—to steer its own course by the Chart and Compass which his holy Word supplies, regulating for itself the Sails and Rudder, according to the winds and currents it may meet with.*   " The Apostles had begun and established precedents, which, of course, would be naturally adopted by their uninspired successors. But still, as these were only the formal means of grace, and not the blessing itself, it was equally to be expected that the church should assume a discretionary power, whenever the means established became impracticable or clearly unsuitable, and either substitute others, or even altogether abolish such as existed . . . . It might seem at first that the apostolical precedents were literally binding on all Ages; but this cannot have been intended; and for this reason, that the greater portion of the apostolical practices have been transmitted to us, not on apostolical authority, but on the authority of the uninspired church; which has handed them down with an uncertain mixture of its own appointments.   How are we to know the enactments of the inspired rulers from those of the uninspired? and if there be no certain clue, we must either bring down the authority of the apostolical usage to that of the uninspired church, or raise that of the uninspired church to that of the apostolical. Now, the former is, doubtless, what was, to a certain extent, intended by the Apostles themselves; as will

* Bishop HIND's *History of the Rise and Progress of Christianity.*

appear from a line of distinction by which they have carefully partitioned off such of their appointments as are designed to be perpetual, from such as are left to share the possibility of change, with the institutions of uninspired wisdom.

If, then, we look to the account of the christian usages contained in Scripture, nothing can be more unquestionable than that, while some are specified, others are passed over in silence. It is not even left so as to make us imagine that those mentioned may be all; but, while some are noted specifically, the establishment of others is implied, without the particular mode of observance being given. Thus, we are all equally sure from Scripture, that christian ministers were ordained by a certain form, and that Christians assembled in prayer; but while the precise process of laying on of hands is mentioned in the former institution, no account is given of the precise method of Church-Service, or even of any regular forms of prayer, beyond the Lord's Prayer. Even the record of the Ordination Service itself admits of the same distinction. It is quite as certain, that, in it, some prayer was used, as that some outward form accompanied the prayer; but the form is specified, the prayer left unrecorded.

What, now, is the obvious interpretation of the holy Dispenser's meaning in this mode of record? Clearly, it is, that the Apostles regulated, under his guidance, the forms and practices of the Church, so as was best calculated to convey grace to the Church *at that time.* Nevertheless, part of its institutions were of a nature, which, although formal, would never require a change; and these, therefore, were left recorded in the Scriptures, to mark this distinction of character. The others were not, indeed, to be capriciously abandoned, nor except when there should be manifest cause for so doing; but as such a case was supposable, these were left to mingle with the uninspired precedents, the claims of which as precedents would be increased by this uncertain admixture, and the authority of the whole rendered so far binding, and so far subject to the discretion of the church. They might not be altered, unless sufficient grounds should appear; but the settling of this point was left to the discretion of the church."*

The Apostles themselves, however, and their numerous fellow-labourers, would not, probably, have been, if left to themselves, so far-sighted as to perceive (all, and each of them, without a single exception) the expediency of this procedure. Most likely, many of them,—but according to all human probability, some of them,—would have left us, as parts of Scripture, compositions such as we have been speaking of; and these, there can be no doubt, would have been scrupulously retained for ever. They would have left us Catechisms, which would have been like precise directions for the cultivation of some plant, admirably adapted to a particular soil and climate, but inapplicable to those of a contrary description. Their Symbols would have stood like ancient sea-walls,

* Bishop HIND's *History of the Rise and Progress of Christianity,* vol. ii, p. 113–115.

built to repel the encroachments of the waves, and still scrupulously kept in repair, when perhaps the sea had retired from them many miles, and was encroaching on some different part of the coast.

There are multitudes, even as it is, who do not, even now, perceive the expediency of the omission; there are not a few who even complain of it as a defect, or even make it a ground of objection. That, in that day, the reasons for the procedure actually adopted, should have occurred, and occurred to *all* the first Christians, supposing them mere unassisted men, and men, too, brought up in Judaism, is utterly incredible.

But besides the reason we have now been speaking of, there is another, perhaps not less important, against the providing in Scripture of a regular systematic statement of christian doctrines. Supposing such a summary of Gospel truths had been drawn up, and could have been contrived with such exquisite skill as to be sufficient and well adapted for all, of every Age and Country, what would have been the probable result? It would have commanded the unhesitating assent of all Christians; who would, with deep veneration, have stored up the very words of it in their memory, without any need of laboriously searching the rest of the Scriptures, to ascertain its agreement with them; which is what we do (at least are evidently *called on* to do) with a *human* exposition of the faith: and the absence of this labour, together with the tranquil security as to the correctness of their belief which would have been thus generated, would have ended in a careless and contented apathy. There would have been no room for doubt,—no call for vigilant attention in the investigation of truth,—none of that effort of mind which is now requisite, in comparing one passage with another, and collecting instruction from the scattered, oblique, and incidental references to various doctrines in the existing Scriptures; and in consequence none of that excitement of the best feelings, and that improvement of the heart, which are the natural, and doubtless the designed result of an humble, diligent, and sincere study of the christian Scriptures.

In fact, all study, properly so called, of the rest of Scripture,—all lively interest in its perusal,—would have been nearly superseded by such an inspired compendium of doctrine; to which alone, as far the most convenient for that purpose, habitual reference would have been made in any questions that might arise. Both would have been regarded, indeed, as of divine authority; but the Compendium, as the fused and purified metal: the other, as the mine containing the crude ore. And the Compendium itself, being not like the existing Scriptures, that *from which* the faith is to be learned, *but the very thing to be learned*, would have come to be regarded by most with an indolent, unthinking veneration, which would have exercised little or no influence on the character.

Their orthodoxy would have been, as it were, petrified, like the bodies of those animals we read of incrusted in the ice of the polar regions; firm-fixed, indeed, and preserved unchangeable, but cold, motionless, lifeless.

It is only when our energies are roused, and our faculties exercised, and our attention kept awake, by an ardent pursuit of truth, and anxious watchfulness against error,—when, in short, we feel ourselves to be doing something towards acquiring, or retaining, or improving our knowledge,—it is then only, that that knowledge makes the requisite practical impression on the heart and on the conduct.

To the Church, then, has her all-wise Founder left the office of *teaching*, to the Scriptures, that of *proving* the christian doctrines: to the Scriptures He has left the delineation of christian *principles;* to each Church, the *application* of those principles, in their Symbols, or Articles of Religion,—in their Forms of Worship, —and in their Ecclesiastical regulations.

And there can be no doubt that every Christian is bound, in duty to his divine Master, to pay obedience to the enactments and ordinances—not adverse to Scripture—of the Church he belongs to, though consisting of uninspired men. For such a measure of obedience is indispensably necessary for the existence of *any* SOCIETY. And it is certain that it is the will of the Lord Jesus that his people *should* be members of those Christian Societies called Churches. . . . .

The religion He introduced was manifestly designed by Him—and so understood by His immediate followers—to be a *social* religion. It was not merely a revelation of certain truths to be received, and of practical rules to be observed,—it was not a mere system of doctrines and precepts to be embraced by each individual, independently of others; and in which his agreement or co-operation with any others would be accidental; as when several men have come to the same conclusion in some science, or have adopted the same system of agriculture or of medicine; but it was to be a *combination* of men who should be "members of the body of Christ,"—"living stones" of one spiritual temple; "edifying" (*i. e.* building up) "one another in their faith,"—and "brethren" of one holy family.

Of this design to establish what should be emphatically a social religion,—a "fellowship" or "communion (*i. e.* community) of saints," there can be, we should think, no doubt in the mind of any reflecting reader of our Sacred Books. Besides our Lord's general promise of "coming unto and dwelling in *any man* who should love Him, and keep his saying," there is a distinct promise also of an especial presence in any *assembly*—even "of two or three—gathered together in his name." Besides the general promises made to prayer,—to the prayer of an individual "in the closet,"—there is a distinct promise also to those who shall "*agree together*, touching something they shall ask." And it is in conformity with his own institutions that Christians have, ever since, celebrated what they designate as, emphatically, *the Communion*, by meeting together, "to break bread," in commemoration of his redemption of his people.

His design, in short, manifestly was to adapt his

religion to the *social* principles of man's nature; to bind his disciples, throughout all ages, to each other, by those ties of mutual attachment, sympathy, and co-operation, which in every human community and association, of whatever kind, are found so powerful.

And it is evident that whoever directs or sanctions the establishment of a Community, must be understood as thereby sanctioning those institutions which belong to the essence of a Community.

Now there are three things which necessarily pertain to every Community or Society, and are implied by its existence; 1st, *Officers;* 2dly, *Rules;* and 3dly, the power of admitting or excluding *Members.*

I. Whatever may be the character and objects of any Society—whether it be a political society [or State,]—or a scientific,—or a mercantile,—or a religious society, such as we call a *Church,*—in all cases, it must have some kind of Government, and consequently, certain Officers to administer that Government; to manage the affairs of the Body, and to exercise some control over the individual members of it.

II. There must also be, in every society, some kind of *Rules;* whether called Laws, or Statutes, or Canons, or by whatever other name: and these rules must be enforced by some kind of *Penalties* against violations of them.

III. And there must also exist, somewhere, a power of determining who shall be *members* of the Society;—what persons shall be admitted or refused admittance into it, or expelled, or restored.

These three things are, as we have said, essential to *every* kind of Society.

As for a Civil Community [or State,] *that* is not a *voluntary* society; but must have, from the very nature of the case, a *coercive* power: it is necessary that all persons residing in each Country, should be *compelled* to submit to the government of that country. And there is no *limit*, except in the justice and wisdom of the rulers, to the punishments denounced against those who disobey the laws.

But in a *voluntary* Society, (such as Christ designed a Church to be,) the ultimate penalty must be expulsion, all others short of this being submitted to as the alternative. "If he refuse," says our Lord, "to hear the Church; let him be unto thee as a heathen man,"—that is, no longer a member of that church.*

And even as a "heathen man,"—one who never belonged to our Society,—has no claim to any of its privileges, nor is subject to its government, or liable to its penalties; so, if one who *has* been a member of it, has renounced its authority, or has been formally

---

* That is, of that particular church whose authority he has renounced. It does not follow that he may not be a member of some other church.

Indeed, it has often happened, amidst the many unhappy dissensions among Christians, that *all* the members of a church that is completely opposed to another, are shut out from christian inter-communion with the other church.

But though we may be justified in saying, such and such a person is not, and cannot be, considered a member of *this* particular church, we have no right to pronounce him thereupon excluded from the Universal Church of Christ.

expelled from it, he is placed on the same footing. It would be unfair, on the one hand, *for him* to claim any of its advantages, or, on the other hand, for *us* to attempt to subject him to its laws and its penalties. He, and that particular Society, have thenceforth nothing to do with each other.*

And here it should be observed that it is necessary not only that every Community should *have* laws, enforced by certain penalties, but also that it should have power to *make* laws, from time to time, not in opposition to the fundamental principles of the society, but for the carrying out of those principles.

For it would be impossible to lay down rules, once for all, so minute and precise as to meet every possible case, and never to need any addition. Even the Mosaic law, which was extremely particular in its directions, was not sufficient without some enactments, made by competent authority, to decide, for instance, what was or was not to be accounted *work*, and consequently prohibited on the Sabbath-day; and many other such points of detail.

* Sometimes it has happened that some church, though claiming no power over a "heathen man," has yet called in what is termed the "secular arm," to punish as heretics, persons who have renounced allegiance to that church, or whom it has excommunicated. But this is in manifest opposition to what our Lord says in the passage above referred to, as well as to his declaration that his "kingdom is not of this world."

Whether those persons were justly or unjustly excommunicated,— or whether they were right or wrong in seceding,—the church which has renounced them, or which they have renounced, has clearly no more rights over them, according to our Lord's express declaration, than it has over a "heathen man."

Our Lord does indeed censure the Jewish rulers for having, in some points, made absurd and frivolous regulations: and in some, having "made the word of God of none effect, through their tradition." In the one case, they had made an *ill use* of the power intrusted to them; in the other they had altogether *exceeded* their power. But nevertheless, He acknowledges that the power did exist in the rulers of the Jewish Church, and that obedience was due to it when their enactments were not at variance with God's laws. "The Scribes and Pharisees," said He, "sit in Moses' seat;" that is, they are his successors in the office of making and enforcing regulations for the Jewish Church ; "whatsoever *they bid you* observe and do, *so do ye;* but do ye not after their works; for they say, and do not."

Now the rules laid down in Scripture for a Christian Church, are (as was remarked above) far less numerous and less precise than those of the Law. So that it was even much more necessary that a christian Church should have that power which our Lord himself acknowledged to have been possessed by the Scribes and Pharisees.

And since it was undoubtedly his design that there should always be christian churches "even to the end of the world," there can be no doubt that He intended these churches to possess all those three requisites above mentioned, without which no community of any kind can subsist. And hence, we may feel assured that the officers of christian churches, and the rules established in them (when not adverse to Gospel

7*

principles), and the penalties which form the sanction of those rules, and the power which every church exercises of admitting or excluding persons as *members*,—all these must, we are sure, have the sanction of our divine Master Himself.

All this we might infer, as has been said, from the mere fact of his having sanctioned the formation of christian communities. But, besides this, He expressly conferred on his Apostles—the first founders and first rulers of christian churches—those very powers just mentioned.

The power of "binding and loosing"*—that is, of making and annulling decisions and regulations—He distinctly conferred on the Apostles; declaring that their decisions should be bound "in heaven," that is sanctioned by Himself. (Matt. xvi. 19.)

This declaration He made first to Peter, as being the person chosen to take the lead in laying the first foundation of a christian church; both among the Jews on the day of Pentecost, and afterwards among the Gentiles. (Acts ii., x.) But subsequently, a little before his departure, He appoints a kingdom to the Apostles generally. (Luke xxii. 29.) In addressing Peter, He mentions the "keys of the kingdom of heaven," that is the power of admitting members into the christian church, and of excluding them. But this is in fact included in the appointment to the kingdom; since the rulers of a church must be intrusted with this power.

* This is the phrase which was and still continues in use among the Jews in that sense.

And He also expressly conferred on the Apostles the power of inflicting and remitting church penalties (John xx. 23), for offences against the society,—what we call *Ecclesiastical* offences. And it is likely, that, besides this, his words had reference also to their office of preaching "baptism for remission of sins," and of administering or refusing baptism, according as each person might appear in their judgment fit or unfit: that is, the qualifications for being admitted into Christ's kingdom, and for being allowed to continue a subject of it, having been laid down by Himself as the Supreme Head, his ministers were left to decide in each case, who was, or was not, thus qualified.

This, doubtless, was our Lord's meaning when He spoke of the "keys of the kingdom of heaven." And it is probably one part of what He meant to include in the power of remitting and retaining sins.

But this, at least, is quite certain, that no mere man can have power to forgive sins *as against* GOD, or to grant or refuse admission into the realms of heavenly bliss; which is the office of the Lord Jesus Himself at the Day of Judgment. By Him his disciples were merely authorised to admit men into his kingdom on earth,—that is, his Church: and to pronounce not what *particular individuals*, but what *kind* of persons should have remission of sins against God, and should attain eternal life,—namely, those whose penitence and faith are seen by Him to be sincere.

He might, had He seen fit, have gifted his apostles and other ministers with the faculty of reading any man's heart, and foreseeing the future course of his life; and He might thus have enabled them to pronounce positively of an individual, that his sins were pardoned by the MOST HIGH, and that he would inherit eternal life. But this gift our Lord did not think fit to bestow on his Apostles, or on any man. They were left, to judge, as they could, of the sincerity of each man's professions, and of the steadfastness both of his faith, and of his whole christian character. And in this they were liable to be deceived; as is evident from the case (among others) of Simon the sorcerer (Acts viii.); for he would not have been admitted to baptism, if it had been perceived at the time that he was " in the bond of iniquity."

But offences *against a society*, that society has a right to pardon; just as an individual may forgive sins against himself. Indeed, our Lord, we know, commanded us thus to forgive. But of course He did not mean that we have power to pardon sins as against God. For *that* belongs to Him alone. If any one does some wrong to us, or to a Society, he also, by doing this wrong, sins against God. It rests with us, or with the society he has wronged, to pardon the *wrong as against his fellow-men*. But God alone can pardon the sin against God.

All those three requisites, then, which we have been speaking of as essential to every Society, our Lord expressly established. He appointed *officers*, and He conferred the power of enacting *rules*, and of admitting and excluding *members*.

And it is plain that what He said to those particular disciples He was addressing, could not be meant as limited to them alone, but as having reference to His Church "even unto the end of the world;" since it is certain He designed his Church not to cease with the lives of its first founders, but to continue permanently.

We may, perhaps, think that, if matters had been left to our judgment and disposal, we should have asked for a continuance of miracles for the conversion of unbelievers, and a continued inspiration in the church, in order to be sure of an infallible interpretation of Scripture. But as there is no promise of anything of this kind, we have no right either to conclude from our own wishes, that it must exist; or again, to reject Christianity for not completely answering our wishes. It is quite otherwise, however, with those things we have been speaking of as *essential* requisites for a Society. We infer that a christian church must have them, not because this is *advantageous* and desirable, but because it is *indispensable* to every kind of Society. Without Officers and Rules of some kind or other, and power of enrolling and excluding Members, no Society could subsist at all. And since our Great Master did sanction the existence of christian societies, we fairly conclude, that by so doing, He sanctioned whatever is essential to the existence of a society, and implied thereby.

Such was manifestly the will of the divine Founder of our religion. And it was also his will that christian communities, the several portions of his kingdom, should continue to subsist under the government of *uninspired* fallible men, having no miraculous powers, nor any infallible guide on earth to appeal to, in case of any doubt as to the right interpretation of Scripture, or the right application of scripture principles.

This may seem to some persons very strange. Not but that we can perceive plainly that there is a *difference* between our case and that of those who lived when the Gospel was first proclaimed. For in order to *introduce* a revelation from Heaven, it was indispensably necessary that certain persons should receive from Heaven a communication of what that revelation was. And no one could have been expected to listen to them, if they had not proved, by the display of miraculous powers, that they really had received such a communication. In after times, on the contrary, the *writings* of those persons may be referred to for a knowledge of what the religion is. And the miracles by which *they* established it, and without which it never *could* have been established, may be appealed to in proof of its divine origin.

But still, if it were left to each Christian's judgment and choice, whether he would or would not have inspiration and other miraculous gifts bestowed on the Church, for the conversion of unbelievers, and for the satisfaction of the doubting, and for the correction of such errors as arise from time to time,—if each man were left to decide on this according to his own judgment and wishes—it is probable that very many would ask for a restoration of those gifts. We should not at least find all Christians agreeing to decline them as no longer needed.

Many there are who would fain have—somewhere

at least on earth—an infallible guide, accessible to all
men, to decide, by evident divine authority, on any
questions that may arise. And some there are who
are even so bent on this, that they resolve to find it,
because they deem it needful, with, or without good
reasons for believing it to exist; and who will accept
the Gospel on no other condition.

The truth is, that there is in the human mind a
craving for infallibility, which predisposes men
towards the pretensions, either of a supposed unerring
church, or of those who claim or who promise immediate inspiration. And accordingly, we find persons
sometimes waver for a time between these two classes
of pretensions, and ultimately give in to the one, or to
the other, and sometimes thus changing more than
once, yet still always clinging to the confident expectation of finding that infallibility we have been speaking of. They are inquiring only after a way of
exempting themselves from all further inquiry. Their
care is only to relieve themselves ultimately from all
further need of vigilant care. They are navigating in
search of a perfectly safe haven, in which the helm
may be abandoned, and the vessel left to ride securely,
without any need of watching the winds and currents,
and of looking out for rocks and shoals. They hope
to obtain, in all ages of the church, that exemption
from all need of vigilant circumspection, which was
not granted even in the age of the Apostles; since we
find that, even when there *were* these infallible guides
on earth, Christians are perpetually warned of the
danger of mistaking "false apostles" for genuine.

And it may be added, that any one who is thus induced to give himself up implicitly to the guidance of such a supposed infallible authority, without presuming thenceforth to exercise his own judgment on any point relative to religion, or to think for himself at all on such matters,—such a one will be likely to regard this procedure as the very perfection of pious *humility*,—as a most reverent observance of the rule of "lean not to thine own understanding;" though, in reality, it is the very error of leaning improperly to our own understanding. For to resolve to believe that God *must* have dealt with mankind just in the way that *we* could *wish* as the most *desirable*, and in the way that to *us* seems the most *probable;* this is in fact to *set up ourselves as his judges.* It is to dictate to Him in the spirit of Naaman, who *thought* that the prophet would recover him by a touch, and who *chose* to be healed by the waters of Abana and Pharpar, the rivers of Damascus, which he deemed better than all the waters of Israel.

But any thing that falls in at once with men's *wishes*, and with their *conjectures*, and which also presents itself to them in the guise of a *virtuous humility;* this, they are often found readily and firmly to believe, not only *without* evidence, but *against* all evidence. And thus it is in the present case. The principle of which we have been speaking,—that every revelation from heaven necessarily requires, as an indispensable accompaniment, an infallible interpreter always at hand,—this principle clings so strongly to the minds of many men, that they are even found still to maintain it, after they have ceased to believe in any revelation at all, or even in the existence of a God.

There can be, we conceive, no doubt of the fact, that very great numbers of men are to be found,—they are much more numerous in some parts of the Continent than among us;—men not deficient in intelligence, nor altogether strangers to reflection, who, while they for the most part conform externally to the prevailing religion, are inwardly utter unbelievers in Christianity; yet still hold to the principle,—which, in fact, has had the chief share in *making* them unbelievers,—that the idea of a DIVINE REVELATION implies that of a universally-accessible INFALLIBLE INTERPRETER; and that the one, without the other, is an absurdity and contradiction.

We have said that it is this principle that has mainly contributed to make these men unbelievers. For when a tolerably intelligent and reflective man has fully satisfied himself, that, in point of fact, no such provision *has* been made,—that no infallible and universally-accessible interpreter does exist on earth —yet still adheres to the principle of its supposed *necessity*, the consequence is inevitable, that he will at once reject all belief of Christianity. The ideas of a REVELATION, and of an unerring INTERPRETER, being in his mind inseparably conjoined, the overthrow of the one belief cannot but carry the other along with it. Such a person, therefore, will be apt to think it not worth while to examine the reasons in favour of any other system of Christianity *not* pretending to furnish an infallible interpreter. This—which, he is fully convinced, is essential to a revelation from Heaven—is by some churches *claimed*, but not *established*, while the rest do not even claim it. The pretensions of the one he has listened to and deliberately rejected ; those of the other he regards as not even worth listening to.

The system, then, of reasoning from our own conjectures as to the necessity of the Most High doing so and so, tends to lead a man to proceed from the rejection of his own form of Christianity, to a rejection of revelation altogether. But does it stop here? Does not the same system lead naturally to Atheism also? Experience shows that that consequence, which reason might have anticipated, does often actually take place. He who gives the reins to his own conjectures as to what is *necessary*, and thence draws his conclusions, will be likely to find a *necessity* for such divine interference in the affairs of the world as does not in fact take place. He will deem it no less than necessary, that an omnipotent, and all-wise, and beneficent Being should interfere to rescue the oppressed from the oppressor,—the corrupted from the corrupter,—to deliver men from such temptations to evil as it is morally impossible they should withstand ;—and, in short, to banish *evil* from the universe. And, since this is not done, he draws the inference that there cannot possibly be a God, and that to believe otherwise is a gross absurdity. Such a belief he may, indeed, consider as useful for keeping up a wholesome awe in the minds of the vulgar; and for their sakes he may outwardly profess Christianity also; even as the heathen philosophers of old endeavoured to keep up the popular superstitions: but a real belief he will regard as something impossible to an intelligent and reflective mind.

We are very far from saying that all, or the greater part, of those who maintain the principle we are speaking of, are Atheists. We all know how common it is for men to fail of carrying out some principle (whether good or bad) which they have adopted;— how common, to maintain the premises, and not perceive the conclusion to which they lead. But the *tendency* of the *principle* itself is what we are speaking of: and the danger is anything but imaginary of its leading, in fact as it does naturally and consistently, to Atheism as its ultimate result.

But whatever our wishes or conjectures might have been, no such choice,—no such offer of infallible guidance—has been set before us. What is required of us is, thankfully to endeavour to make the best use of the advantages we *have*, instead of conjecturing or wondering why it is that we have not more. We are not called on to explain to the satisfaction of all men, or of ourselves, the reasons, in each instance, for God's having dealt with us as He has. What we are to say, in reference to any such inquiries, is, "Even so, Father! *for so it seemed good in Thy sight.*"

To Him, then, it seemed good, that after the departure of the Apostles, no successors to them in the Apostolic office should arise. As *members* indeed, and as *ministers and rulers* of christian churches, they were succeeded by others, down to this day. But as *Apos-*

tles of Jesus Christ, they have no successors. As personal attendants on Him, and eye-witnesses of his *resurrection*—as both possessors and *dispensers* of *miraculous* gifts (Acts viii. 14), and as *inspired oracles* to make known the divine will,—in all these points, which were what constituted the apostolic office, they left none to succeed them. In all that relates to christian churches, and also in that for the sake of which churches were instituted, the conduct of individual Christians in *all* the concerns of life,—men are now, by the decree of Providence, left to act (according to their own best discretion) in conformity with Gospel *principles*, as recorded in Scripture.

The Holy Spirit, indeed, " who helpeth our infirmities," is promised to those who earnestly seek it, and who strive to profit by it. This aid is needed by us, and is promised to us, both for the establishment of our *faith*, and also for the guidance of our judgment, and of our *conduct*, whether in matters connected with the Church, or in anything else. But how far any one is really " led by the Spirit " in each instance, there is no authority on earth to decide. It is the office of that Spirit to guard us both from *error* and from *sin*. But we must not pretend to be either free from sin, or exempt from error; since of *that* we cannot be infallible judges. If it be right to say, " Who can tell how oft he offendeth?" we ought to add also, " Who can tell how oft he mistaketh?"

A christian church, then, being a Society, instituted under Christ's sanction, for the purpose of keeping up and extending the knowledge and practice of his religion, and of thus making men faithful and obedient subjects of his kingdom, the rulers of such a Society are bound to act, according to the best of their power, with a view to this object. They are to keep in mind, that is, that it is *Christ's* kingdom and not their *own*, in which they hold office. "We preach not ourselves," says the Apostle, "but Christ Jesus our Lord; and us, your servants, for Christ's sake."

The powers, therefore, which He has entrusted to a Church are to be exercised in strict conformity with the principles laid down by Him and his inspired servants.

No Church has power to alter, or to add to, the terms of gospel salvation as laid down in Scripture; or to keep back from its members anything revealed in Scripture; or to encourage, or willingly leave them, in ignorance of it. For its very office is, in the words of Christ Himself, to " teach them to observe *all* things whatsoever I have commanded."

It is, indeed, allowable, and proper, that a Church should employ, for the instruction of its people, convenient Summaries and Expositions of Scripture doctrine, such, for instance, as Catechisms. For this is to supply an omission, which (as above observed) was purposely left in Scripture. But then these Catechisms, &c., must contain the very doctrines of Scripture, and none other. And being the compositions of uninspired men, no authority must be claimed for them, except from their agreement with Scripture. And the same rule applies to Forms of prayer and to Creeds.

Creeds, which have been sometimes called "Symbols," sometimes "Confessions of Faith," or "Articles of Religion," are statements of such doctrines as must be acknowledged by any one who would become, or remain, a member of the Church which adopts that Creed. In different Churches, in the earliest times, different Creeds were in use; and alterations were made in them from time to time. Not that any Church had a right to alter the christian Faith; but that it was necessary to meet, and guard against the particular religious errors which arose in various Ages and Countries. But as none of these creeds is to be found in Scripture, so, there is none that can claim any authority, except from its conformity to Scripture.

The *doctrines*, then, which a christian Church teaches, and is bound to teach, are to be those of the christian Scriptures; neither more nor less.

But, on the other hand, Church *ordinances* and *regulations* are only required to be not *at variance* with Scripture. For it is indispensably necessary for a Church to make enactments on many points respecting which nothing is precisely laid down in Scripture; but only the general principle, "let all things be done to edifying."

For instance, assembling for public joint Worship is enjoined in Scripture; but the times, places, and mode of conducting the worship are not specified. The Sacraments, again, as instituted by Christ, are to be celebrated; but the mode of celebration is not prescribed. It is not even ordered that the Elders [Clergy] are to administer the Sacraments; though this, (very naturally and properly,) has been the rule of every Church.

In these, and in several other points, a Church is not only authorized, but compelled, to make regulations; because we are enjoined to do things which *must* be done in *some* regular specified mode, and the mode is not laid down in Scripture.

For instance, since Christians are commanded (as has just been observed) to *assemble* (Heb. x. 25) for divine worship, it is necessary that the times for doing so should be fixed by authority. And, accordingly, certain days have been, in all ages of Christianity, set apart by every Church, for this purpose. Thus every one knows what is called Christmas-day has been set apart to commemorate the birth of Jesus Christ; the day called Good Friday, for his crucifixion; and Easter-day in each year, and also the first day in each week (thence called "the Lord's Day"), to celebrate his resurrection.*

---

* Hence, the Sunday, being (like the Jewish Sabbath) one day in every seven, is sometimes called the Christian Sabbath; though kept on a different day of the week from the Jewish Sabbath, and in a differeut manner, and to commemorate a different event.

Neither the foutrh Commandment, nor any other law enjoining the observance of the seventh day of the week in memory of the close of the creation, is regarded by Christians as binding on them. For if it were, they would be bound strictly to obey it, as it was given. For the Apostles,—who, themselves, as Jews, kept the Sabbath-day, and also, as Christians, assembled for worship on the Lord's Day,—never made a *change* of the Sabbath from the seventh day to the first. And no Church, consisting of uninspired men, has any right to change any divine ordinance designed for them. But the Mosaic Law having come to an end, and, moreover, having never been binding on Gentiles, a

And in the observance of "the Lord's Day," after the example of the Apostles (though no express command of theirs to that effect is recorded), all Churches, from the earliest times, have, very properly, agreed.

A Church that should act otherwise, would be *making an ill use* of the powers bestowed on it; but it would be presumptuously *exceeding* its powers, if it should dare to enact anything at variance with Scripture. For instance, either, on the one hand, to abolish the Sacraments ordained by Christ, or, on the other hand, to depart from that celebration of the Lord's Supper which He Himself appointed, and to administer the bread without the cup, which He directed *all* the Disciples to drink of, is what no Church can have any right to do.

And it would be equally against Scripture, and that in a most important point, to attempt to convert christian Ministers into *sacrificing* Priests: because Scripture plainly teaches that, under the Gospel, this office belongs to Christ alone.

But christian Ministers for the performance of such duties as are described in Paul's Epistles to Timothy and to Titus, and elsewhere, every church clearly has a right to appoint, for the reasons already given. And there is no reason to doubt that the Elders ordained in each Church by Paul, or any other Apostle, did themselves, in turn, ordain others to assist or to succeed them; and these again, others, and so on in perpetuity, down to the present day.

christian church is left to determine what days shall be set apart, as above mentioned.

But then, it is from the Church that Ministers (as well as Church ordinances) derive all their authority. Whether in sending fresh labourers into the Lord's vineyard, or in any of their other functions, they must act as *authorised* by the Society, and as representing it; not as possessing independent powers, as individuals. For it is to a Church as to a Society that those rights we have been speaking of belong; and whatever is done by the regular Officers of a Society, conformably to its constitution, is to be considered as done by the society.

When, therefore, Bishops, or any others, are spoken of as *ordaining* persons to the Ministry, it must be understood that, being empowered by their Church so to do, according to the rules of that Church, they are its *representatives*, and their acts are its acts.

And if any Minister were regularly deprived of his office, he would no longer have any power either to ordain, or in any way to officiate; unless he were admitted into some other Church, and taken into its service as one of its Ministers.

The rights, then, conferred on christian Communities by our divine Master Himself, being such as we have described, no one need be distressed by doubts and fears respecting some possible irregularity in the ordination of some minister, which may possibly have occurred at some time or other, in the course of eighteen centuries.

Amidst the wars and tumults and general confusion which took place at various times during that space, and especially during what are called "the dark ages," when ignorance and barbarism, as well as lawless violence, were so prevalent, it may have happened, more than once, that some person who had never been regularly ordained, or, perhaps, even baptized, may have contrived to intrude himself into the ministerial office; and to have even attained the rank of a bishop; and may thus have been the ordainer of others, the successors of whom may possibly be among ourselves at this day.

There is no christian Minister now existing that can trace up, with complete certainty, his own ordination, through perfectly regular steps, to the times of the Apostles. And, accordingly, if the reality of the ministerial Office were made to depend, not on a man's being an acknowledged Minister of a christian Church, but on a certain mysterious sacramental virtue, transmitted from hand to hand, in unbroken succession from the Apostles, there would be a most distressing and incurable uncertainty in each Christian's mind, whether he were really baptized, really ordained, or really partaker of any christian privileges.

But as it is, there is no ground for any such perplexing doubts. A christian Community, formed on Gospel principles, confers on its recognised Officers the rights of christian Ministers; who are to be regarded as having Christ's commission, and as successors of the Apostles in the ministerial office. We are bound, indeed, to do our very best to prevent irregularities of any kind, in ordinations, and in every thing else connected with our religion. But we need not fear that any accidental or unavoidable irregularity that may ever have occurred, can have the effect of shutting out whole Bodies of sincere disciples from the Gospel covenant and christian ordinances, or from any privilege granted by Christ Himself to those who should be "gathered together in his name."

It is to be observed, however, that although no *one individual christian Minister* can, with complete certainty, trace his own succession in an unbroken chain from the Apostles, and prove that there was no flaw in any link, the case is different when we look to *the Clergy* generally. For there can be no reasonable doubt that *such an Order of men* did always exist, from the times of the Apostles, continuously, to this day. We may be as sure of this as we are that great numbers of the English nation are descendants of the Saxons, who settled in Britain in the fifth and sixth centuries, though there is probably no one man who could trace his descent from any of them. For, christian Ministers held office in the churches as immediate successors of others who held the same office, and who in like manner professed to be the immediate successors of others, &c., whose predecessors had been appointed by the Apostles themselves.

Now, if, a century ago, or ten centuries ago, or at any other time, a number of men had arisen, claiming to be the immediate successors (as above described) of persons holding this office, when, in fact, *no such Order of men had ever been heard of,* such an absurd pretension would have been immediately exposed and derided.

There must always, therefore, have existed such an

Order of men, from the time of those Apostles who professed to be eye-witnesses of the Resurrection, and to work sensible public miracles in proof of their divine commission. And, consequently, the christian Ministry is a standing *monument* to attest the *public proclamation* of those miraculous events at the very time when they are said to have occurred.

Now, at that time there must have been great numbers of persons able and willing to expose the imposture, had there been any.

And this argument for the truth of the Sacred History is quite independent of any particular *mode* of appointing christian Ministers. If, for instance, these had always been elected by the People, and had at once entered on their office without any ordination by other Ministers, still, if they were but appointed (in whatever mode) as immediate successors of persons holding the same office, the argument would be the same.

That mode, indeed, of admitting men into the Ministry which was practised by the Apostles (1 Tim. iv. 14, and v. 22) has, in fact, been retained in all ages of Christianity. But the argument we have now been considering is quite independent of this. It turns entirely on the mere fact of *the constant existence* of a certain Order of men.

And it is worth observing, that the LORD's DAY is a monument of the same kind. It is kept all over the world, by different and even hostile Bodies of Christians, in memory of the Resurrection of Jesus Christ. And not only so,—for this alone would not be a decisive proof,—but it is observed by them as a day which has been *always* thus kept, from the very day when the Lord Jesus is recorded to have risen, and to have appeared to his Disciples. Now, if it had *not* been thus constantly kept, from the first, but the observance of it introduced in some later age, those among whom it was thus introduced would have been able to testify that they had never heard of such a festival before.

CORRUPTIONS OF CHRISTIANITY.

It was observed in the preceding Section, that if all things relating to the Christian Church had been ordered by Divine Providence in the way that *men* would have been likely to conjecture as the most probable, and to wish for as the most desirable, there would have been some infallible guide left on Earth, to decide all questions that might arise, and to guard us against all possible religious error. There would have been a *perpetual inspiration* lodged in some person or persons, endued with such manifest *miraculous* powers as could leave no doubt as to their inspiration. And these infallible interpreters would have been universally and readily *accessible*.

But it is notorious, that such was *not* the design of Providence: and that no such guide does exist. Of all the persons who have claimed infallibility, there is none who has displayed (as Paul did) "the signs of an apostle," that is, such palpable and undeniable miraculous powers, as to leave no doubt in any candid mind, of his being really inspired. And since the very purpose for which an infallible guide is supposed to be needed, is, the removal of all reasonable *doubts*, it is plain that if God had thought fit to provide us with such a guide, He would not have left it at all *doubtful* where we were to look for that guide.

It seems to have been his design that part of Man's trial on Earth should consist in his being required to "prove (Δοκιμάζειν), [that is, try and examine] all things, and hold fast that which is right." We are called on to inquire carefully, and humbly, and piously, after truth; and to embrace whatever appears, to the best of our judgment, to be the truth.

To complain of this,—to reject or undervalue the revelation God has bestowed, urging that it is no revelation to us, or an insufficient one, because unerring certainty is not bestowed also,—because we are required to exercise patient diligence and watchfulness, and candour, and humble self-distrust,—this would be as unreasonable as to disparage and neglect the bountiful gift of eyesight, because men's eyes have sometimes deceived them; because men have mistaken a picture for the object imitated, or a mirage of the desert for a lake; and have fancied they had the evidence of sight for the sun's motion; and to infer from all this that we ought to blindfold ourselves, and be led henceforth by some guide who pretends to be himself not liable to such deceptions.

The two great volumes,—that of Nature, and that of Revelation, which God has opened before us for our benefit, are in this respect analogous. Both are in themselves exempt from error; but they do not confer complete exemption from all possibility of error on the student of them. As the laws of nature are in themselves invariable, but yet are sometimes imperfectly known, and sometimes mistaken, by natural philosophers, so the Scriptures are intrinsically infallible, but do not impart infallibility to the student of them. Even by the most learned, they are in many parts imperfectly understood; by the "un-learned and unstable" they are liable to be "wrested to their own destruction."

But still, if no errors or dissensions had arisen in the Church during the days of the Apostles, and then, when these inspired teachers were removed, heresies and schisms (σχίσματα, divisions) had arisen for the first time, we might have felt as if God had forsaken us, and as if Christians were exposed to such trials as had not been originally designed. Or we might have imagined (as indeed some persons *have* imagined) that God would still grant us inspiration, attested by miraculous signs, if we were not wanting in faith, and in earnest supplication for such gifts.

And accordingly, in almost every Age of Christianity, there have been persons who have persuaded themselves that miraculous powers and inspiration actually are bestowed on themselves or on their

Church; and these pretensions are believed by such as decide according to their own wishes and conjectures, without any rational proofs.

But when we come to examine Scripture History, we find that, even in the times of the Apostles, false teachers did "arise, speaking perverse things, to draw away disciples after them,"* and that Christians were thus divided into rival sects. And this, the Apostles teach us, is a part of the appointed trial to which we are to be subjected here on earth. "There must needs be heresies, that they which are approved may be made manifest" (1 Cor. xi. 19), that is, that men may have to exercise their care and candour in chusing between truth and error.

And since God did think fit that christians should have to encounter such trials, He mercifully provided that they should be forewarned "to take heed to themselves." The errors and corruptions introduced, even in the days of the Apostles, are recorded in our Sacred Books, on purpose, no doubt, to put us on our guard; to prepare us to be watchful against corruptions of Christianity in all other Ages of the Church; and also to prevent our being disheartened at finding ourselves exposed to such a trial.

It is not the design of this Dissertation, nor indeed would its limits permit, to give an historical account of each of the various corruptions of Christianity which have taken place in different Ages and Countries. It will be sufficient to give a sketch of the principal *sources* from which they arose, and of the

* Acts xx. 28, *perverted* doctrines, διεστραμμένα.

means by which, in many instances, they were encouraged and kept up.

These two general rules, then, are to be kept in mind :—

1*st*, That whatever *opposed* Christianity at the outset, afterwards tended to *mix* itself up with the Religion, and corrupt it.

2*dly*, That as far as any corruptions depended on *local* and *temporary* circumstances, so far, they would be likely soon to die away, without spreading widely; but so far as they were connected with *Human Nature*, we may expect to find them appearing again and again, in various countries.

I. First, then, we have said that the causes which, at the beginning, led to open hostility against the Gospel, afterwards operated to corrupt it. All those human faults and follies—all those prejudices, and infirmities, and vices—which originally disposed men to reject the Christian religion, found their way *into* it, in proportion as it prevailed.

At first, almost all those whose notions and whose dispositions were wholly adverse to Christianity, rejected it altogether, and endeavoured to put it down: though even from the very first there were exceptions to this rule; as we see in the instances of Iscariot, and of Simon the Sorcerer. But as the Religion spread, and became less and less unpopular, and the number of disciples multiplied more and more, there was a continually increasing number of persons who, though members of Christian churches, had not fully understood the character of the Gospel, nor imbibed the

8*

spirit of it. And these introduced *into* the Religion the same kind of errors and wrong principles as had originally been openly arrayed *against* it.

The chief opposition to the Gospel arose from (1.) Judaism; (2.) Pagan Superstitions; (3.) Heathen Philosophy; (4.) Immorality of Character; and, (5.) Worldly Policy.

And the spirit of Judaism, of Paganism, &c., afterwards found their way *into* Christianity, and tended to corrupt it.

(1.) It has been pointed out in an earlier part of this Dissertation, how much opposed the prevailing Jewish notions and prejudices were to the religion of Jesus Christ.

And accordingly, one of the very earliest attempts to corrupt Christianity was made by the Judaizing teachers, who were continually endeavouring to bring the Gentile believers under the yoke of the Mosaic Law. (Acts xv., Gal. ii., Phil. iii.)

(2.) Then, again, of the opposition of the Pagan worshippers to the Gospel, we find many instances mentioned in the Book of the Acts of the Apostles; especially in chap. xvi. 20, 21; and xix. 27.

And we find, from time to time, attempts made to incorporate into Christianity superstitions borrowed from Paganism, or of a similar nature.

The earliest, perhaps, of these corruptions of Christianity, was that introduced by those very ancient heretics, the Gnostics, whom the Apostle John was particularly occupied in opposing, both in his Epistles and in the opening of his Gospel.

These men, it is well known, blended with christian doctrines many of the notions of the Pagans, of the Persian, and some other Eastern Nations. The religious system of these Nations consisted in acknowledging and reverencing two beings of equal power,—a good and an evil god,—whom they called Ormuzd and Ahriman. And some of their descendants, in the same regions, at this day, are said to retain this faith, and to be worshippers principally of the evil god.

The Gnostics accordingly taught, among other things, that the world was not created by the Supreme God, but by an Evil Being, or by a certain inferior god.*

But, as has been above said, various other Pagan errors, or errors resembling those of Paganism, have, from time to time, crept into the christian Church.

(3.) The ancient heathen philosophers again, who believed little or nothing of the popular superstitions, were no less opposed to the Gospel, which they derided as " foolishness." And many of them, when they afterwards embraced Christianity, endeavoured to reconcile it with their philosophical speculations, and thus to be wise above that which is written.

It is evidently to this danger that Paul is alluding, in many passages; especially when he warns the Colossians, " Beware lest any man spoil you through philosophy and vain deceit, after the rudiments of the world, and not after Christ." (Col. ii. 8. See also 1 Cor. i. 20–28.)

It appears, therefore, that even in the Apostolic

* Thence denominated by them Δημιουργός.

Age, men had begun to introduce into Christianity presumptuous speculations on matters not revealed in Scripture, and to make the Gospel a field for the exercise of their philosophical ingenuity. But in later ages this evil prevailed to a far greater degree.

(4.) As for moral depravity, no one can doubt how much this must have led many persons to shut their ears against the evidences for a religion which required them to reform their lives.

The description given of Felix, the Governor, would no doubt have suited a great number of others: " When Paul reasoned of righteousness, temperance, and the judgment to come, Felix trembled, and said, Go thy way for this time; when I have a convenient season I will call for thee."

But when persons of this character did become members of the Church, as it appears many did, even in the time of the Apostles, they naturally sought to accommodate the religion to their own corrupt characters. This seems to have been more particularly the case with those Gnostics above mentioned. For they taught that men are to be saved by what they called " knowledge* of the Gospel," while living the most immoral life, and yet having no sin (that is nothing imputed to *them* as sin) but being accounted righteous without " doing righteousness." (1 John iii.) And this it was that made the Apostle John so vehement in his censure of them.

But there are many allusions in the Apostolic Epis-

---

* Hence their title of "Gnostics;" that is, persons *knowing* the Gospel.

tles, to others besides these Gnostics, who sought to "hold the truth in unrighteousness." (Romans i. 18.)

(5.) Lastly, *worldly policy* was evidently one of the chief causes which, in the outset, acted as a hindrance to the reception of Christianity. It is plain, from the very nature of the case, that all views of worldly ambition,—all desire of worldly profit or advantage of any kind,—all considerations of supposed political expediency,—must have been, at first, arrayed in opposition to the Gospel. And every part of the sacred narrative confirms this. We find the Jewish rulers influenced by the fear that " the Romans would come and take away their place and nation." (John x. 48.) We find them urging before Pilate, that " whosoever maketh himself a king, speaketh against Cæsar." And we find the same sort of plea repeatedly used to the Roman governors, and often with effect. (See Acts xvii. 7, and xix. 23.)

And again, the poverty, hardships, and persecutions, which the early Christians had been so earnestly forewarned of by our Lord (John xvi. 1, 2), and to which they were actually exposed, must have operated very strongly in prejudicing all men of a worldly character against the religion.

Of course, in proportion as Christianity became less unpopular, and more generally received, this cause would less and less operate in making men *reject* the religion, and would be more and more likely to *corrupt* it. In proportion as worldly-minded men became members of the Church, they would naturally endeavour to wrest the Religion to their own views of ambition or of profit.

This could not be expected to take place to the same extent in the earliest Ages as afterwards. Yet we find that even in the days of the Apostles, men had crept into the church who were tainted with avarice or worldly ambition, and who corrupted the christian doctrines so as to favour their own views. For we find Paul cautioning Timothy against "perverse disputings of men of corrupt minds and destitute of the truth, who regard religion as a source of profit."*

All the principal causes, then, which occasioned *opposition* to Christianity, at the outset, led afterwards to the *corruption* of the Religion; and accordingly, some of the principal corruptions which have, at various times, been introduced, will be noticed under the same five heads under which we have, just above, treated of the sources of the original opposition to the Gospel. Those causes, which had begun to operate even in the days of the Apostles, had, of course, more of this corrupting influence in later times. In proportion as the dangers to the Church from *without* were diminished, by the increasing prevalence of the Religion, the dangers from *within* naturally increased. For, the number must of course have become greater, of members of the Church who were such merely because they had been brought up as children of Christian parents, or because Christianity was the prevailing religion; and who *would* have rejected it when first

---

* 1 Tim. vi. 5. Ν μ ζώντων πορισμὸι εἰναι τήν εὐσέβειαν

preached, from their having an unconverted heart, and being strangers to the true spirit of the Gospel. And such persons will always be likely to aim at bringing their religion into a conformity with their own characters, instead of conforming their own characters to the Religion.

II. The second general rule we laid down was, that so far as any human fault or folly was peculiar to *some particular time or Country*, its effects may be expected soon to have passed away without spreading very far; but so far as it belonged to *human nature* in general, we must expect to find the evil effects of its reappearing again and again, in various forms, in all Ages, and in various regions.

And for the most part it will be found that the prejudices and evil dispositions of men which have introduced religious error, and accordingly the religious errors themselves thence arising, are different in their *outward form* according to the peculiar circumstances of each time and place; but that in *substance* and at bottom, they are nearly alike, always and everywhere.

For, example, the prejudice of the Jews in favour of their own nation and institutions, gave rise to that very early heresy above noticed (see Acts xv., and Gal. ii.), of those who taught that all Christians were bound to keep the Mosaic Law; or at least, that such as did so had attained a superior degree of sanctity. The violation of the UNITY [ONENESS] of Christ's religion, by thus dividing Christians into two classes, admitted to different degrees of religious privilege, has been already noticed. The sect of Judaizing Christians, however, thus founded seems not to have lasted long. The destruction of Jerusalem and its Temple appears to have soon put an end to it. But the *general* tendency towards this violation of Christian Unity, being not peculiar to the Jews, but a part of human nature, has shewn itself again and again, under various forms, in various portions of the Church.

What are called the "Monastic Orders," which have long existed in many Churches, are a striking instance of this. Though the great mass of Christians have been solemnly dedicated to Christ at baptism, wherein they engage to be his "faithful soldiers and servants;" yet many have thought fit to take on themselves a new and distinct engagement, not binding on Christians generally, but only on such as have professed this new and superior kind of Christianity. The members of such Orders are often called the "religious;" and there is one well-known order called the "Society of Jesus;" as if the Church itself were not the *Society of Jesus*, and all its members bound to be *religious*. And the members of these Orders are supposed to possess a certain extraordinary kind of holiness, from their imposing on themselves certain restrictions, and privations, and other sufferings, according to rules laid down, not by Scripture for all men, but by particular founders for their own Order. Now this is clearly in violation of the ONENESS of Christ's religion.

Again, one may find persons dividing Christians into "Elect," and not Elect—those who are, and those who are not "God's people:" accounting some Christians "Saints," and others not; some "Evangelical," and others not. Though "Saints" was the very term used by the apostles to denote what we call " Christians ;" and though it is plain that since *Christianity* is the religion of the " *Gospel* " [Evangelium], all doctrines and all persons must be *Evangelical* or not, exactly in the same sense, and in the same degree, that they are, or are not *Christian.**

Those, also, who regard christian Ministers as *sacerdotal* Priests, acting as a kind of *mediators* between God and the People, are evidently going very far towards such a distinction between Clergy and Laity as is at variance with the Apostolical view of Christian-Unity.

And, it may be added, that there is a considerable number of persons who make a division of christians into the two classes of Communicants and non-Communicants. For there are very many of these latter, who, though far from disregarding christian duty altogether, or absenting themselves from public worship, yet consider that, so far from being a duty, it would be a *wrong* thing for *them* to attend the Lord's Table, unless they were determined to become Saints in some peculiar manner, different from what is expected of christians generally. And this they think it would be presumptuous for *them* to pretend to. They regard themselves, in short, as an *inferior class* of christians.

---

* There are, indeed, some persons who confine both the terms " Christian " and " Evangelical " to those who exactly agree with them in all points, and belong to their Party ; regarding all others as excluded from the Gospel covenant. But there are, again, some who make the distinction above alluded to.

. And, it is to be observed, that the division of worshippers into different classes in respect of religious privileges, belonged, even much more, to the Pagan religions, than to the Jewish. For among the Pagans, certain persons were "initiated" into such "Mysteries" of their religion as were carefully kept *secret* from the vulgar. And this was not the case with the Mosaic religion.* The division, therefore, of Christians into such classes, is what the heathen converts, no less than the Jewish, would be inclined to. And it is, moreover, something so natural to man, that, in one shape or another, it has appeared in almost all parts and Ages of the Church.

And so it is with most of the other corruptions of Christianity. The particular *form* in which each has appeared, will have generally been determined by *local* and *temporary* circumstances; and, when these circumstances are changed, that particular corruption will die away, to reappear (so far as it pertains to the character of the " natural man,") under some new shapes, in various countries.

It is to be observed, however, that those corruptions of Christianity which arise from the mixing up of Judaism with it, are, for one reason, likely to be more lasting than most others, and to be oftener revived. Christians acknowledge that the Mosaic Dispensation came from God. And that, and also the Christian

---

* Josephus remarks, as a distinction between the Pagan and the Jewish religions, that this latter made known to all the People the mysteries of their religion, while the Pagans concealed from all but those specially "initiated " the mysteries of theirs.

Dispensation, are contained in the volume which we call the Bible. Now, any one who regards the Bible (which many Christians do) as *one book*, containing divine instructions, without having formed any clear notions of what does and does not belong to each Dispensation, will, of course, fall into the greatest confusion of thought. He will be like a man who should have received from his father, at various times, a great number of letters containing directions as to his conduct, from the time when he was a little child just able to read, till he was a grown man; and who should lay by these letters with care and reverence, but in a confused heap, and should take up any one of them at random, and read it without any reference to its *date*, whenever he needed his father's instructions how to act.

Accordingly, many erroneous notions, wholly or partly drawn from Judaism, have again and again found their way into the christian Church.

For example, there have been in almost all Ages of the Church, persons who have taught that Jesus Christ is to come upon earth and reign in great worldly splendour at Jerusalem for a thousand years; which period is thence called Millennium. And superior privileges, as God's peculiar People, are then to be restored (according to this doctrine) to the Jews; that is, to such Jews as shall have continued *unbelievers;* not to the descendants of those great multitudes of them who embraced Christianity in the days of the Apostles, and since, and who thereupon soon became blended with the Gentile Christians. But the remnant of the Jews who shall have obstinately rejected the Gospel up to that time, are then to be restored to their own land, and to have a superiority in God's sight over men of Gentile race. And the Temple at Jerusalem is to be restored, and to be again the place of peculiar holiness, whither all men are to resort to worship.

Now these expectations of a Christ, who is to be a great and victorious temporal king, and of a kingdom of earthly glory, and of the restoration of the Temple, and of the exaltation of the Jews above all other people, are precisely those which the Jewish nation were so wedded to when our Lord came, and which led most of them to reject Him.

There are several other religious errors which have arisen from the same cause,—the practice of confusedly blending together the Law and the Gospel. Thus, some persons, as we had before occasion to remark, represent temporal rewards and punishments as a part of the sanction of the Christian Dispensation; and again, future rewards and punishments as a part of the sanction of the Mosaic. And this, as we have already said, destroys all clear notions of either system, and leads to great and dangerous practical errors, besides exposing our Scriptures to unanswerable objections from infidels.

And again, the introduction into Christianity of sacerdotal Priests,* Altars, Sacrifices, and Temples,

---

* Our word "Priest" is formed from Πρεσβύτερος; which is translated an "Elder," in our version of the Bible. But the word which our translators have rendered "*Priest*" is, in the original Greek,

which is so utterly repugnant to the whole character
of the Gospel, may be traced both to Judaism and
to Paganism. For all these things were common to
them both; though the Jewish Priests offered sacrifices to the true God, and the Pagan Priests to idols.

The Priests of the Israelites were appointed by the
Almighty Himself, for the express purpose of offering
sacrifices, in the name and on the behalf of the people;
they alone were allowed to make oblations and burn
incense before the Lord; and it was through them
that the People were to approach Him, that their service might be acceptable. A very great portion of
the Jewish religion consisted in the performance of
certain ceremonial rites, most of which could only be
duly performed by the Priests, or through their mediation and assistance; they were to make *intercession*
and *atonement* for offenders; they, in short, were the
mediators between God and Man.

And among the Pagans, whose institutions appear
to have been, in great measure, corrupt imitations of
those of the Patriarchal religion, we find, in like man-

'Ιερεὺς, in Latin SACERDOS, and is always applied to a sacrificing minister. And the word is never applied to any one under the Christian
dispensation, except Jesus Christ alone, our great and only High Priest,
who offered up Himself a sacrifice for man's redemption.

Now we may be sure that, if the Apostles had ordained any one to
the office of a *sacerdotal* priest, or had designed that there should be
any such in the christian Church, there would have been mention made
of it in the Book of Acts, and in the Apostolic Epistles.

Whenever the title of priest ['Ιερεὺ,] is applied to any Christians,
it is applied to *all* Christians (Rev. v. 10, and 1 Pet ii. 9) as offering
up themselves to God.

ner, Priests, who were principally, if not exclusively, the offerers of sacrifices, in behalf of the State and of individuals,—intercessors, supplicating and making atonement for others,—mediators, as before, between Man and the object of his worship.

The office of priest, then, in that sense of the word which we are now considering, viz., as equivalent to 'Ιερεύς, being such as has been described, it follows that in *our* religion, the *only* priest, in that sense, is Jesus Christ Himself; to whom consequently, and to whom alone, under the Gospel, the title is applied by the inspired Writers. He alone has offered up an atoning *sacrifice* for us, even the sacrifice of his own blood; He "ever liveth to make *intercession* for us;" He is the "one *Mediator* between God and man;" "through Him we have access to the Father; and no man cometh unto the Father, but by Him."

As for the Ministers whom He, and his Apostles, and their successors, appointed, they are completely distinct from Priests in the former sense, in office, as well as in name. Of this office one principal part is, that it belongs to them (not exclusively indeed, but principally and especially) to preach the Gospel,—to instruct, exhort, admonish, and spiritually govern, Christ's flock. His command was to "go and teach all nations;"—to "preach the Gospel to every crea-ture;" and these christian Ministers are called in the Epistle to the Hebrews, "those that bear rule over them, and watch for their souls, as they that must give an account." Now it is worthy of remark, that the office we are at present speaking of made no part of the especial duties of a Priest, in the other sense, such as those of the Jews, and of the Pagans. Among the former, it was not so much the family of Aaron, as the whole tribe of Levi, that seem to have been set aside for the purpose of *teaching* the Law; and even to these it was so far from being in any degree confined, that persons of any tribe might teach publicly in the synagogues on the Sabbath-day; as was done by our Lord Himself, who was of the tribe of Judah, and Paul, of the tribe of Benjamin, without any objection being raised; whereas an intrusion into the Priest's office would have been vehemently resented.

And as for the Pagan Priests, *their* business was rather to conceal, than to explain, the mysteries of their religion;—to keep the people in darkness, than to enlighten them. Accordingly the moral improvement of the people, among the ancients, seems to have been considered as the proper care of the legislator; whose laws and system of public education generally had this object in view. To these and to the public disputations of philosophers, but not at all to the Priests of their religion, they appear to have looked for instruction in their duty.

That the Christian Ministry, on the contrary, was appointed in great measure, if not principally, for the purpose of giving religious instruction and admonition, is clearly proved both by the practice of the Apostles themselves, and by Paul's directions to Timothy and to Titus.

Another, and that a peculiar and exclusive office

of the Christian Ministers, is, the administration of the Sacraments of Baptism and of the Lord's supper. But this administration does not at all assimilate the Christian Priesthood to the Pagan, or the Jewish. The former of these rites is, in the first place, an admission into the visible Church; and therefore very suitably received at the hands of those whose especial business is to *instruct* and examine those who are candidates for baptism, as adults, or who have been baptised in their infancy; and in the second place, it is an admission to a participation in the gifts of the Spirit, which constitute the Church "the temple of the Holy Ghost." The treasury, as it were, of divine grace is then thrown open, to which we may resort when a sufficient maturity of years enables us to understand our wants, and we are inclined to apply for their relief. It is not, let it be observed, through the mediation of an earthly Priest that we are admitted to offer our supplications before God's mercy-seat; we are authorised, by virtue of this sacred rite, to appear as it were in his presence ourselves; needing no intercessor with the Father, but his Son Jesus Christ, both God and man. "Having therefore," says Paul, "*boldness* to enter into the holiest by the blood of Jesus, by a new and living way, which he hath consecrated for us, and having an High Priest over the house of God, let us draw near with a true heart, in full *assurance* of faith, having our hearts sprinkled from an evil conscience, and our bodies washed with pure water."

The Sacrament of the Lord's Supper, again, is not,

as the Romanists unwarrantably pretend, a fresh sacrifice, but manifestly a celebration of the one already made. And the rite seems plainly to have been ordained for the express purpose (among others) of fixing our minds on the great and single oblation of Himself, made by the only High Priest "once for all;" that great High Priest who has no earthly successor. And *all* the communicants are alike partakers, spiritually, of the Body and Blood of Christ (*i. e.* of His Spirit), of which these are the emblems, provided *they themselves* are in a sanctified and right frame of mind. It is on the personal holiness of the Communicant, not of the Minister, that the efficacy of the sacrament depends; *he*, so far from offering any sacrifice himself, refers them to the sacrifice already made by another.

Such being, then, the respective offices of these two Orders of men (both now commonly called in English, "Priests," but originally distinguished by the names of *Hiereus* and *Presbyteros*), we may assert that the word in question is *ambiguous;* denoting, when thus applied to both, two things essentially distinct. It is not merely a comprehensive term, embracing two species under one class, but rather an equivocal term, applied, in different senses, to two things of different classes. At least, it must be admitted, that what is most essential to each respectively, is wanting in the other. The essential characteristic of the Jewish Priests, was (not their being *ministers* of religion; for that, in a certain sense, all the Levites were, but) their offering *sacrifices*, and making atonement and intercession for the people; whereas, of the Christian Minister, the especial office is religious instruction, and the administration of rites altogether different in their nature from the offering of sacrifices; totally precluding the idea of *his* being himself the mediator between God and Man.

And the contrast in this point, between the christian religion on the one hand, and all that exist, or ever existed, besides it (including the Jewish), on the other, will afford, if we rightly consider when, and by whom, our faith was introduced, one of the most powerful evidences of its truth.

The Apostles, though attentive to the regular government of the churches they founded, ordaining, for various services, Elders, and other Ministers, male and female, (the latter being known by the title of "Widows,") yet appointed no order of Priests in the sense of *Hiereus* (familiar as they must have been with the name), answering to the sacrificing Priests of the Jewish and of the Pagan religions. The same observation will apply to the Temple. The term was familiar to the New Testament writers; but it is never once applied by them to a christian place of worship; always to the worshippers themselves collectively;—to the christian congregation; as *e. g.* "Know ye not that ye are the temple of the Holy Ghost, which dwelleth in you?" "Your body is the temple of the Holy Ghost." "Ye, as lively stones, are builded together into an holy temple," &c.

All this is indeed perfectly intelligible to any one who understands the character of our religion. It is perfectly consistent with the Gospel scheme; but it is utterly at variance with the notions which would naturally have occurred to the unassisted mind of Man.

A further proof of this, if further could be needed, is furnished by the changes which were introduced in after ages. The very institution which Christianity in its pure state had abrogated, was grafted into it, as it became corrupted with human devices. An order of Priests in the ancient sense, offering pretended sacrifices, on a pretended altar, in behalf of the People, was introduced into the christian scheme, in such utter contradiction both to the spirit, and the very letter of it, that they were driven to declare the bread and wine of the Eucharist miraculously changed into literal flesh and blood offered up day by day repeatedly; although the founders of our religion had not only proclaimed the perfection of the one oblation of our Lord by Himself, but had even proved the imperfection of the Levitical sacrifices, from the very circumstance of their being repeated "year by year continually;" inasmuch as they would have *ceased* (says the Apostle) "to be offered," if, like the sacrifice of Christ, "once for all," they could "have made the comers thereunto perfect." Now, if when the religion *had* actually been established *without Altar, without Sacrifice, without Priest on earth*, all these were introduced into it, in opposition to its manifest character, through the strong craving (if we may so speak) of "the natural man" after them; how much more might we expect—with what complete certainty—that men brought up Jews, and having never *seen or heard of* any religion, true or false, without Priests, would have instituted, had they been left to themselves, an order of sacrificing Priests in their new religion? And how certain, that, since they carefully abstained from this and provided against it in the terms they employed;—how certain—that they were *not* left to themselves, but proceeded under the guidance of a divine director?

The corruptions then subsequently introduced into Christian churches, in respect of the Priesthood, do in reality, by shewing what the tendency of *human nature* is, go to prove the *superhuman* origin of the original institution. These have, however, afforded ground for cavil against Christianity itself, to those who, ignorantly or designedly, confound the religion itself with this perversion of it.

The Greek and Romish, and some other Churches have, in fact, in some great degree, transformed the *Presbyteros*, the Priest of the Gospel Dispensation, into the *Hiereus*, or Levitical Priest: thus derogating from the honour of the ONE great High Priest, and altering some of the most characteristic features of his religion, into something more like Judaism or Paganism than Christianity.

To enter into the detail of this perversion, would lead to a discussion not only too long for our present purpose, but which in fact must have been forestalled by any one who is at all acquainted with the abuses formerly prevailing among us.

Before the Reformation of our Church, the Priest professed, like the Jewish, to offer sacrifice (the sacrifice of the Mass) to propitiate God towards himself and his congregation: the efficacy of that sacrifice was made to depend on sincerity and rectitude of intention, not in the Communicants themselves, but in the Priest; he assuming the character of a mediator and intercessor, prayed not *with* but *for* the people, in a tongue unknown to them, and in an inaudible voice; the whole style and character of the Service being evidently far different from what the Apostle must have intended, in commanding us to "pray for one another." The Priest undertook to reconcile transgressors with the Almighty, by prescribing penances, to be performed by them, in order to obtain *his* absolution; and, profanely copying our only High Priest, pretended to transfer to them his own merits, or those of the Saints. He, like a Pagan, rather than a Jewish, Priest, kept hidden from the people the volume of their faith, that they might, with ignorant reverence, submit to the dominion of error, instead of being "made free by the truth," which he was expressly commissioned to make known; thus hiding the "candle under a bushel," which was designed to "be a light to lighten the nations."

In short, whoever will minutely examine, with this view, the errors of our unreformed Church, will find that a very large and important portion of them may be comprehended under this one general censure, that they destroyed the true character of the Christian Priesthood, substituting for it, in great measure, what cannot be called a Priesthood, except in a different sense of the word. These errors, in short, go far towards changing the office of *Presbyteros* into that of *Hiereus.*

There is another point in which superstitions, very much like those of the Pagans, have corrupted the worship of many Christians. We had occasion to remark, in an earlier part of this Dissertation, that many of the Pagan gods were deceased MEN, whom they had deified on account of some supposed extra-ordinary excellence of character, and eminent services to mankind, or to their countrymen.

Some of these they worshipped as gods; others under the title of demi-gods, or heroes. Any man whom his countrymen had been accustomed to vene-rate very highly in his lifetime, they naturally first *wished*, and then *hoped*, and lastly *believed*, might be elevated after death to such an exalted state as to en-able him to hear them, and to do them services, either by himself, or by making applications on their behalf to some superior god. And just as persons in hum-ble life generally apply to a king or other great man, not directly, but through his ministers and other at-tendants, so, a large portion of the Pagan worship was addressed to some whom they accounted inferior gods.

But, moreover, they supposed each of these inferior deities to have a special regard for his own country. Thus Romulus (Quirinus) was the *tutelar* god of Rome, and Theseus of Athens, &c. And even private fami-lies had gods of their own, who among the Romans were called "Lares," and "Penates." And the supe-rior gods also were supposed to have partialities for particular regions or races. Thus Minerva [Pallas] was tutelar goddess of Athens; and Diana [Artemis] of Ephesus: and Juno, of Argos and Samos, &c. The *power* also of many of their gods was supposed to be limited to particular places, or to particular offices. Thus, we find the Syrians fancying that the God of Israel was the God of the *hills* (1 Kings xx. 23), and would not be able to succor his People on the plains. And Castor and Pollux were supposed to protect sailors, &c.

And moreover, there were certain images and temples, which were supposed to have a superior sanctity above other images and temples of the same god. And again, some particular temples were resorted to by those who had need of some particular kind of service. Thus, oracles were supposed to be given by Apollo, not in every one of his temples, but only in those at Delos, and Delphi, and some others. And it was the like with respect to various other benefits sought for from several of the gods.

Such, then, being the natural tendency of mankind, the consequence was that many Christians, though they did not introduce into the christian Religion the worship of the *very same* gods which were worshipped by their pagan forefathers, yet fell into the same kind of superstitions.

Their deep reverence for the Blessed Virgin, and for the Apostles and other eminent Christians, led them to hope, and then to believe, that these persons were able after their departure from Earth, to hear any one who called on them, and to make prayers of intercession for them. And the evil of this practice of invoking departed Saints, was,—and still is, to many

Christians—disguised by their overlooking the difference between asking the prayers of the *living* and of the departed. No doubt many persons entreated (as Simon the Sorcerer did, Acts viii.) Peter or other Apostles to pray for them. And James expressly exhorts Christians to pray for one another (Jas. i. 16). No Christian need scruple to ask any one whom he considers to be a pious and worthy man to pray for him. But when it came to be believed that a holy person, when *removed from the Earth*, can hear the addresses of thousands and millions of his votaries calling on him in all parts of the world, and know the secret dispositions of mind in each several person that invokes him, this belief did in fact *deify* him.

Whatever subtle explanations may be attempted of the way in which glorified "saints" are able to hear, from various regions, and to repeat, more prayers in the day than there are minutes in the twenty-four hours, it is plain that at least the great mass of their worshippers must regard them no less as gods than the ancient pagans did the Beings they worshipped.

The consequence was, that the chief part of the worship which is due to the "JEALOUS GOD" came to be paid to the Virgin Mary, and those other "Saints" (amounting to several hundreds), who were, from time to time, enrolled on the list.

And thus did Christians introduce into their Religion, under new names, almost every one of the ancient pagan superstitions just above noticed. They knelt before *images* and pictures of the saint they invoked. They attributed peculiar holiness to some particular image, or chapel, above others dedicated to the same saint. They had patron saints (answering to the tutelar gods of the Pagans) presiding over particular nations, or classes, or persons. One saint, again, was supposed to be peculiarly powerful in procuring some particular kind of relief or benefit; and another, in another kind. In short, we have only to look back to what has been just said of the Pagan worship, and we shall see how closely it corresponds in every point (besides many more which might have been added) with the worship which has been, in some Churches, introduced into Christianity.

And, on the other hand, if we look to the Scriptures, we shall plainly see that it is not *thence* that the invocation of Saints could have been derived. They not only contain nothing to warrant it, but they seem framed purposely to guard all who are sincerely desirous of following Scripture, against this very corruption. Though we find in the Book of Acts narratives of the death (Acts vii., xii.) of the two martyrs, Stephen, and James the Apostle, the brother of John, there is no mention of their being invoked after death. And when God saw fit to convey his commands to Cornelius, and again to Paul (Acts x., xxvii.) by a created Being, it is not either of these blessed martyrs, but an Angel, that is sent.

The Virgin Mary, again, is hardly so much as named throughout the Acts* and Apostolic Epistles. Now this silence respecting her is utterly inconceiva-

* Once very slightly, in Acts i.

ble, supposing it had been the practice of the early Christians to pray to her. In the Gospels, again, she is but rarely mentioned.

Even John, her adopted son, though in all likelihood he must have long outlived her, does not record her death, nor give any particulars of her life; and yet he wrote, as is universally believed, purposely to supply the omissions of the other Evangelists. And it is remarkable that we gather from him *incidentally*, and only *incidentally*, that Mary had usually resided with Jesus, who, at his death, committed her to the care of the Beloved Disciple; and "from that time he took her to his home." Why this sparing and unfrequent mention of her whom "all generations should call blessed," and who must have been personally so well known to many of the most eminent disciples?

Humanly speaking, this seems to us impossible. We are left,—we are driven, to suppose that the divine Spirit which guided the sacred Writers, led them, whether consciously or unconsciously, to suppress what they would naturally have recorded, in order to guard against that superstitious veneration for the Virgin Mary, to which, as experience shews, there is naturally so strong a tendency in the minds of Christians. And the few passages which do allude to her, furnish a strong confirmation of the soundness of this conclusion. They are chiefly such as are calculated, and apparently designed, to repress superstitious veneration. One of them records that, when the mother and other kindred of our Lord were announced as desiring to speak with Him, He took occasion to point out that these had no claim, on that ground, to especial reverence; He turned to his disciples, and said, "Behold my mother and my brethren!"   Upon another occasion, when a woman exclaimed—"Blessed is the womb that bare Thee, and the paps that Thou hast sucked"—He replied, "Yea, *rather* blessed are they that hear the word of God and keep it."   One of those who *did* so, was, we may be sure, his mother herself; but the mere circumstance of her being *his mother*, did not, as He declares, imply a blessedness equal to that of the humblest of his faithful hearers.   Does not the record of *these* allusions to one of whom so little is recorded, seem expressly designed to guard against that superstitious error, to which the tendency is so natural, and, as experience has shewn, so strong?

Once more, it is mentioned in the narrative contained in the second chapter of St. John's Gospel, that the mother of Jesus was invited, as well as himself, and his disciples, to the marriage-feast at Cana.   She seems to have been apprised of his design to perform the miracle; for she applied to him when the wine was deficient.   His answer has not that roughness, indeed, which our English translation gives it, from the use of the term " woman."   The word in the original is one which denotes no disrespect; being found in the classical Greek writers applied even to a queen.   But He plainly forbids her interference, telling her that the time is not yet come for the display of his miraculous power.   Now, why is her application to him, and his reply,—why is even her presence on this occasion at all,—mentioned in this place?

Evidently, for the purpose of shewing that he would *do no miracle at her bidding;* that his filial reverence did not extend to his admitting her interference in anything connected with his ministry. It is a warning to all who *will* be warned by Scripture, that they must not be led by their veneration for the mother of Jesus, to look for her intercession for them with her Son. "There is one mediator between God and Man," Jesus Christ—between Him and Man—none. He is himself ever at hand; and if any man will seek to do his will, "He will come unto him, and make his abode in him by his Spirit."

Any one, therefore, who carefully follows the teaching of the Evangelists and Apostles, will be preserved from such errors as we have been speaking of. But it was the disposition of "the Natural Man" that originally led the Pagans to corrupt the Religion revealed to the earliest generations, and to "worship the creature more than the Creator." And that very same disposition has led many of those Christians who neglect the guidance of Scripture, to introduce like corruptions into Christianity.

III. In addition to these sources of corruption, the tendency already mentioned to introduce philosophical speculations into Christianity has shewn itself again and again under various forms, in all ages of the Church, and has given rise to a multitude of heresies.

Philosophy is not at all opposed to true Religion, as long as men confine their speculations to matters which properly come within the Province of Reason.*

But in what relates to Divine Revelations, Reason should be confined to these two points:—1*st*, To judge of the grounds on which any professed revelation should be received or rejected, as being "from Heaven, or of men;" and 2*dly*, To determine what it is that we are enabled and required to learn from the Revelation which God has actually given.

The restless spirit of philosophising, however, was not easy to be subdued, or to be confined within these limits. Even during the times of the Apostles, and still more after their departure, many philosophers, on embracing Christianity, transgressed their proper limits, and sought to exercise their ingenuity on that subject—one of so much interest and importance—in order to maintain their superiority over the vulgar, even in the knowledge of divine mysteries. They acknowledged, for the most part, that the christian revelation had made known things pertaining to God, which could not otherwise have been known: but these things they seem to have regarded as fresh *materials* for human reason to work upon; and when the illumination from heaven—the rays of revelation— failed to shed full light on the Gospel dispensation, they brought to the dial-plate the lamp of human philosophy.†

* It is remarked by Locke, that those who are for laying aside the use of Reason in matters pertaining to Revelation, resemble one who should *put out his eyes* in order to make use of a *telescope.*

† Some persons have been so much struck with the resemblance

Accordingly, we find in very early times, curious questions raised concerning the incarnation, and the nature and person of the Lord Jesus. One system so ancient as to be alluded to by John in his Epistle, represented Jesus Christ as not really "come in the flesh," but as a man in appearance only. Other systems made *Jesus* to have been born a *mere human being*, on whom, at his baptism, a certain emanation (which they called *Christ*) from the divine fulness, descended and dwelt in Him. And endless were the questions raised, and the different hypotheses set up, as to the *manner* in which the divine nature was united with the human in Jesus Christ; whether He was properly to be called *one* person, or two; whether the Virgin Mary were properly to be styled the Mother of *God;* whether Christ should be regarded as of *one substance*, or of *like* substance with the Father; whether the Deity *suffered* at the crucifixion; in what way the sacrifice of Christ was accepted as a *satisfaction* for sin; *why* this sacrifice was *necessary;* besides (in later times) an infinite number of equally subtle speculations as to the nature of the Trinity,—the divine *decrees*,— and, in short, everything pertaining to the intrinsic nature of the Supreme Being, and the

between some of Plato's speculations, and those of certain ancient Theologians, respecting the Trinity, as even to imagine that he must have received some revelation from Heaven!

But instead of concluding that Plato had imparted to him by inspiration knowledge beyond what was communicated to the Apostles—or at least beyond what they were commissioned to teach—we ought rather to infer that those Theologians had corrupted the simplicity of the Gospel by mixing up with it Plato's philosophy.

explanation of all his designs and proceedings. And yet the motions of the earth, and the circulation of the blood, were not discovered till many ages after. The cause of the vital warmth in animals, philosophers are not even yet agreed on; nor is it decided whether light, heat, and electricity, are substances, or qualities of bodies. But as to the *substance* of the Supreme Being, and of the human soul, many men were (and are still) confident in their opinions, and dogmatical in maintaining them; the more, inasmuch as in these subjects they could not be refuted by an appeal to experiment.

All these various systems of philosophical theology were discussed in language containing technical terms more numerous than those of almost any science; some of them taken from the sacred Writers (we may say, in every sense of the phrase, *taken from* them," since hardly any theologian confined himself to *their* use of the terms), and others not found in Scripture, but framed for each occasion. These were introduced professedly for the purpose of putting down heresies as they arose. That they did not effect this object, we know by *experience;* which, indeed, would lead us to conclude, that heresies were by this means rather multiplied. We are inclined to think, that if all Christians had always studied the Scriptures carefully and honestly, and relied on these more than on their own philosophical systems of divinity, the Incarnation, for instance, and the Trinity, would never have been *doubted,* nor ever *named.* And this at least is certain, that as scientific theories and technical phraseology gained ground, party animosity raged the more violently. The advocates of the several systems did not, like the ancient heathen philosophers, carry on a calm and friendly dispute, but (to the disgrace of the Christian name) reviled, and (when opportunity offered) persecuted each other, with the utmost bitterness. For each of them having not only placed the essence of Christianity in faith, but the essence of faith in the adoption of his own hypothesis, and strict adherence to his own use of the technical terms of his theology, was led hence to condemn all departures from his system, as involving both blasphemy against God, and danger to the souls of men. And they employed, accordingly, that violence in the cause of what they *believed* to be divine truth, which Jesus Himself and his Apostles expressly forbade in the cause of what *they knew* to be divine truth. " The servant of the Lord," says Paul, " must not strive, but be gentle unto all men, in meekness instructing them that oppose themselves, if God, peradventure, will give them repentance, to the acknowledging of the truth." (2 Tim. ii. 24, 25.) But those who lose sight of the real character and design of the Christian *revelation*, generally lose also the mild, patient, and forbearing *spirit* of the Gospel.

There is no one of the numberless systems we have alluded to that has not been opposed, and strongly condemned, by the advocates of some different one; but they have not usually been condemned on what appears to us to be the right ground.

The proper objection to the various philosophical systems of religion,—the different hypotheses or theories that have been introduced to *explain* the Christian Dispensation,—is, not the difficulties that have been urged (often with good reason) against *each* separately; but the fault that belongs to *all* of them equally. It is not that the Arian theory of the incarnation, for instance, is wrong for *this* reason, and the Nestorian for *that*, and the Eutychian for *another*, and so on; but they are *all* wrong alike, because they *are theories*, relative to matters on which it is vain, and absurd, and irreverent, to attempt forming *any* philosophical theories whatever.

And the same, we think, may be said of the various schemes (devised either by those Divines called the Schoolmen, or by others) on which it has been attempted, from time to time, to explain other religious mysteries also in the divine nature and dispensations. We would object, for instance, to the Pelagian theory, and to the Calvinistic theory, and the Arminian theory, and others, not for reasons *peculiar* to each one, but for such as apply in *common* to *all*.

Philosophical divines are continually prone to forget that the subjects on which they speculate, are, *confessedly*, and by their *own* account, beyond the reach of the human faculties. This is no reason, indeed, against our believing any thing clearly *revealed in Scripture;* but it *is* a reason against going beyond Scripture with metaphysical speculations of our own. One out of the many evils resulting from this, is, that they thus lay open Christianity to infidel objections, such as it would otherwise have been safe from. It is too late, when objections are alleged from the difficulties involved in some theory, to reply, that the whole subject is mysterious and above reason, and cannot be satisfactorily explained to our imperfect faculties. The objector may answer, "Then you should have *left* it in the original mysterious indistinctness of the Scriptures. *Your own explanations* of the doctrines of your Scriptures you must not be suffered to make use of as far as they are admitted, and then, when they are opposed, to shelter them from attack, as sacred mysteries. If we enter on the field of philosophical argument, we cannot be allowed afterwards to shrink back from fair discussion on philosophical principles."

It is wiser and safer, as well as more pious and humble, and more agreeable to Christian truth, to confess, that, of the mysteries which have been so boldly discussed by many who *acknowledge them to be unfathomable*, we know nothing beyond the faint and indistinct revelations of Scripture; and that if it had been possible, and proper, and designed, that we should know *more* of such matters, more would have been *there* revealed.

And we should rather point out to objectors that what *is* revealed, is *practical*, and not speculative:— that what the Scriptures are concerned with is, not the philosophy of the Human Mind in itself, nor yet the philosophy of the Divine Nature in itself, but (that which is properly *Religion*) the *relation* and connection of the two Beings;—what God is *to us*,—

what He has done and will *do* for us,—and what *we* are to be and to do, in regard to Him.

How great must be the errors arising from men's overlooking, or not carefully attending to, this circumstance, it is hardly necessary to point out. The rustic, who persists in maintaining that the sun itself actually moves, because he sees it rise and set, *i.e.* sees that it is in different *positions relatively to himself;* and the child, who, while he is sailing in a ship, fancies that the land flies from him, or advances towards him; are not more completely mistaken in their notions, than those theologians who reason upon the accounts which the Scriptures give us of the Deity, as if these were intended to explain to us what He is, absolutely, in Himself, and not merely what He is in relation to ourselves.

And the liability to error is greatly increased by this circumstance; that even the relations in which God stands to his creatures are so imperfectly comprehensible by our understandings, that it is necessary to explain them by analogical language, and by the use of such types and comparisons, as may furnish to our minds a kind of picture or image of heavenly things, whose correspondence with the original cannot of course be in all points complete ; any more than a picture can, in all respects, resemble the solid body which it is designed to imitate. If, therefore, we extend the analogy further than was intended, and conclude, that the things which are represented as corresponding in some points, must needs correspond throughout,—or if, again, we conclude, that the things must be *alike*, because they are analogous, and bear similar relations to something else,—we shall fall into the grossest absurdities; such as we often see in children, when they interpret literally the analogical explanations which are given them.

If any one will be at the pains to collect instances for himself, from recollection of his own infancy, and from what he has observed in other children, of the mistakes which are in this way continually committed by every child, and will carefully reflect on these, not as a mere source of amusement, but with a view to his own instruction, they will serve as a mirror to shew what sort of mistakes he himself also has to guard against, in the notions he forms respecting the Almighty.

To take one out of innumerable instances; how many there are who speak and reason concerning the *glory* of God (that being a phrase which occurs in Scripture), as if they supposed, that the desire of glory did literally influence the divine Mind, and as if God could really covet the admiration of his creatures: not considering that the only intention of this expression is to signify merely, that God's works are contrived in the same admirable manner, as if He *had* had this object in view: and that we are bound to pay Him the same reverent homage and zealous obedience, as if He were really and literally capable of being glorified by us. And yet it is chiefly from a literal interpretation of this phrase of " the glory of God" that some Divines have undertaken to explain the whole system of Divine Providence, and to establish some very revolting and somewhat dangerous conclusions.

The difference between *Religious* knowledge properly so called, and what may be more properly styled theological *Philosophy*, may be thus illustrated. Different theories, we know, have prevailed at different times, to account for the motions of the planets, and of the moon, and other heavenly bodies,—the tides, and various other subjects pertaining to natural philosophy. Several of these theories, which supplanted one another, have now become obsolete; and modern discoveries have established, on good grounds, explanations of most of these points. But the great *mass of mankind* cannot be expected to understand these explanations. There are, however, many points of daily *practical* use, which they *can* understand, and which it is needful for them to be informed upon. Accordingly, there are printed Tables, showing the times of the sun's rising and setting at each period of the year,—the appearances of the moon,—the times of eclipses,—the variations of the tides, in different places, and the like. And all these are sufficiently intelligible, without any study of astronomy, even to plain unlearned men. The practical knowledge thus conveyed involves no astronomical theory, but may be equally reconciled with the Ptolemaic or the Copernican systems of the universe. It is not the less possible, nor the less useful, for any one to know the times when the sun gives light to this earth, even though he should not know whether it is the sun that moves, or the earth.

Now it is just such practical knowledge as this that the Scriptures give us of the christian Dispensation. They afford practical directions, but no theory. But there is this important difference between the two cases. The human faculties could, and at length did, (though it is beyond the great 'mass of mankind,) discover the true theory of the appearances and motions of the heavenly bodies. In matters pertaining to divine Revelation, on the contrary, though there must actually *be* a true theory, (since there must *be* reasons, and those known to God Himself, even if hidden from every *creature*, why He proceeded in this way rather than in that,) this theory never can be *known* to us; because the whole subject is so far above the human powers, that we must have remained, but for Revelation, in the darkest ignorance concerning it. Many curious and valuable truths has the world discovered by philosophy, (or as our translators express it "wisdom;") but " the world" (says Paul) " by wisdom knew not *God.*" of which assertion the writings of the ancient heathen philosophers, now extant, afford sufficient proofs.

And, we would further remark, that if it had been possible and allowable for us to follow up by metaphysical researches, the view opened to us by Revelation, and thus to enlarge our knowledge of God's dealings with Man, Paul (as well as the other Apostles) would not have censured, but favoured, such researches, and would have set us the example of so speculating. And if he *had* done this, even in those discourses of his which are not recorded in writing, we may be sure that his Gospel would *not* have been considered as "foolishness" by the Greeks, even those of them who did not fully agree with him. This, therefore, supplies a useful practical rule in judging of anything we may read or hear: whenever we meet with such a representation of Christianity as would *not* have been a stumbling-block to the Jews, or such as would not have been *foolishness* to the Greeks, we may at once conclude that *this cannot be the Gospel which Paul preached.* For he would not have been opposed as he was, had his doctrine favoured either men's pride and worldly ambition, or their spirit of presumptuous speculation.

It may be remarked, as another reason for condemning such presumptuous explanations, and metaphysical theories of Christianity, as we have alluded to,—all of them equally,—that if such speculations be allowed, it is evident Christianity must be not one, but *two* religions;—that for the few profound theologians, and that for ordinary men ; such as the humble shepherds to whom the holy Angels announced the birth of Jesus,—the fishermen and publicans who associated with Him,—and "the common people" who (we read) "heard Him gladly." Now there is nothing more characteristic of the Gospel Dispensation than its *oneness ;—one* Lord,—one faith,—one hope,—in short, one and the same religion proposed to all who will heartily receive it.

All such speculations, then, we should reject, if we would (in the words of the Apostle Peter) " desire, as new born babes, the sincere (ἄδολον, *unadulterated*) milk of the Word, that we may grow thereby." If we would learn the very gospel which the Apostles taught, just as it was received by their hearers, we must in heart and spirit accompany the simple shepherds in their visit " to Bethlehem, to see" (not what human philosophy has devised, but) " what the LORD hath made known to us."

IV. Many corruptions, again, of Christianity have been either introduced, or favoured and kept up, by *moral corruption* in the members of christian Churches. For it belongs to the true Gospel to purify and also to elevate the moral character. Hence, there is a complete and constant opposition between genuine Christianity and all the evil and base propensities of man's nature. This is what Paul means when he says, " Walk in the Spirit, and ye shall not fulfil the lusts of the flesh; for the flesh lusteth against the Spirit, and the Spirit against the flesh; and these are contrary the one to the other, so that ye cannot do the things that ye would :" that is, he who has within him two contrary tendencies, cannot at the same time yield to both.*

Every kind of depravity or moral defect, therefore, predisposes men either to reject Christianity altogether, or else to introduce, or to accept, some erro-

---

* Ταῦτα δὲ ἀλλήλοις ἀντίκειται, ἵνα μὴ, ἃ ἂν θέλητε, ταῦτα ποιῆτε. Gal v. 17. More exactly translated—" these are so opposed to each other as to be an obstacle to your doing what ye desire to do."

By the expressions which are rendered " flesh," and " fleshly lusts," and "a carnal mind, which is enmity against God," Paul does not mean merely *sensual* excess, but *all* evil dispositions of the natural man. For he expressly charges the Corinthians with being "carnal" on account of their "*strifes* and *divisions*."

neous views of it. And there is no kind of religious corruption against which men are usually less on their guard. They are well aware, indeed, that there is a danger of men's falling into sin in *violation* of the precepts of religion. And they are not ignorant that a religion which is altogether *false* may have a bad moral effect on the worshippers. But they consider that a man who has embraced a true Faith, and who is of a religious disposition, will necessarily be *made*, by his religion, a good moral man; or at least such a man as will be accepted as righteous by the God he worships.

Now, this is true, only if we suppose him to observe diligently the caution of Paul, "that they who have believed in God should be *careful* to maintain good works," (Tit. ii. 14, and iii. 8;) "giving all *diligence*," (2 Pet. i. 5) (as Peter exhorts us), to add to his faith, virtue, &c. But if he takes no vigilant *pains* in the improvement of his moral character, the result will be, that, instead of his religion improving his character, his moral deficiencies, on the contrary, will tend to corrupt his religion. The rain itself, which falls pure from the heavens, will not continue pure if it be received in an unclean vessel.

And this kind of corruption took place—as has been above said—even in the days of Paul; who speaks of some, "who having cast away a *good conscience*, concerning [the] Faith, have made shipwreck." (1 Tim. i. 19.)

It will be sufficient to mention some of the principal errors of this class, that have crept into the Church, without entering into a full examination of any of them.

1*st*, The notion that a Priest has power to forgive sins as against God is evidently a doctrine very acceptable to such persons as have a sense of religion combined with a great dislike to the practice of christian virtue; and who, accordingly, are glad of any contrivance for being religious without virtue.

2*dly*, The same may be said of the doctrine, that fasting and other penances,—or pilgrimages to certain holy places,—or prayers and sacrifices offered up in behalf of the deceased,—or rich gifts bestowed on the Church, can atone for sin, and help to obtain for a man final salvation.*

3*dly*, Of a like nature is the doctrine, that if a man who has led a thoroughly unchristian life shall on his deathbed receive the Lord's Supper, or the rite of "Extreme Unction," professing sorrow for his sins, and faith in Christ, we are authorised to pronounce, that (supposing his professions to be, at the moment, sincere) his salvation his certain.

Now, the utmost that Scripture can warrant, in such a case is, that we are not forbidden to *hope*. But the Scripture-*promises* are all made to those who "bring forth *fruits* meet for repentance." And any one who presumes to hold out confident promises where Scrip-

---

* It is very remarkable that in all religions either devised by men, or corrupted by human inventions, there is a tendency to set aside certain particular *seasons*, or particular *persons*, for what is called "mortification,"—that is, *self-torture* as a kind of set-off against the toleration of general licentiousness at other times, or in other persons.

ture does not, is evidently guilty of preaching, not the true Gospel, but one of man's invention.

4thly, The heresy of the ancient Gnostic Antinomians has been already alluded to, as being held in such detestation by the Apostles. And some Antinomian doctrines much like theirs have been found in every Age of the Church.

For example, That because " by grace we are saved through faith, and not of ourselves, but by the gift of God," (Eph. ii. 8,) and " without the works of the Law," therefore, we may safely " continue in sin that grace may abound," (Rom. vi. 7 ;) that certain persons may know and feel themselves set apart as " God's People," and that these are certain of salvation, though continuing in the practice of known sins, because God will not impute sin to *them*, do what they will; and that they ought not to be at all uneasy at any sins they may commit, because He purposely suffers " his own people to fall into very grievous sins, in order to show them their own weakness, and to *humble* them !" though in reality such a doctrine is calculated to puff up a man with spiritual *pride*, in addition to all his other vices; since nothing is more flattering to a proud heart than the notion of being *privileged* to do without censure, or without danger, what *others* would be condemned for.

All these shocking absurdities, so utterly at variance with Scripture, have found their way into Christianity through the depravity of Man. And when we consider, that besides the mischief done by such teachers to their own followers, they bring a scandal on Christianity itself, we cannot wonder at the abhorrence shown by the Apostles, of the Antinomians of their own day. They raised a prejudice against the Religion, as being far worse than no religion at all; because the doctrine they taught tends to silence the suggestions and the reproaches of natural conscience, and represents God as the encourager of vice.

5thly, Besides these avowed Antinomian doctrines, there are others which are liable to be so understood as to lead practically to the same consequences; though these consequences are not designed or foreseen by those who incautiously teach such doctrines. For example, there are some good, well-meaning men who represent Paul as describing, in his Epistle to the Romans, (chap. vii. 9–25,) his own actual condition. If they would read the whole chapter through, (especially verse 9,) and then go on to the eighth chapter, they will see that this is impossible; and that the Apostle is evidently describing the condition of a man under the Law, and not under the Gospel—sensible of the requirements of God's Law, but not under the influence of the Grace of the Gospel.

Now, any man who is living a life of gross vice, while he approves and admires virtue, will not be likely to be at all alarmed, or to consider moral reformation as needful, or indeed as possible, if he believes himself to be just in the *same condition with the Apostle Paul*, and all the other most eminent Christians that ever existed. And he will be likely to regard all that is said in Scripture about holiness of life, as a kind of *theory* which no one is expected to bring into practice.

Again, the doctrine that "nothing a man can do can forward his own salvation," is indeed true, in the sense that no good works of ours can establish a claim of merit in God's sight; and also in this sense, that we cannot lead a life of true christian virtue, of ourselves, and without the aid of the Holy Spirit, which "helpeth our infirmities." But if the doctrine is earnestly and continually taught *without* these explanations, the greater part of the hearers will understand it in a sense exactly opposed to Paul's exhortation, to "work out our own salvation with fear and trembling;" and they will also conclude, that if to *keep* God's commandments cannot *further* a man's salvation, to *break* them cannot *hinder* his salvation. At least, the Christian is not incited to endeavour to "grow in grace," and to "go on unto perfection." And thus the doctrine becomes, in its consequences, completely Antinomian.

Again, some teach that Christ's obedience to the divine law is imputed to believers in Him; so that the good works He performed are reckoned in God's sight as performed by *them*. This doctrine, though not warranted by Scripture,* is taught by some who are themselves striving to lead a virtuous life. But

---

* Our Lord seems to be expressly guarding against this notion in the Parable of the Marriage-feast. The Wedding garment (which represents the "righteousness of Christ,"—that is, the moral character which his Spirit enables us to attain to) was provided—according to the Oriental custom—by the king But the guest who refused to put it on was cast out without being allowed to plead—" *You* are clad in the wedding garment; your wearing it may be *imputed* to me, and may serve instead of my putting it on."

their hearers will be likely to conclude, "if Christ's *suffering* for us and in our stead, is to exempt us from suffering in *our own* persons, then, by parity of reasoning, his performing in our stead good works which are imputed to us, as if *we* had performed them, must exempt us from all need of keeping God's commandments ourselves." And though this may not be an inevitable conclusion, and explanations may be given which will avoid it, still, we may be sure that there *will* be a danger of men's drawing such an inference. And for this danger those teachers will be responsible who set forth a doctrine not clearly taught in Scripture.

And some there are who dwell exclusively on the efficacy of faith; teaching (which is quite true) that genuine christian faith will not fail to bring forth the fruit of a christian life. But if they do not at the same time teach, as our Lord and his Apostles do, the necessity of "*running*,"—"*striving*,"—"*watching*,"—being "*careful*," (1 Cor. ix. 24; Luke xiii. 24; Mark xiii. 33–37,) in their christian course, their hearers will conclude that they have only to take care of their faith, and leave christian virtue to follow of itself. And being once convinced that they have embraced the true faith, they will feel themselves in the condition of a man who has embarked on board a safe *ship*, bound to the right port, who has nothing to do but sit still, and let himself be *carried* thither. And the consequence of their thus taking no pains or care in the moral cultivation of their mind, will be, (as has been observed above,) that their religion, instead of improving their moral character, will be itself corrupted by it; and having "cast away a good conscience, they will make shipwreck of the faith." (1 Tim. i. 19.)

The above are a part, and only a part, of the religious corruptions which have been introduced or fostered by moral corruption.

V. Lastly, worldly policy has greatly helped to promote some of the worst religious errors. The same kind of men who would, most of them, have opposed Christianity, from covetous or ambitious views, when it was first preached, were disposed, afterwards, to distort the religion, so as to suit those views.

Thus, any worldly men who found their way into the Ministry, were tempted to favour any kind of superstitious error that tended to bring them profit and power. The People were often disposed to fancy that the Priests could serve God in their stead, and that there were mysteries in Religion which the Priests understood, but which the Laity need not know anything of, and ought not to inquire into. And hence they were ready to follow blindly the guidance of the Priests in religious matters; just as a man trusts, in legal concerns, to his Lawyer, and in medical concerns, to his Physician; doing what they direct, and not considering it necessary himself to study Law or Medicine.

All these, and many other such erroneous notions, have been encouraged by worldly-minded Priests for the increase of their own power and wealth.

Again, ambitious and worldly-minded Rulers are generally glad to make use of Religion as an instrument for securing the submission of the People to tyrannical oppression, and for aiding their ambitious views when they seek to subdue their neighbours, under the pretext of propagating the true Faith. Such men are disposed, like the Jews of old, to "take Jesus by force to make Him a King;" that is to make his a "kingdom of this world."

Such men perceive a political advantage in having the same religion professed by all their subjects; and they endeavour to secure this object by force. They make laws for the punishment of heretics: or to exclude from civil rights every one who is not a member of their Church; or they seek to compel every one to have his children taught their Faith.

All these are so many different forms in which the spirit of PERSECUTION shows itself, in varying degrees of violence.

Now, it is of course most desirable that all men should agree in true christian faith and practice. But then, this profession of the Religion should be *sincere* and *voluntary*. It is utterly contrary to the spirit of Christ's religion to attempt to maintain or to propagate it by force. But it belongs to the "natural man" to feel jealousy and dislike to those who differ from us in opinion on important points; and, when we fail to convince them, to wish to force them to submission; or at least to keep for ourselves what is called a "political ascendancy" over them. And those who have a zeal for what they consider true religion, but who are strangers to the genuine spirit of the Gospel, persuade themselves that they are seeking God's glory and the good of mankind, in carrying out their own intolerant principles. Since Governments, they say, ought to seek the *good,*--universally,—of the subjects, and true religion is the greatest good, it must be the duty of the Civil Magistrate to insist on his subjects adhering to a true religion.

But they overlook two circumstances: 1st, that since the Magistrate must, by this rule, be himself the Judge *what* religion is true, it would follow that the Jewish Rulers had a right to forbid the Apostles to preach the Gospel; and that the Apostles were bound to obey; and, 2dly, that though the *sincere* acceptance of true religion be the greatest good, an outward profession, in obedience to the laws, of what a man does not really believe, is no good at all, but a great evil.

Yet all this is overlooked by those who "have a zeal towards God, but not according to knowledge" of the true Gospel.

In addition, however, to mistaken religious zeal, there can be no doubt that men's minds are often biassed towards this particular corruption of Christianity, by worldly policy. The love of power and worldly pre-eminence helps to give their turn to their religious zeal. And thus they so far mistake the real character of Christianity, as to imagine it allowable, and even a sacred duty, to put down religious errors by force, or to secure a monopoly of civil rights in behalf of the members of their own Church.

The above, then, are the chief sources from which corruptions of Christianity have sprung. And they correspond to those from which, as we have seen, originated the chief part of the early opposition to the religion, viz.: mistaken adherence to the Mosaic Law; superstition; misapplied philosophy; moral depravity; and worldly policy.

As for the *means* by which various religious errors have been kept up and spread, one of the principal is that employment of *coercion* which has been just noticed. As a general rule, a resort to restrictions, and to force of every kind, must be, on the whole, more favourable to error than to truth, in all subjects: because it tends to take away the great *advantage* which truth has over error. Truth being in itself stronger than falsehood, may be expected to gain a superiority when there is free discussion. But Laws and Penalties may be on the wrong side as well as on the right. Those, therefore, who resort to these, may, not unfairly, be presumed to have themselves, some distrust of the goodness of their cause, since they remove the trial from a Court (that of Reason) in which truth has an advantage over falsehood, and appeal to brute-force, in which truth has no such advantage. A fair and *free trial* is what, generally speaking, the intelligent advocates of truth, in all subjects, will be likely to call for, and the advocates of error to deprecate. Moreover, in regard to religious questions, the resort to coercion proves a person to have totally mistaken the character of Christianity as to *one* most important point; so that there is a probability that he will have mistaken other points also.

That erroneous view, again, of christian *Unity*, which has been already noticed, has tended very much to keep up and to extend other errors. For if a man is once convinced that all Christians are bound to belong to some one Community on earth, he will dread nothing so much as separation from that Church, whatever it may be, which he considers as having the best claim to *be* that one community.

And thus, a *majority* will be enabled completely to dictate to the understanding, and to domineer over the conscience, of all the rest. For, whatever strong reasons a man may see for condemning any corruptions which that Church may have sanctioned, he will labour to stifle his convictions, and to believe any absurdity, or approve of any abuse, rather than exclude himself, as he supposes, from the true Church. So also, a mistake as to the true limits of Church-authority is one which tends to foster other mistakes. If a Church assumes the right of setting aside the precepts of Scripture, or of giving any interpretations whatever of them to suit its own views, or of "making the Word of God of none effect through their tradition," a man will be led to submit to all this against his better judgment, if he is persuaded that he is only submitting to the authority which Christ has appointed for his guidance in all that pertains to religion.

And lastly, the prevalence of this error leads to the neglect of the study of the Scriptures, and even to their being left untranslated, and inaccessible to the People. For as no one need study medical books, himself, if he is placed under the care of a skilful physician, so there seems no need for any one to study Scripture, if he has others to do it for him, whose interpretations, after all, he is bound to receive, and who are ready to tell him what he is to believe and do.

And thus *general ignorance* will soon prevail; which is the greatest encourager and supporter of every kind of error and abuse. For when the light of the Gospel which was given for the illumination of the World, is thus "put under a bushel," men are thenceforward left to grope in darkness, without any means of distinguishing truth from falsehood, or genuine Religion from the grossest superstitions.

REFORMATIONS IN RELIGION.

WE have seen that corruptions of christianity have existed, from the days of the Apostles, downwards; and that these inspired teachers warned men to be on their guard against this danger. They exhort us to "take heed to ourselves," on account of "deceitful teachers," and to "prove all things, and hold fast that which is right." Christians, then, are evidently bound to be carefully watchful against any corruption of the "simplicity of the Gospel." And whenever they shall find that any unscriptural doctrines or practices have crept in, it is their duty to exert themselves for the correction of the evil. And, accordingly, it appears that almost every one of the corruptions which have prevailed in christian Churches, was opposed, more or less, at its first introduction. Yet, on the whole, this opposition was, for many centuries, so far ineffectual, that the religion of the greater part of the Christian world degenerated more and more from its original purity.

It is not our design to give an account of the various attempts made (with or without success) to resist the introduction of corruptions, or to drive them out. It will be sufficient to point out:

I. What are the principal hindrances that have stood in the way of a successful opposition to errors and abuses, and of needful reformations.*

II. What are the faults that reformers are chiefly liable to, and against which, consequently, men ought to be especially on their guard.

[I.] There are three mistakes frequently committed by Christians, each of which has contributed to prevent successful opposition to corruption, and correction of them.

(1.) Some have attached too much importance to

---

* In modern language one sometimes hears of "reforming abuses.' But this is an impropriety. It is an *institution* that is *reformed:* abuses are to be *remedied.*

matters not essential, and have contended too earnestly about them.

(2.) Others—and sometimes, indeed, even the very same persons—have acquiesced in very serious corruptions, through a mistaken anxiety for what they consider *Christian Unity* and concord.

(3.) A third cause, tending to the same effects, is a mistaken *dread of innovations*. Those who are on their guard *only* against *sudden* corruptions, and overlook such as creep in silently and gradually, will be disposed to resist as innovations what are, in truth, *restorations;* and to maintain what are, in reality, *very great and mischievous* innovations.

(1.) When men are once engaged in a *contest* on any question, their eagerness is apt to increase as the debate goes on; and they often come to regard some matter that is really of very small consequence, as if it were of the greatest. Thus, their attention is often drawn off from things far more important. For example, there have been fierce controversies among Christians about the proper time for celebrating the festival of Easter. And this is one of the many cases in which the attempt to unite all Christians under the government of *one single community on earth*, has led to discord instead of concord. For, it is necessary that in any *one* Church, the times for celebrating religious festivals, should be fixed by authority; however unimportant it may be *what* shall be the time fixed. But two or more independent Churches may differ in this, and in several other non-essential points, without hostility and strife. Such questions, however, immediately become a source of strife, as soon as it is thought necessary to unite these Churches into one. And the same may be said of that most bitter dissension which arose between the Eastern and Western Churches as to the use of leavened or unleavened bread at the Lord's Supper. And at the very time when these controversies about such comparatively insignificant points were raging with the utmost fury, the unscriptural practice of applying to the Virgin and other saints as mediators (besides many other superstitions), was spreading widely among Christians.

So also, in later times, and even in our own day, there have been vehement debates on the question, whether a clergyman should preach in a black dress or a white one. And the attention of many persons has thus been called off from the far more important question as to the soundness of the doctrine preached. While occupied about the colour of a vestment, they have overlooked the serious corruptions of the faith introduced by such as were " teaching for doctrines the commandments of men."

And, again, the schism of the Donatists, which gave rise to one of the most furious contentions that ever existed among Christians, originated merely in a question as to the regularity of the appointment of a certain bishop.* These persons having taken up that notion respecting " apostolical succession" which has been noticed in a former part of this Dissertation, they would not allow that the ministers ordained by the bishop whose succession they disputed, were ordained

* Cæcilian, elected Bishop of Carthage, 311.

at all; or that any whom these baptized were really Christians, &c. And while this fierce contest lasted, which was nearly two centuries (from the fourth to the sixth), men's attention was drawn off by it from essential points; and various corruptions were allowed to spread, unchecked and unnoticed. Moreover, one effect of such contests is, that many men are apt to become, at length, so weary of strife, as to be ready to purchase peace at any price, and to acquiesce in various abuses and errors in important points, rather than run the risk of exciting any controversy.

Now we ought certainly to prefer peace and christian concord to everything *except* the essentials of Gospel-truth and pure worship. But these must not be given up even for the sake of peace.

For, religious *agreement* is not that christian concord which it is so important to aim at, unless it be agreement in the *genuine* Religion of the Gospel. There may be an agreement in error as well as in truth.

But, vehement and long-continued disputes about matters of minor importance which are not worth so much contention will often drive men into the opposite extreme, and make them ready to consent to anything for the sake of peace and unity.

(2.) And thus they are led to commit the second of those mistakes above adverted to, and to resist all correction of abuses for fear of unsettling men's minds, disturbing the peace of the Church, and violating its Unity.

And this is especially the case when men have adopted that view of Christian Unity which represents it as consisting in having *one community on earth*, to which all Christians belong, or ought to belong, and to whose government all are bound to submit.

It is true, the same kind of feeling may influence the members of *any* Church, even one which does not claim to be "*the* universal church." For men are undoubtedly bound to be very careful not to "cause divisions" hastily, or on slight grounds. Whatever christian Church they find themselves belonging to, they are bound to give no occasion of any schism— any unfriendly separation from it, unless they are fully convinced on deliberate reflection that its doctrines or practices are at variance, in essential points, with Scripture, and that there is no reasonable hope of reform. But, on the other hand, if the rulers of any Church, force a part of its members to separate from it, by maintaining what is really thus unscriptural (and of this the All-Wise God alone can be the infallible judge), the guilt of the schism lies with those rulers.

The questions, however, what *is* or is not Scriptural? and *what* points are essential? are to be very carefully and candidly considered, under a sense of awful responsibility to God; and are questions on which different men often come to different conclusions.

And hence, while some are guilty of hastily causing divisions on wrong grounds, or on insufficient grounds (as if each man were free to consult his own fancy or convenience in such matters,) others sometimes fall into the opposite extreme. For there are persons who will bring themselves to acquiesce in something which they perceive to be fundamentally wrong, for fear of being guilty of causing a schism.

Now this latter fault, men are much more liable to, who consider "the true Church" to be, necessarily, one community under a *single government on earth.* For all Christ's promises being made to his CHURCH, they feel that a separation from that community which they regard as the Catholic Church, would be to renounce the Gospel Covenant. And thence they are led to infer, either that Christ allows this Church to depart in important points from the written Word, or else that what plainly appear *to be* departures from it, are somehow reconcilable with it. They would, perhaps, be glad if the governors of their Church could be prevailed on to remedy such and such an abuse. But if these resolve, in compliance with the wish of the majority, to retain it, such persons consider that they have only to submit, rather than forfeit (as they imagine) *all* their Christian hopes at once. To oppose or question the decisions of the Church which they regard as the divinely-appointed Authority and Guide for all Christians in whatever pertains to religion, they consider as a rebellion against Christ. And thus they in time force themselves to believe their Church *infallible*—to assent to and uphold the grossest corruptions —and to resist all attempts at correction.

This mistake as to the nature of christian unity is one which could hardly arise in the days of the Apostles. For *they* manifestly founded many distinct Churches, agreeing indeed in Faith, but quite independent of each other, and having no common Head on Earth. And the Bishops which they appointed for the government of most (if not all) of these Churches, differed as much from the Bishops of later times, as a Sovereign prince does from a colonial governor. Each was the Head Presbyter, to whom was intrusted the chief power in an entire Church.

It was indeed allowable and desirable that delegates from these several Churches should assemble, from time to time, to hold a Council, (or, as it is called in political affairs, a *Congress*,) for the purpose of conferring together on religious questions, and concerting measures for putting down false doctrines and abuses. This did not necessarily destroy the independence of the Churches; any more than Sovereign-States surrender their independence when they send ambassadors to a Congress to deliberate concerning a treaty. But ambitious men, when they obtained a majority in any of these Councils, naturally encouraged the notion that the minority were bound to submit to their decisions, whether they would or no. This, so far, tended to combine all these Churches into one. And when the chief part of the Roman Empire became christian, the Emperors always sought to favour this combination, in order that they might the more easily and the more completely control it.

And that this worldly policy of theirs had a principal share in the uniting of the several distinct christian communities into one, is plain from the circumstance that it was not *Jerusalem*—the earliest christian Church, and from which all others were offsets—but *Rome*, the *political* Capital of the Empire, that came to be regarded as the seat of government, and centre of the Universal Church.

There is not, indeed, any rule laid down by divine authority, as to what is to be the greatest extent of a single Church. It cannot, therefore, be said that there is in Scripture any direct prohibition of Christians all over the world uniting themselves into one single community. But the example left us by the Apostles, in founding many distinct Churches, independent of that of Jerusalem, and of each other, shews that they did not consider a very extensive Church as either a necessary or a desirable thing.* And the inconvenience is so manifest and so great, of placing under one Church-government men of different nations, far distant from each other, and differing in language and in customs, that we may be sure no such thing would ever have been thought of, except either for reasons of worldly policy, or else from a misconception of the character of Christ's kingdom. The ruler of a great empire, containing many provinces, may naturally wish that all his subjects should be members of the same Church; and the supreme rulers of any Church are likely to be tempted by ambition to extend that church as widely as possible. Those, again, who make the mistake above alluded to, respecting the true meaning of christian-unity, will readily enter into these views. And some will be likely to fancy that the governors of a single Church comprehending all Christians, will be likely to prevent such errors as might spring up

* Not only were there several distinct Churches in the one province of Macedonia, and in that of Achaia, but the one Epistle to the Galatians is addressed to "the *Churches*" of Galatia.

in some out of a multitude of independent Churches, and thus preserve the purity of Gospel truth. But this is to suppose that the governors of the universal Church are to be *infallible*. Else, it is plain that they may fall into error as easily as the governors of a smaller Church, and may employ their extensive power in maintaining and spreading such error. And, accordingly, all who contend for a Universal Church, in the sense of a single community under one government on earth, always lay claim,—more or less distinctly,—to infallibility as belonging to that Church.

But as no such infallibility can be proved, or does exist, the result has been that all attempts to give universal dominion to a single Church have increased the difficulty of checking and of correcting corruptions.

For example—one great abuse, and that the parent of many others, the keeping of the Scriptures and of the public Service in a dead language, was doubtless much favoured by the great extent of a single Church. The abuse was not one that originated in very early times. For it was not caused by men's having from the first a superstitious dread of any attempt to translate the Scriptures at all, and consequently leaving them in the original Hebrew and Greek. On the contrary, they were *translated* into Latin, when that was the prevailing language, on *purpose* that they might be accessible to the people. And afterwards, when Latin gradually ceased to be spoken in the Provinces, and at length, in Rome itself, the Latin Bible and Prayer-Books continued in use after they had ceased to be understood by the mass of the people. No one could point out the precise time when a new translation first became necessary; because the change of Latin into Italian, Spanish, &c., was gradual. And men had a sort of superstitious veneration for the language which they and their fathers had been accustomed to hear employed in divine Service.

And this is evidently an error which it served the purpose of an ambitious Church to keep up.* All over the world, as far as the dominion of that Church extended, the Priests had a language of their own, not understood by the common people, in which alone the Sacred Books could be studied. And thus the People could know little or nothing of their Religion, except just what these Priests chose to tell them.

Now it is true, indeed, that the same error might find its way into each of several independent Churches, however small. It is conceivable, for example, that independent Churches in various parts of the world might have retained, some, an ancient Gothic translation of the Bible, some, an Anglo-Saxon, &c., long after those languages had ceased to be spoken. But then it is far less likely that *every one* of forty or fifty independent Churches should persist in this error, than that *one* should do so. And if *some* of those

---

* The enforcement of celibacy on the clergy, (for which there is no warrant in Scripture,) was also manifestly favourable to the ambitious views of a supreme central government, as it tended to keep the clergy unconnected with the people.

Churches, or even any one of them, had made new translations of the Bible to meet the wants of the People, the others would have been shamed into following their example in a thing so evidently reasonable.

And this is proved by what has actually taken place. It is well known that at the time of Luther's Reformation, and long before, the translating of the Scriptures into modern languages was most earnestly opposed by those who adhered to the Church of Rome. The Scriptures, which were originally addressed to Christians of all classes, including slaves, were represented as unfit for the perusal of the common people. But since then, the Roman Catholics have in some measure followed the example of those Churches which they denounce as heretical.* They have among them now, (though not in perfectly free circulation,) translations of Scripture into English, French, Italian, and other languages. And some of them have also Prayer-Books, with the Latin and their own language printed in parallel columns, so as to enable them to understand the Service that is going on.† There can be little doubt, therefore, that

* This great and important *change* completely disproves what is maintained by the advocates, and by the bitterest enemies, of the Church of Rome—the *unchangeable* character of that Church. But there is nothing so grossly and notoriously false as not to gain credence, if maintained by both of two opposite parties.

† As for the celebration of Divine Service in Latin, it has ever been made a matter of boast by the Roman Catholics, that in a foreign Country, a priest going thither ignorant of its language, can at once perform Service, as at home; and that a traveller equally ignorant of

this would have been done long before, if there had been all along numerous independent Churches, such as the Apostles established.

It is true, indeed, that before the time of that Reformation, and indeed, in a less degree, for a good while after it, the prevailing ignorance was such, that few besides the Clergy could read at all. But then it should be remembered, first, that to have the Church-Service—including the reading of the Scriptures—in a language understood by the People, is a most important benefit even to those who cannot themselves read; and secondly, that this gross ignorance would not have *existed* if the Clergy had all along done their duty in presenting to the People the Scriptures in their own language, and encouraging them to learn to read, for the very purpose of studying those Scriptures as they ought.

It is plain, therefore, that the abuse we have been speaking of was left much the longer unremedied in consequence of the dominion of *one* Church of vast extent.

And the same may be said of many other abuses. A reform that is evidently needed, is more likely to be resisted by *one* community, than by *every one* of many independent communities. Any one out of

the country, can attend the Service of his Church, which is the same everywhere; while a member of any other communion would be at a loss. This is as if a blind man should make it a matter of boast that he is not incommoded by the short days of winter, and has no occasion for candles. That day and night are alike to him, would indeed be an advantage, if he could see in *both*; but not, when the case is that he can see in *neither*.

several distinct Churches, when it corrects something that is manifestly wrong, sets an example which others are not unlikely to follow. And this advantage is wanting, when all or nearly all Christians are put under one single government.

The causes above mentioned have proved, in very many instances, great hindrances to needful reforms. Nevertheless, many attempts were made, in the earlier Ages of the Church, to introduce errors and abuses, which were vigorously and often successfully resisted. We have on record many varieties of false doctrine and corrupt worship, (most of them now nearly forgotten,) which were generally condemned and expelled as heretical.*

Unfortunately, indeed, it often happened that the mode in which many of the ancient heresies were opposed, was such as to have the effect of giving rise to fresh heresies. But it was with good reason that

---

* It should be observed that a "Heretic" properly signifies a person who maintains some false doctrine condemned by the *Church of which he is a member*. No *Church*, therefore, can be, in strictness of speech, *heretical*, though it may be erroneous. Accordingly, the Church of England, for example, pronounces the Church of Rome to have "erred;" but does not apply the term "heresy" to its errors, because it acknowledges the Church of Rome to be a distinct, independent Church. The Romanists, on the other hand, pronounce the Church of England "heretical," because they reckon all Christians as members—even though disobedient and rebellious members—of their own Church. Those of them at least who do *not*, (for there is a good deal of uncertainty on this point,) cannot maintain that their own Church *is* Universal [Catholic] in the ordinary sense of the word, namely, as *actually* comprehending *all* Christians. They should rather call it "the Church which *seeks* to be Universal."

the majority of the early Christians—and, indeed, of Christians in all ages—always opposed (though not always wise in their mode of proceeding) every *innovation* in doctrine. They justly considered, that anything *new* (in essential points) introduced into Christianity must be wrong.

But then, they often committed the fault of being on their guard *only* against *sudden* corruptions;—against any innovation brought in *openly* and all at once. They overlooked (as men are apt to do in all subjects) the principle so well laid down by Lord Bacon, that "*Time* is the greatest innovator;" that it "introduces changes so silently and gently as to escape notice;" and that "since things alter for the worse *spontaneously*, hence, if they be not altered for the better designedly, there will be no end of the evil." To resolve that *no* changes should take place, is to talk idly. One might as well forbid the winds to vary, or the tides to flow. But to resolve that no changes shall take place *except* such as are *undesigned* and accidental, is to determine that though a clock may gain or lose indefinitely, we will take care that it shall never be regulated.

What is called "the change of the *style*," is a striking instance of a seeming *innovation*, which was really a *restoration*, being a return to the right course, by the sudden correction of a great error that had resulted from the accumulation of imperceptibly small ones.

In religious matters, a remarkable instance of a *gradual* corruption, and a *sudden* reform, is the point already noticed,—the keeping of the Scriptures in a language unknown to the People. This was a most enormous *innovation ;* since the Sacred Writers manifestly addressed themselves to Christians of all ranks. But it was overlooked, because it was no *sudden* innovation. The Latin language went out of use *gradually.* No one can fix the precise day or year on which a fresh translation was first needed. But when men did perceive the need, and translated the Bible into modern languages, this was a great and palpable *novelty.* And, as such, it was vehemently opposed; though, in reality, it was, in spirit, a *restoration* of the original state of things; the placing of the Scriptures before the People in a language which they understood.

So, also, there can be no doubt, that the change of christian Ministers into *Sacerdotal Priests*, making offerings on an altar, and also the custom of invoking saints, and most of the other corruptions already noticed, crept in gradually and insensibly.

The fond veneration for the memory of any holy martyr led men to visit his tomb, and to preserve carefully his garments, or other relics, and also images or pictures of him. They naturally prayed to God, with these images before them, for grace to follow the good example of such a holy man. And thence they were gradually led to beg for his intercession, and, in fact, to worship him.

Then, when this had become a long-established corruption, and when men were called on at once to renounce it, and to pray to none but the all-present

God, many were startled at the *innovation*, and resolved to keep to "the *old* religion," and to worship
as their ancestors had done for centuries, rejecting as
heretical all new doctrines. For, to *them*, the observance of the first and second commandments *was* a
novelty; though, in reality, it was only a *return* to
the primitive worship.

And so it was, no doubt, with the greater part of
the corruptions that crept into Christianity. Men
were not sufficiently on their guard against them,
because they came in by little and little. And then,
when correction was attempted, many resisted it, and
would not allow that these *were* corruptions, because
no one could point out the precise time when they
arose.

But if we look to SCRIPTURE, and compare with
this the doctrine and practices of some christian
Churches, it will be plainly seen that their religion
has been corrupted; though we may not be able to
say exactly *when*, or by what means.

And this is the only safe course of proceeding.
For when a book, for instance, is often reprinted, the
only way to insure accuracy is to collate carefully
each edition with the original copy. Sometimes this
is neglected, and the second edition is printed from
the first, and the third from the second; and so on,
down to perhaps twenty or thirty editions. And the
result has generally been, that though each edition
has but a very few fresh misprints, and differs but
very little from the preceding, yet the twentieth or
thirtieth edition will be found, when compared with

the original, to be excessively incorrect, through the accumulation of a multitude of small errors.

In like manner, if we would keep our Religion pure, both from new and from old corruptions, we must go straight to the very fountain-head itself, and observe what is or is not agreeable to the inspired Word.

[II.] From the causes, then, which we have been speaking of, the correction of various abuses was so much impeded and so 'ong delayed, that thorough *Reformation* (or as it might have been more wisely called—a *Restoration*) became necessary.

By the "reformation" of a Church is generally understood a *fundamental change* in doctrine and worship, as distinguished from slight alterations. And we use the word reformation in a corresponding sense, in reference to any other Institution also. It is like the pulling down and *rebuilding* of a great part of a house, as distinguished from the many small *repairs* which are made every year by a prudent man, and the occasional small improvements he may see need for. Those repairs and improvements he makes on purpose that he may be saved from the far greater cost and inconvenience of rebuilding, which is an evil in itself, though a necessary evil when timely repairs have been neglected.

So also, every reformation is an evil, on account of the general disturbance and agitating alarm it tends to produce. But this is a less evil than the utter corruption of Christianity. And there is no other alternative when errors and abuses have been long suffered to accumulate, and all timely remedies have been obstinately rejected.

But many persons are led by their dread of the evils and dangers of a reformation, to oppose it as long as possible, and to endeavour to delay it; not considering that the longer it is deferred, the more violent and dangerous it is likely to be.

The principal dangers to which reformers are liable, may be classed under these two heads :—

(1.) They are apt to feel too secure against falling into the faults of the system they are reforming. They often *retain* several of their former wrong notions; and accordingly commit some of the same errors, in substance, though in some new shape—as those they undertook to remedy.

(2.) And, secondly, they are apt not to be sufficiently on their guard against *reactions*. In their abhorrence of what is wrong, they have often rejected what is right along with it, and have often rushed from one extreme to the other; not considering that there may be two errors quite opposite to each other, and that men in their eagerness to avoid one fault, will often be blinded to the danger of committing a contrary fault, that is, perhaps, even worse than the first.

(I.) When men feel a very strong abhorrence of any fault in the particular form in which they have been used to see it, they are apt to feel too much self-confidence in reference to that fault; and not to be on their guard against falling into (substantially) the same fault in some other shape.

For example—the detestation felt by the early Christians for the pagan worship of the images of Jupiter and Juno, and other gods and goddesses, made them feel secure against any danger of idolatry, in a christian Church. And this absence of self-distrust contributed to their falling into similar superstitions under different names, by paying adoration to images of Beings whom they do not call *gods and goddesses*, but male and female *Saints*.

So also, in the present case, reformers often retained some of the erroneous principles which had led to the abuses they were correcting; and thus they frequently themselves committed like errors, though in a different shape.

For example, they were fully convinced that the claims of the Church of Rome to *infallibility* are unfounded. But many still clung to the notion that infallibility must be lodged *somewhere* on Earth. They still thought a divine *Revelation* necessarily implied an unerring guide for the right *interpretation of that Revelation*.

Some of them, accordingly, fancied that there must be somewhere, though not at Rome, an infallible Universal Church; though they sought in vain to find any person or Body of men having acknowledged power of any kind, over all Christians, and entitled to represent and to dictate to the whole christian World.

And there are, even now, not a few persons, members of reformed Churches, who suffer themselves to be mystified by the vague and obscure language of artful leaders, and to be deluded into a belief in the infallibility of a certain Universal Church, consisting of all the "orthodox," that is, all those who agree in opinion with those leaders. And thus they fancy themselves bound to receive as gospel truth whatever they are told by those leaders, whom they regard as most *profound* theologians. For as muddy water is often supposed to be *deep*, from one's not being able to see to the bottom of it, while that which is exceedingly clear is thought shallower than it is, so, weak men are apt to admire as very profound, in Theology or in Philosophy, what they cannot clearly understand, and to despise as shallow, whatever is made very plainly intelligible.

Others, again, of those who cling to the notion of an infallible interpreter of Scripture, have concluded that every sincere Christian, or that they themselves, or that certain persons whom they look up to as preeminently holy, do possess this unerring guide, in the inspiration of the Holy Spirit. Whatever is really dictated by that Spirit, they justly concluded must be infallibly right. And they found in Scripture promises of the aid of that Spirit. They inferred, therefore, that whatever occurred to their minds, after having prayed for this spiritual aid, must be the true interpretation of Scripture; which, consequently, all men are bound to acknowledge and submit to.

It is remarkable that most of the persons who put forth such claims, do not pretend to exemption from *Sin*, though they hold themselves to be exempt from the possibility of *doctrinal error*. To suggest a doubt as to the truth of any *doctrine* they maintain, they regard as questioning the truth of God Himself. But for any man to account himself *impeccable*, they consider as an impious presumption. And yet the office of the Holy Spirit is to lead us, not only "into all *truth*," but also into "all *righteousness;*" for "the fruit of the Spirit is in all goodness, and righteousness, *and* truth." And though both are highly important, most persons would allow that this latter is the more so. If a man were offered the choice,—supposing he could not have both,—of being completely secured, either from all *mistakes* in doctrinal points, or from all *sin*, he would hardly hesitate to acknowledge that the latter would be the more valuable gift. Yet the very same persons who make no claim to *unerring rectitude of conduct*, and exemption from *sin*, will hold themselves to have attained unerring rectitude of *judgment*, and exemption from *error;* and will regard any doubt on *that* point as a distrust of God's promises. And yet they are no more promised infallibility than impeccability.

Some, however, there are who seem to think that both in doctrinal questions and in moral questions also, their *judgment* is infallibly right; and that though, in practice, they are liable to go wrong, this can only be when they offend *against* the dictates of their own conscience. This is to claim a great superiority over the Apostle Paul, and to reverse his procedure. For *he* says, "I judge not mine own self; for I know nothing against myself;"* (that is, I am not conscious of any wrong;) "yet am I not hereby

* Οὐδὲν γὰρ ἐμαυτῷ σύνοιδα. 1 Cor. iv. 4.

justified: but He that judgeth me is the Lord." *Ile* therefore did *not* set up his own conscience as an infallible standard of right and wrong.

A circumstance, however, which is still more remarkable, is this; that many of those who thus in reality lay claim to "*inspiration*" and "*infallibility*," yet carefully keep clear of those *words.* They do not *call* themselves inspired or infallible. And yet it is plain that a man who feels quite certain that his interpretations of Scripture are suggested by the very Spirit which dictated that Scripture, is, so far, claiming just as real an inspiration as the Sacred Writers themselves possessed. If he feels quite certain that he is *unerringly following* an *infallible guide*, he must in reality regard himself as infallible.

In this, as in many other cases, men are misled by *names.* They mistake for two different doctrines what are in reality only two different expressions of the very same.

When, however, a large portion of the christian World which had been under the dominion of a single Church, had thrown off that yoke, the danger of falling into the mistake of looking for an infallible guide on earth was much diminished. For those inclined to such a notion would naturally, as long as they were under *one* Church, look to that Church as the seat of the infallibility. But when they were separated into several distinct communities, the error tended—if one may so speak—to cure itself.

For then, several *conflicting* claims to infallibility were of course put forth, by persons teaching *different* doctrines, yet who each professed (and doubtless often with truth) to have earnestly prayed for inspiration; and as it was plain that *all* these claims could not be well founded, this naturally put men on inquiring whether *any* of them were so. And then, all sober-minded men perceived that the only *proof* of inspiration, and that which must necessarily accompany it— the display of *miraculous* signs—was wanting in *all* the claimants; and consequently, that no infallible guide on Earth has been provided.

But the error, though greatly checked, is still to be found among weak-minded enthusiasts, who cannot, or will not think accurately.

It is kept up in them in great measure, by their confounding together the infallibility of the guide in *itself*, and *our* infallibility in following that guide. For instance, if, on the one hand, the mariner steers by a *chart*, then, even though he conform to it quite exactly, yet if this chart itself be at all incorrect, he may be misled by it. If, on the other hand, he steers by a star, he is sure that his *guide* cannot be wrong; but yet he may be misled if he mistakes one star for another. If, however, he is convinced that this is totally impossible, and that he is *infallibly following* an infallible guide, it is plain he reckons himself infallible.

And even so, though the Scriptures and the Spirit of God cannot themselves err, no one has a right to pronounce confidently that he is exactly conforming to them, unless he is favoured with some sensible miraculous signs from Heaven to assure him of this. Without such a sign, " if we say that we have no sin"

—or that we have no error —"we deceive ourselves." For even, if in some point, our judgment or our conduct *be* in point of fact perfectly right, still, as we cannot with perfect certainty *know* this, during our state of trial on Earth, we have no right confidently to claim it.

Another wrong principle which has been retained by many reformers, is that of *persecution*. By the *principle* of persecution, we mean the notion that it is allowable and right to use secular coercion in religious matters, or to maintain what is called the political "ascendancy" of those who profess the true Faith; so that they should monopolize civil rights and privileges.

The reason why we speak not of *persecution* itself, but of the persecuting *principle*, is that where this principle is the most thoroughly carried out, there will be no *actual* persecution. In any country where all who dissented from the Established Faith have been either killed, or banished, or compelled to conform, there is no longer any one to be persecuted. No tree is destroyed by the scorching drought of the African Deserts, or by the intense frost of the Polar regions, because no tree can grow there. And in the most intolerant Countries on the Continent, no heretics are burnt, because there perescution has finished its work.

And accordingly all persons agree in professing (and generally, no doubt, with sincerity) to be averse to persecution. Nebuchadnezzar, who condemned Shadrach, Meshech, and Abednego to the flames, and those Roman Emperors under whom so many christian

Martyrs suffered, wished them rather to save their lives by worshipping the heathen gods. And it is the same with all, down to this day, who hold the persecuting principle.

Now, that principle was not renounced by most of the earliest Reformers. They complained, indeed, of the persecutions they *themselves* were exposed to. But this was not from any doubt that heretics ought to be punished, but because they denied that *they* were heretics. Persecution they considered as consisting in penalties inflicted on those who profess the *true* Faith, which, of course, they held theirs to be. To put to death such as are really heretics, was, in their view, no persecution.

By degrees it came to be perceived, that this principle leads to a war of extermination among all persons of different persuasions. And men began to adopt notions more humane, but not at all consistent either with the Gospel, or in themselves. They considered it as too severe to *burn* heretics, or even to put them to a less cruel *death*. But they thought it right to punish them by fine and imprisonment, either for refusing to profess what they did not believe, or for persisting in teaching doctrines which they felt themselves bound to propagate. (See Acts v. 28.)

And others, again, went further, and were for inflicting no punishment on those who do not hold the true Faith, but only excluding them from the rights of citizens; so as to secure to the "true believers" a monopoly of civil power.

But all these different classes of persons agreed in

the erroneous principle which goes to make Christ's, a "kingdom of this world."

Many persons imagine that there is a necessary connection between these views and a belief in the infallibility of a certain Church, and of the impossibility of salvation out of it; as if no one could think it right to persecute for religious error unless he thought himself exempt from all possibility of error; and again, as if every one who does think this, must be a persecutor.

But this is quite a mistake. For, on the one hand, a man may be confident that his is the only saving Faith, and that his Church is infallible—which was *actually* the case with the Churches under the immediate care of the inspired Apostles—and yet may be convinced, like those very Apostles, that coercion in religious matters is utterly unchristian.

And, on the other hand, a civil Ruler may so far misconceive the true character of the Gospel as to think it right to compel all his subjects to profess what appears to him to be the best religion; yet without thinking his Church or himself infallible in religious matters, any more than he is infallible in *secular* matters. Now in secular matters no Kings or Senates pretend to infallibility. They make such laws as they deem most expedient, and alter them from time to time as they see cause. But as long as those laws are unrepealed, they consider themselves (and very rightly) authorised to enforce them by penalties. If, then, they regard Religion as coming *under the province of the civil Magistrate*, they will of course apply the same rule to that also. They will feel themselves bound to take care, not only of the persons and property, but also of the souls of their subjects. They will prescribe what, in their judgment, shall appear to be the best regulations for traffic, and for keeping the peace, &c., and also the best for Religion.

And perceiving the convenience of a uniformity of Worship for all their subjects, they will be likely to regard all who do not conform to that which they have established, as enemies of the State ; and thence to expel or to degrade them as politically dangerous. And thus, without making any claim to religious infallibility, any more than to general legislative infallibility, they will change Christ's kingdom of Heaven into an earthly kingdom.

It is, indeed, true that any persons whose notions in morals or in politics are such as to make it impossible that they can be peaceable and loyal citizens, may allowably be excluded, not only from civil rights, but from the right of residing at all in the Country. And if there be absolutely no other way of fixing on such persons, but by their professed religion, it is necessary (as long as such continues to be the case) to submit to the very great evil of making their religion a test to exclude them.*

If, for example, any one is fully convinced—in opposition to all reason and to all experience—that no Jews can possibly be good subjects, he ought to urge (not that the most unprincipled of them should

* See PALEY'S *Moral Philosophy.*

be bribed by the hope of civil privileges to profess Christianity, but) that none of the Jewish Race should be allowed to reside in the Country.

But to make the profession of a certain Faith a necessary qualification for civil privileges, on the ground that it is the *true* Faith, and that the Magistrate is bound to uphold the true Faith, and to make the Church and the State *one community*, &c.; all this is evidently making Christ's a Kingdom of this World.

Gradually, juster views of the true character of that Kingdom prevailed more and more both among Protestants and Roman Catholics. But even now, these views are far from being universally acknowledged.

To the instances that have been noticed, others might have been added, of the same class; that is, instances of reformers retaining or reviving some of their former wrong notions, or practices, in some different shape. But what has been now said is sufficient to shew how careful men ought to be not to flatter themselves that when once they have reformed a corrupt system, or renounced a corrupt Church, they are thenceforward safe from like corruptions. If the corruptions are such as have their origin in the nature of Man, and (as is generally the case) are rather the *cause* of the faulty system, than the *effect* of it, it is against the infirmities of human nature that we should the most watchfully guard.

(II.) The other class of errors formerly mentioned as likely to be committed by reformers, are those which arise from what we called the tendency to *reaction;* to "mistake reverse of wrong for right," and thus to rush from one fault into another fault of the contrary extreme.

For example, many christian doctrines having been corrupted by "philosophy and vain deceit," and mixed up with presumptuous and absurd speculations, the result has been, that some have been led to reject the doctrines themselves as taught in Scripture.

Thus, the doctrines of our Lord's divine Nature, and of his Atonement, have been by some reckoned among the early corruptions of Christianity. This was doubtless caused, in a great measure, by men's being disgusted with the rash metaphysical explanations of those doctrines which have been given by some who were accounted profound theologians; and which others, equally rash, have confounded with the doctrines themselves. And some have even gone so far as to represent the Apostles as having mistaken their Master's meaning as to these points, or mixed up their own fancies with his revelations; so as to have preached a different Gospel from what He designed, and to have led their followers into idolatry. For, the arrogant pretensions to a perpetual inspiration *in the Church,* and its consequent infallibility, having been found utterly groundless, a reaction ensued, which led some to deny the inspiration of Paul himself, which he established by the miraculous "signs of an Apostle."*

* The Religion of Mahomet may be reckoned as one of the corruptions of Christianity, and as owing, in some degree, its origin

Some, again, have fallen into an extravagance which prevails a good deal at the present day; that of interpreting any part of Scripture they please, *allegorically*, as being what they call a "Myth," though stated by the Sacred Writers as a simple fact. According to these persons, Scripture is true indeed, but true only in the sense which they chuse to put on it, and utterly untrue in the sense in which it was understood for many centuries, and in which the Writers *knew* it was understood. To call this a *Revelation* is a manifest contradiction. But what such persons really mean, or really believe, no one can decide. For, by their own shewing, they have so low a moral principle as to think it allowable for a man to teach what he is conscious is false in the sense in

or at least some part of its wide diffusion, to a reaction against opposite corruptions. For the Mahometans, though they account Mahomet a greater prophet than Jesus Christ, yet confess Jesus to be the Christ, —to have been really sent from God,—to have been superior to all who came before Him,—and to have established his claim by miracles. And the chief part of the fables which they have mixed up with the Gospel-history, they borrowed from some of the earliest heretics. This religion, in short, is evidently a corrupted offshoot of Christianity.

At the time when Mahomet arose, a great part of the Christian world had fallen into saint-worship, and the adoration of pictures and images; and had also corrupted the doctrine of the Trinity into something very nearly approaching to Tritheism Against these errors he vehemently protested, dwelling strongly on the Divine Unity, and on the duty of renouncing every kind of idolatry. But the principle of persecution—already admitted by most Christians,—he retained and vigorously carried out. And along with the errors he rejected, he discarded also great part of the fundamentals of Christianity besides introducing much false doctrine of his own.

which he *knows* it will be understood; this being the conduct they attribute to Writers whom they regard as God's messengers commissioned to instruct mankind.*

Others, again, justly considering Holy Scripture as the only sure foundation of christian doctrine, and perceiving that to set up the authority of Church-tradition as an infallible interpreter of Scripture, might make Scripture say anything whatever, so as to render "the Word of God of none effect,"—and perceiving also that to shut out the People from the reading of Scripture is a monstrous abuse,—were led into an opposite extreme. They were for discarding all catechisms, and other human statements of christian doctrine, and depriving every Church of the office of teaching. They were for simply putting the Bible into each person's hands, and leaving him to make out, by his own unassisted study of it, whatever religion he could for himself. They forgot that, of all the books of the New Testament, there is not one that was written for the purpose of making known the christian Religion to those who were *quite strangers* to it. On the contrary, all those books were evidently written for the use of such as were already Christians, who had been carefully instructed [catechised] (See Luke i. 4), and examined in the christian Faith.

It is the office of a Church to *teach*, and of Scripture to *prove*. We should study the Sacred Books carefully, as alone possessing divine authority in matters of faith. But we should study them with the

* See Dr. WEST's "Discourse on Reserve," and Essay i. on the "Kingdom of Christ."

best helps we can obtain; and with care not to mistake the character of them, and the purposes for which they were written. In short, we should imitate the Bereans of old, who did not refuse to hear the teachers that came among them, but "searched the Scriptures daily, to see whether those things were so" which were taught them (Acts xvii. 11).

Human teaching bears the same relation to Scripture, that what is called "paper currency" does to the precious metals. Bank-notes and Bills of Exchange, though of no *intrinsic* value, are a very convenient circulating medium so long as they really *represent* gold or silver, and are payable in coin on the demand of the holder. But if these notes are made a legal tender, and are required to be received in payment, by the decree of the very government which issues them, and on its bare word, without being convertible into gold and silver, the result is, that those metals soon disappear, and men are cheated of their goods in exchange for worthless bits of paper.

Even so, as long as human teaching is really a *representative* of Scripture, and Scripture proof is always ready to be given, of whatever is taught, then, and then only, we are secured against the danger of having God's word superseded by "doctrines which are commandments of men."

Then, again, some men's horror of the doctrine, that good works can claim merit in God's sight, and that pilgrimages to certain supposed holy spots, and various kinds of self-torture, can atone for sins, led them into the Antinomian error of the ancient Gnostics.

They taught the doctrine of justification by faith, in such a sense as to contradict the Apostle James (ii. 17–26), or at least to leave their hearers utterly careless about christian holiness of life.

Other instances might be given of corruptions of christian doctrine, arising in great measure out of a reaction against opposite corruptions.

With respect to religious *ordinances* again, the burdensome and often superstitious rites with which christian worship has been in some Churches overlaid, have created such a reaction, that some have even gone so far as to reject the Sacraments distinctly appointed by Christ himself, and administered according to his direction by his Apostles, (1 Cor. xi. 23–26.) And the perversion of the office of christian Ministers by those who have made them Sacerdotal Priests, has driven some into a rejection of a regular christian Ministry altogether.

Others again, not going quite so far, have yet thought themselves bound to reject all institutions and ordinances that are not expressly enjoined in Scripture. There had been a manifest abuse of church-authority in introducing *ordinances* and *customs* that are *contrary* to Scripture; and again, in teaching *doctrines* that are not *contained* in Scripture. And this produced a reaction which led men to confound these two things together, and to deny the power which manifestly belongs to a church, of making bye-laws respecting matters intrinsically indifferent, and in which Scripture gives no commands.

And some reformers seem to have been led by their deep detestation of the corruptions they have protested against, to endeavour to be as *unlike* as possible to the Church from which they have revolted, even in matters indifferent: altering for the sake of change. They ought to have considered that the *presumption* is always against a change; that is, since change is not a good in itself, none should be introduced unless it can be shown to be needful, and to be a change for the better.*

It is true, we may very rightly alter or reject things, good or harmless in themselves, when they are found to be very liable to *abuse*, or when they cause unnecessary offence. Thus "Hezekiah brake in pieces the brazen serpent which Moses had made," when he found that the Israelites burned incense before it. And the Apostle Paul, though he decides that there was no harm in eating meats offered to idols, yet forbids the Corinthians to do so, when their eating it would be misapprehended and cause offence. So, also, a statue or picture of Christ, or of any eminent Christian, is not an evil in itself. But when it is found that the vulgar pay adoration to images or pictures, or that others apprehend them to be doing so, then such images should be removed from places of worship, as being a snare to weak brethren.

This, however, is no exception to the above rule, but an application of it. For in such a case, there *is* a good *reason* for the change.

Lastly, the usurpation and extravagant claims of a

---

* See Preface to the Book of Common Prayer

Church have driven some persons to set at nought Church-government altogether, and to overlook entirely the sanction which our Lord Himself gave to christian communities, and the powers which he conferred on them. The erroneous and over-strained notions of Church-unity which have been above noticed as having contributed to maintain corruptions and to hinder reforms, afterwards led to such a violent reaction, that many thought nothing of the guilt of Schism, and seemed even to forget that there was such a thing. And this, in turn, has sometimes produced a contrary reaction. The disgust and alarm caused by those who revolt against all rules, and discard the very notion of a christian community, have driven others to submit to the grossest abuses of Church-authority, for the sake of good order and peace. It is just so, that, in political affairs, also, there is a constant reaction between tyranny and anarchy; each in turn tending to produce the other.

Many more instances might be adduced; but what have been noticed are sufficient as specimens, to shew how watchful reformers ought to be against the tendency to reaction—against suffering incautious zeal to hurry them from one extreme into another.

We shall now proceed to treat somewhat more fully of the questions relating to Church-unity.

CHURCH ALLEGIANCE AND SEPA-RATIONS.

IT has been pointed out that the correction of abuses and corruptions in Religion has been, in most instances, resisted and long delayed; partly from an undue attention having been directed to points of *minor importance*, which has drawn off men's thoughts from very serious errors; partly from mistaken notions respecting *Church-unity;* and partly from a mistaken dread of *innovation*, causing men to overlook what are in reality the greatest innovations.

From these and other causes, various corruptions have often been allowed to go on unchecked by timely remedies, and to increase, till a thorough reformation was necessary; and indeed much longer. And the longer a reformation is deferred, the more difficult, and the more dangerous and violent, it is likely to be.

In particular, a reformation very long delayed is the more liable to those two classes of evils mentioned above; [I.] the danger of retaining some of the former wrong principles, so as to revive, under a new form, the faults which had been corrected; and [II.] the danger of *reactions*, leading men from one extreme into another.

[I.] For, the longer any corruption has been allowed to prevail, the more it will have wrought itself into men's character, so as to have affected their mind throughout, and become, as it were, a part of themselves. And then, the same fault, substantially, will be the more likely to reappear in a different shape.

Thus, for instance, when the principle of persecution, above adverted to, had been so very long acted on, that men all over the world had been familiarised to the putting down of heresies by sword and fire, and the enforcement of the profession of the true Faith by the Civil Magistrate, as an indispensable religious duty, the consequence was, that reformers, even when exposed to persecution themselves, still clung to the faulty principle. They considered persecution, (as was before observed,) as consisting in punishing those who maintained the *truth*. And it was long before they came to perceive,—what Scripture so very plainly points out,—the inconsistency with Christ's Religion of all use of coercion in his cause. And some remain blind to this, even down to the present day.

And, again, when *ignorance* of the true character of Christianity, resulting from the non-translation of the Scriptures, had been very widely spread and long continued, and then, persons who had very little mental cultivation, and who had been trained from childhood in most erroneous religious notions, suddenly came to the perusal of the Scriptures, (often without any assistance,) it naturally happened that many of them fell into gross mistakes as to the meaning of what they read. In particular, they often mixed up together confusedly the Law and the Gospel; and often read *detached passages*, taken at random, without any reference to times, places, persons, and occasions. And thus among many, ignorance of the true character of Christianity continued, in a great degree, to prevail, though in a new shape.

This has been often brought forward by the opponents of the Reformation, as a proof of the danger of putting the Scriptures into the hands of the People. But if christian Ministers had all along done their duty in training the People to an intelligent and profitable study of Scripture, this evil would have been, for the most part, prevented. Instead of this, they had kept them ignorant and uneducated, generation after generation. And mankind had been so long blindfolded that they could not see clearly when the bandage was removed.

[II.] And again, the longer and the more obstinately any needful reform has been resisted, the more fierce in general will be the spirit in which it is at length effected. Abuses which have been maintained long after they have been exposed and complained of, men are apt to correct with an angry and indiscriminate violence, which often leads them to rush into extremes, and to reject what is true and right, along with what is erroneous and faulty. Thus, one may sometimes see long-continued tyranny succeeded by revolutionary anarchy; and a long reign of ignorant superstition, even by avowed Atheism.

Many, also, of the evils which are apt to accompany any great religious reformation, have been increased by the *too great extent* of a single Church.

The Apostles appear to have founded a distinct Church in each considerable city; as at Philippi, Thessalonica, and several other cities in Macedonia, and elsewhere. Now, if some corruption had found its way into these Churches, and one of them—suppose Philippi—had reformed itself, although it is likely that some degree of jealousy and disapprobation would have at first arisen in the other Churches which were as yet unreformed, and though the Philippians might have been censured as having taken a rash step, at least they could not have been denounced as schismatical *revolters.* No one could have complained that they had *separated* from a Church of which they were subjects. They could not have been viewed in the light of *rebellious children*, throwing off the yoke of an authority they had been subject to.

But when a multitude of Churches were united into one vast Community, comprehending many great Nations spread over extensive Regions, then any reformation not embracing the *whole* of this great Church, necessarily implied *revolt* and separation.

Any branch of that Church which resolved to correct abuses that were obstinately retained by the supreme central Authority, was compelled to throw off submission to that Authority, and to assert its independence. And then, those who adhered to the Church which claimed to be the Universal Church, naturally regarded the others as not only erroneous, but Heretics, and Schismatics.

And such they undoubtedly *would* have been had they separated on insufficient grounds. They had done that which *would* have been sinful, if it had not been justified by the corruptions in essential points of Faith and Worship, which the supreme central Authority had obstinately refused to correct. This refusal transferred the sin of causing the division, from the revolters, to those who made the revolt necessary.

But of course a separation thus effected gave rise to much more hostile feelings on both sides than would have been likely to exist between Churches that had been *originally* distinct, and had always continued so; neither claiming any control over the other. Such Churches might, indeed, have been to a certain degree alienated from each other by differences in Doctrine or Discipline; but there would not have been the additional provocations of a revolt, and an unfriendly separation on the one side, and a claim of supremacy on the other.

And, accordingly, it was on the very ground of the Reformed being *Heretics* and *Schismatics* that the *secular power* was called in to reduce them by force to submission. Princes were not called on to wage war against *religious error*, merely as such; but they were urged to reduce to obedience those who had *revolted* against the Church to which they were bound to be subject. And thus religious wars, and fierce persecutions, and mutual hatred were introduced, far beyond what would have been likely to arise if the original independence of numerous Churches had always continued.

When several distinct Churches had been *established in revolt*—the members of them having been compelled to *secede* from the Community they had belonged to, on account of a *disagreement* as to the fundamentals of Christianity—the result was, that the ideas of *distinctness*, and of *disagreement*, often came to be, in some measure, blended together in men's minds. There was a sort of presumption created, that any Churches *independent* of each other may be expected to be at *variance*. That mutual friendly feeling and free inter-communion which prevailed in the earliest ages—when an Ephesian Christian, for instance, going to settle at Corinth, or at any other place where there was a christian Church, and bringing proper testimonials, was at once received as a member of that Church—were much impaired, and sometimes forgotten.

And, moreover, when men had become familiarly *accustomed* to separation, from having been forced into it, they were in danger of becoming *careless* about it, and disposed to think lightly of the sin of Schism.

Something similar takes place in many other cases. For instance, those who have been placed in such circumstances as to make the shedding of blood an unavoidable evil, are in danger of gradually losing their original repugnance to it, and becoming so far hardened, as to think little of sacrificing human life, even *without* necessity.

It is the same in the matter now before us. There is always a danger that *necessary* separations may lead to others not necessary, and may have prepared men's minds to make every little difference, even on points of no vital importance, a ground for setting up new sects. The colour of a Minister's vestment,—the names of the months, and of the days of the week —the mode of conducting Church music,—the using or not using of a ring in matrimony,—on these and such like matters, differences of opinion have been made a plea for separation.

Now, it is much less likely that this would have occurred in Churches which had not broken off from any other, but had been all along distinct Communities. For though, in any such Church, differences of opinion on minor points might have arisen, it is likely that men would have agreed to some compromise, rather than occasion hostile divisions.

It is true, indeed, that in almost every question, however insignificant, there is a better and a worse decision; and the decision of each man's own judgment will, of course, appear to himself to be the better. But in matters not essential, it is evidently a duty to yield, or to adopt a compromise, rather than endanger christian concord. For if each person were to draw up what might appear to himself the very best form of Church Government, and the best possible mode of expressing each christian Doctrine, and the most perfect Ritual for divine Worship, and should resolve not to belong to any Church that did not exactly adopt all these in every particular, it is plain that there would be almost as many Sects as families, and that no christian community at all could subsist for a single year.

But, as has been above said, when unfriendly separations had been once begun, through a necessity caused by the obstinate retaining of abuses, causeless divisions often ensued from men's having become familiarised to divisions, and almost entirely regardless of Church-union.

And again, abhorrence of such divisions has led some Christians to adopt the system of making a State and a Church *one Community*, and assigning to the Civil Magistrate the entire control in spiritual matters, and the right of dictating to the consciences of all the citizens. And thus under the name of " making the State religious" and " providing for the greatest good of its subjects," they make Christ's a kingdom of this world.

With this fault, and with the endless divisions which have contributed to cause it, Reformers are often exultingly reproached by the advocates of the system of having one great Church which is to comprehend all Christians, and to dictate to them their faith and practice. See, they say, what are the consequences of once allowing any separation from the Church on any grounds whatever! When you have once begun, you cannot tell where to stop.

Now, in truth, that very Church from which the Reformers revolted, was (as has been above pointed out) the original cause of all these evils. In the first place, by obstinately adhering to an accumulated mass of gross corruptions, it made a thorough reformation necessary. And secondly, by having absorbed into *one* Community a multitude of distinct Churches, it made *separation* a necessary part of *reformation*. And thus it not only *retarded* needful reformations, and made them more *difficult*, but also made them, when they did come, much more *hurtful*, and more exposed to the dangers which are attendant on any great reformation.

As for what are, and are not, such essential points as to warrant separation, it would of course be unsuitable to our present purpose to enter on the discussion of such a subject. But every one should be warned, that in each question of the kind that may arise, he is bound to inquire and examine seriously, carefully, and dispassionately; not as if it were merely a matter of taste, fancy, or convenience. We are responsible to God for the exercise of our best discretion in forming a decision. And we are bound in duty to Him, to take care neither to sacrifice the essentials of Christianity for the sake of peace, nor again, lightly and wantonly to cause divisions.

All separation, in short, and all resistance to Church-authority, must be either a *duty* or a *sin*. Which of the two it is, in each particular instance, each must decide according to the best of his judgment; which is, after all, fallible. And in no case are we authorised to pronounce our neighbour guilty of an *unpardonable* sin. But though christian charity requires us to make allowance for those who appear to us blameable, it is no part of charity to confound the distinctions of right and wrong; nor indeed would there be any *room* for the exercise of *charity* in judging of those whom we do not consider to be acting wrongly.

On these and several other important questions connected with religion, some persons are so distrustful of what they call "private judgment,"—that is, the judgment of the generality of men, and of themselves, —that they resolve to renounce altogether the exercise of private judgment on all religious questions, and to submit themselves in every thing to the judgment of their Church. They dwell much on the incompetency of most men to decide rightly on difficult points; and consider that there is a pious humility in determining not to exercise their own judgment at all.

But they quite forget that, in the course they adopt, they do decide on one most important and difficult point. A man who resolves to place himself under a certain guide to be implicitly followed, and decides that such and such a Church is the appointed infallible guide, does decide on his own private judgment, *that one* most important point, which includes in it all other decisions relative to Religion. And if, by his own shewing, he is *unfit to judge* at all, he can have no ground for confidence that he has decided it rightly. And if, accordingly, he will not trust himself to judge even on this point, but resolves to consult his priest, or some other friends, and be led entirely by *their* judgment thereupon, still he does, in thus resolving, exercise his own judgment as to the counsellors he so relies on.

There is no need, therefore, to dispute about the *right*, or about the *duty*, of private judgment. For there is plainly an unavoidable *necessity* of private judgment, on any subject wherein we *take any serious interest*. The responsibility is one which, however unfit we may deem ourselves to bear it, we *cannot* possibly get rid of, in any matter about which we really feel an anxious care. It is in vain to discuss the questions whether we *may*, or whether we *ought*, to exercise private judgment, since we *must* do so, whether we will or no.

That which often misleads men in this matter, is, that we *can* refrain from exercising private judgment *on this or that particular point*, by *transferring* our judgment to some other point. For example—A sick man who is conscious of his own want of knowledge of medicine, may refrain from exercising any judgment as to the remedies he should use, and may put himself wholly in the hands of a physician; that is, he *judges* that a physician is needful, and that such and such a practitioner is worthy of confidence. Or, supposing he distrusts his own judgment on this point also, then he consults some friend whom he *judges* to be trustworthy, as to *what* physician he shall employ. In one way, or else in another, he cannot but exercise private judgment. So, also, if a man inherit a great fortune, and have a strong sense of the great responsibility attending it, and of his own unfitness to dispose of his wealth, he may resolve to make it all over to trustees, to distribute in charity at their discretion. He may have judged rightly in so doing; but it is evident he *does* judge, and does exercise an act of ownership once for all, in thus divesting himself of his property. And if he deem himself incompetent even to the task of selecting trustees, and relies on the judgment of some friend as to what persons he shall appoint trustees, still he is exercising his judgment in the selection of that friend. The responsibility is one which he cannot shake off, do what he will.

The man who in the course of God's providence comes into the possession of wealth, is by that providence, entrusted with the stewardship of that wealth, however ill-qualified he may seem, to us, or to himself, for such a charge. And instead of murmuring or wondering at God's dispensations, or trying in vain to shake off the responsibility thus laid on him, he should set himself to do the best he can towards the fulfilment of the duty imposed on him.

And it is the same in all cases. We do and must exercise our judgment, on one point or on another, in all matters except those in which we *take no interest,* and which do not occupy our thoughts. In most of the causes, for instance, which are tried in a court of justice, we do not trouble ourselves to exercise any judgment, if we know or care nothing about either plaintiff or defendant, and feel no interest in the decision.

Accordingly, if any one resolves that he will not exercise any judgment on religious matters, and really does consistently keep to that rule, not deceiving himself (as many do) in the way just above noticed, by judging on one point instead of another, he will find that there is only one possible way of complying with that rule—namely, by *withdrawing his attention* as much as possible from the whole subject, except as far as regards outward forms and observances, and refraining altogether from considering the questions, what the christian Religion is, and whether there is any truth in it.

And there are not a few who really do, in this way, abstain from exercising any judgment at all in religious matters, and are content to do and say just what they have been accustomed to, without any serious reflection on the subject. But even so, they do not escape responsibility. For we are responsible, not only for doing, but also for leaving undone; else, the servant who hid his Lord's talent in the earth would have escaped condemnation.

Of course it is not meant that on any important point a man ought to make up his mind, unassisted, and without consulting those whom he may consider to be intelligent, and well-informed, and upright advisers. Only, let him not deceive himself by imagining that he *can* forego *all* exercise of his own judgment in any matter about which he has a real and anxious care.

And, on the other hand, we should guard against the opposite mistake of supposing that whatever is left to our own *discretion* is, therefore, left to our *caprice*, and may be decided on at random. We may *have a right* to do many things which we should not *be right* in doing. For instance, when any bill is brought into Parliament, each member has an undoubted right to vote for it or against it; but it would be absurd to say that he would *be equally right* in doing either. It is in such cases, and in such alone, that there is room for the exercise of any such quality as good sense, wisdom, discretion, &c. For, in matters quite *indifferent*, there is clearly no exercise of judgment in deciding. Nor, again, is there any room for it in matters that are already decided for us, and in which we have *no choice:* as, for instance, when a Judge has to declare what the law *actually* is on such and such a point. But when a Legislator is called on to decide what the law *ought* to be, and, in short, in every case where we have to decide, and where there may be a better or a worse decision, it is then, and then only, that there is room for the exercise of good sense.

We should keep in mind, then, that as the exercise of our own judgment (in matters in which we feel a deep interest) is, on the one hand, *unavoidable*, so it is, on the other hand, *responsible*. We are bound to use, to the best of our power, such faculties and opportunities as God's providence may have bestowed on us, in judging of any question pertaining to Religion; and among others, in any question as to separation.

But though, as we have already said, much blame attaches to those who hastily, and on slight grounds, separate from their Church; a Church, on the other hand, is not exempted from a share of blame, which *narrows* too much its terms of communion. *Some* terms, of course, are indispensable; since persons differing as to the fundamentals of christian Doctrine and Worship cannot possibly be members of the same christian Community. But care should be taken not to go beyond what is necessary. If possible, none should be excluded of those who can join in christian Worship together, and receive instruction together in the essential truths of the Gospel. To multiply Articles of Faith and Ordinances, unnecessarily, manifestly tends to create divisions.

And it is not enough to say that these Articles are, all, such as we are convinced are scriptural, and that none of our Ordinances are contrary to Scripture, and that the scruples of those who object to them are unfounded and frivolous. All this may be true; and it may be true that those are to blame who on such grounds separate from the Church; yet this does not clear from blame those who put a stumbling-block in the way of weak brethren by insisting on points that are not essential, and on which persons may differ who are yet capable of worshipping together as Members of the same christian Church. "Him that is weak in the Faith, receive ye, but not to doubtful disputations." (Rom. xiv. 1.)

It is to be observed, however, that when we speak of points that are and that are not "essential," we mean, in this place, essential as terms of *communion;* not, of *salvation.* For there are some points of disagreement which would completely prevent men from being Members of the same Church, though hardly any, of either party, would regard the other as under a fatal error.

For example, there are persons irreconcilably opposed on the subject of Church-endowments. Some of the advocates of what is called "the voluntary system" consider it as not only objectionable, but utterly unlawful, to attend what they call a *hired* Ministry*

---

* More properly called *unhired;* being supported, not like a labourer by the wages of his employer, but by endowments similar to those of many Hospitals, Colleges, &c.

—that is, one maintained by endowments. And the other party, though not holding it absolutely *unlawful* for a Minister to be dependant on the voluntary contributions of his People (since "the labourer is worthy of his hire,") yet consider this so very *undesirable*, that they would feel bound to support and promote the system of endowments. Now these two parties could hardly continue members of the same Church. And yet neither need regard the other as having abandoned the fundamentals of Christianity.

The same may be said of an irreconcilable disagreement as to the use of *extemporary* prayer, and of stated *forms*, in Public Worship. Some consider the use of any form, even the Lord's Prayer, as not allowable. Others, again, believe that a special promise is made to the "common" prayers of a Congregation who "*agree together* touching something they shall ask in Christ's name;" and that, accordingly, they are bound to pray *together*, (either audibly or mentally,) and not merely to *listen* to the prayers offered up by another. And they hold it to be impossible, in most cases, that a Congregation (at least, the *whole* of it) can so constantly go along with all that is said by an extemporary speaker, as to *accompany*—properly speaking— his prayers; that is, so as not only to *understand* and *approve* what he says, but to make his prayers *their own prayers also* at the moment. These prayers, accordingly, will generally be, they conceive, rather of the character of exhortations addressed to the People by the Minister, than of joint-prayers addressed by the People to God.

Now persons strongly impressed with these opposite notions could not be united in one Church, though they may not regard each other as fatally in error.

It has been above said, that a man is deeply responsible for the sin of Schism, if he should, without evident and strong necessity, separate from his Church. But some have doubted *what* Church it is that has this general claim to his allegiance; whether that which is established by *law;* or that which his *ancestors* formerly belonged to; or that in which he *himself* has been brought up.

As for the first of these, the Religion established by law, has not, on *that* ground, any claim on the conscience. A member, for example, of the Church of England becomes a *dissenter* if he settle in some part of the Empire where some other form of religion is established. But if he is conscientiously a member of his own original Church, and sees no reason to consider it unscriptural, he has no right to forsake it on political grounds.

As for the Church to which one's ancestors may have belonged, no one should think himself bound to investigate obscure and difficult questions of history, and to judge of all the acts of those who founded or reformed his Church, perhaps several centuries ago, in order to decide whether he is permitted or whether he is bound, to continue in the Church in which he was brought up. If those founders separated unreasonably, *they* indeed were chargeable with the sin of Schism. But it would be to create a fresh Schism, if he were to forsake the Church he was brought up in, not from feeling any objection to its Doctrines or Worship, but merely on the ground that its original formation was not justifiable.

And a like principle is universally recognised in all civil affairs. Else, indeed, the whole World would be filled with perpetual rebellions and civil wars. For example, every one knows that Norway was formerly united, not to Sweden, but to Denmark—that, in like manner, Normandy, and other provinces of France, and also the North American States, formerly belonged to England; and that Ireland at one time consisted of several independent Kingdoms. But if a Norman were to hold that he owed no allegiance to the French Government, or an American to that of the United States, and so on, unless every such separation and annexation could be proved originally justifiable, and if every man were to think himself authorised on such grounds to raise revolt, there would be hardly such a thing as a peaceable Government on Earth.

Each man, therefore, owes allegiance, generally, to the Church in which he has been brought up, unless he find this incompatible with his reverence for God's Word, and his obedience to the divine Will.

Independently, however, of any *disagreement*, a separation may take place with the consent of all parties, of one Branch of a Church from the rest, merely from reasons of convenience, and without any interruption of harmony and inter-communion, any more than among the several distinct Churches originally founded by the Apostles. For example, this took place with the American Episcopalian Church, which formerly was a portion of the Church of England. When the American States became politically independent, the inconvenience of having one Church whose members were citizens of different political Communities, was so plain to all parties, that a friendly separation was agreed on. And if this had been done long before, by mutual consent, merely on the ground of the inconvenient *distance* between the two Countries, no one could have had any right to find fault with the measure. For, any union or separation that is made by mutual consent, is evidently a matter which the parties concerned have a full right to determine for themselves.

But difficult questions may arise when both parties do *not* thus agree; those who desire to form themselves into a distinct Church being opposed by the rest. Suppose, for instance, that on the occasion just alluded to, the English Church had refused to consent to the independence of the American, and had insisted on retaining control over them. In any such case, those desiring to secede should, in the first place, satisfy themselves, on careful consideration, that the evils they seek to remedy are not only real, but great, and likely to interfere with the objects for which Churches exist. Next, they should respectfully, and in a spirit of kindness, set forth their reasons, and listen candidly to what may be urged on the opposite side. And if they see no reason to alter their opinion, they should still remonstrate earnestly and perseveringly, before they take the extreme step of seceding without the consent of their brethren.

In these, however, and in all similar matters, it is impossible to lay down rules such as will at once apply to every case that may arise. There must always be room for the exercise of sound judgment and candour, in deciding on each particular question.

There is one principle, however, which should always be kept in mind, and which, obvious as it is, men often lose sight of in practice; namely, that a *necessity* imposed by external circumstances, and for which we are not responsible, will justify, and call for, such measures as *would* be sinful if there were no such necessity. We should be careful, therefore, not to commit either the error of censuring men for doing what would, in ordinary circumstances, be wrong; or the error of supposing ourselves at liberty to do, at any time and under any circumstances, whatever has, in some particular case, been justifiably and rightly done.

In the ordinary affairs of life, this principle is, in general, well understood and acted on. For example, for a number of men, citizens of any State, to assemble, and by their own authority, declare themselves a Senate, and proceed to elect Magistrates, and enact Laws, and establish a Government, would justly be regarded as a most heinous act of rebellion; and all their laws, (however good in themselves,) would be evidently null and void. But if a number of persons were to find themselves wrecked on a desert island, or the sole survivors of a pestilence, or in some other way left to themselves, no one would contend that they were bound thenceforward to live in a state of anarchy, because they had no legitimate Rulers or Laws. They would be authorised, and bound, to agree as well as they could, in establishing some sort of Government. And the Laws and Magistrates thus appointed would have as good a claim to obedience as those of any Country in the World; because it is plainly necessary to human welfare, and agreeable to the divine Will, that men should live under a regular Government. Yet this case would afford no precedent for any persons who should take upon them to break up an existing Community, and to revolt against "the Powers that be."

So also, if the persons thus situated were to find themselves without regularly ordained Clergy, or without any except such as they were fully convinced had abandoned the genuine Doctrines of the Gospel, it would be absurd to suppose it could be the Will of their Heavenly Master, that they should remain for ever destitute of a christian Ministry and Church-ordinances. They would clearly be conforming to the spirit of his injunctions, in forming themselves into a Church, and appointing various Orders of Ministers, selecting the best qualified persons they could find, for each office, and establishing Church-regulations according to the best of their judgment. And the necessity under which they were placed, would justify, and render valid, all their acts and appointments; supposing them always not to be in themselves superstitious or unscriptural. But such a case would afford no fair precedent for persons differently circumstanced, who should take upon themselves, wantonly and without necessity, to ordain Ministers, and set up themselves as a new Church.

So, also, there may be extreme cases of such cruel and intolerable oppression as to justify subjects in revolting against an established Government. But extreme cases do not destroy the authority of a general rule, though they may authorize an exceptional departure from it, And it is undoubtedly true, as a general rule, that we are in duty bound to submit to existing Governments.

Again, if the loyal portion of a garrison were to revolt from a general, who had turned traitor, and was betraying the city into an enemy's hands, so far from being treasonable in thus revolting, they would have been abettors of treason if they had not. And yet the general rule is, that soldiers are bound to obey their commander.

In like manner, submission to Church-authority, and the preservation of Church-union, are the rule; and resistance, or separation, the exception. The burden of proof lies with those who undertake to justify a departure from a rule. And if they do thus justify themselves, their case affords no fair precedent for those who would introduce general discord and confusion.

It is to be observed, however, that when we speak of the general claim to obedience, which the Laws of any Community—civil or ecclesiastical—have on its Members, this does not imply such a blind veneration as should withhold us from seeking any needful amendment. Any one who scorns the absurdity of attributing infallibility to human Beings, would be himself guilty of a still greater absurdity, if, while considering all men as fallible, he should yet act as if they were *in*-fallible, by insisting that all their institutions and regulations should be like the Laws of the Medes and Persians, which could never be changed; and that no one should even inquire whether amendment in any point be possible, and needful. All wanton and hasty changes, indeed, should, in all subjects, be avoided; the presumption being, as has been above said, against every alteration. And a man's veneration for any existing Constitution—whether in Church or in State—may reasonably lead him to deprecate any fundamental change. But the best security against this,—-in short, against revolution,—is, the constant correction of abuses, and the introduction of improvements as they are needed. It is the neglect of timely *repairs* (as was remarked above) that makes *rebuilding* necessary.

And, moreover, the amendment of any Law that is faulty, tends (beside the immediate benefit) to increase men's confidence in those that are left unchanged; and in this way contributes to the stability of the whole system. For it creates a presumption that what is left unchanged, is so left for some good and sufficient *reasons*, and not from a mere blind determination against *any* change, whether for the worse or for the better.

Some persons, however, there are, who are far from thinking all existing laws (civil or ecclesiastical) faultless; and who, on that ground, hold themselves at liberty to disobey or evade any that they think objectionable. But if these very persons are called on to exert themselves to procure, in a regular way, a remedy for the evil, they will shrink from the trouble, or expense, or odium, they might thus incur for the public good. There are many, for example, who from their disapprobation of the existing revenue laws, or game laws, &c., will violate these without scruple, when they can do so with impunity. But when urged to exert themselves in perseveringly calling the attention of the Legislature to these laws, they will plead that it is no concern of theirs, but only of their Rulers.

And they act in the same way with respect to Church-regulations; disregarding without scruple any that they disapprove; but refusing to take any pains for the regular correction of anything they complain of.

But a truly conscientious and right-minded man will pursue exactly the opposite course. As long as a law *exists*, he will feel bound to obey it, as far as he can with a safe conscience. But if he consider it an *unwise* law, he will exert himself to have it amended by competent authority; or, if necessary, to have some competent authority *appointed* for the purpose of rectifying whatever may be amiss. These exertions may, perhaps, cost him much more trouble and discomfort than he, individually, suffers from the existing state of things. But he will not hesitate to sacrifice his own immediate personal comfort and ease, for the lasting benefit of his Countrymen and fellow-Christians. For a true Christian is most emphatically and pre-eminently public-spirited. "NONE OF US," says the Apostle Paul, "LIVETH UNTO HIMSELF." (Rom. xiv. 7.) And he who is the most sedulously occupied in working out, on Gospel principles, his own salvation, will always be found the most devotedly active in promoting the welfare of his brethren.

THE END.

A

CATALOGUE OF BOOKS

PUBLISHED BY

WILLIAM GOWANS.

"Ignorance is the curse of GOD; knowledge the wing wherewith we fly to heaven."
SHAKESPEARE.

"Without books GOD is silent, justice dormant, natural science at a stand, philosophy lame, letters dumb, and all things involved in Cimmerian darkness." .... BARTHOLIN.

Nos. 81, 83, AND 85 CENTRE STREET.

NEW YORK:

1860.

CATALOGUE

OF

WILLIAM GOWANS' PUBLICATIONS.

Plato's Phædon;

Or, a Discussion on the Immortality of the Soul. Translated
from the Greek by Charles S. Stanford. A new edition, enriched
with Archbishop Fenelon's Life of Plato; the Opinions of ancient,
medieval, and modern philosophers and divines, on the Soul's
Immortality; together with Notes, historical, biographical, and
mythological. To which is added a Catalogue of all the works
known to have been written on a Future State. With a beau-
tiful and accurate portrait of Plato. 12mo. pp. 309. Price
$1.00.   1854.

Ancient Fragments.

Namely:—The Morals of Confucius, the Chinese Philosopher;
The Oracles of Zoroaster, the founder of the Persian Magi; San-
choniatho's Theology of the Phœnicians; The Periplus of Hanno,
the Carthaginian Navigator and Discoverer; King Hiempsal'
History of the African Settlements; The Choice Sayings of Pub-
lius Syrus; The Egyptian Fragments of Manetho; The Similitudes of Demophilus, or Directions for the Proper Regulation of
Life; and The Excellent Sayings of the Seven Wise Men of
Greece. Translated into English by various authors. 12mo
pp. 298 $2.00.   1835

Denton, Daniel.

A Description of New York, formerly called New Netherlands, with the places thereunto adjoining. Likewise a Brief Relation of the Customs of the Indians there. By DANIEL DENTON. A new edition, with an Introduction and copious Historical Notes, by GABRIEL FURMAN. 8vo. pp. 74. $1.00. 1845.

The Same Work.

Large Paper. 4to. Only 100 were printed. $3.00. 1845.

Cupper, R. A.

The Universal Stair Builder: being a new Treatise on the Con struction of Staircases and Hand-rails, showing plans of the various forms of stairs, method of placing the risers in the cylinders, general method of describing the face-moulds for a hand-rail, and an expeditious method of squaring the rail. Useful, also, to stone-masons, constructing stone stairs and hand-rails; with a new method of sawing the twist part of any hand-rail square from the face of the plank, and to a parallel width. Also, a new method of forming the casings of the rail by a gauge. Preceded by some necessary Problems on Practical Geometry, with the sections of Prismatic Solids. Illustrated by 29 Plates. 4to. pp. 30. $6.00.

*** By competent judges this book is accounted the best that has, as yet, appeared on the subject of Stair Building.

Colton, C. C.—Lacon;

Or, Many Things in Few Words, addressed to These Who Think. By the Rev. C. C. COLTON. Revised edition, with an Index, and Life of Colton. 8vo. pp. 504. $2.00. 1849.

The Same Work.

In one vol. 12mo. pp. 504. $1.25. 1849.

Allyn, Avery.

A Ritual of Freemasonry, illustrated by thirty engravings. To which is added, a Key to the Phi Beta Kappa, the Orange, and Odd Fellows' Societies. With Notes and Remarks. By AVERY ALLYN. 12mo. pp. 269. $5.00. 1831

Jachin and Boaz;

Or, an Authentic Key to the Door of *Freemasonry*, both Ancient and Modern, calculated not only for the Instruction of every New-Made Mason, but also for the Information of all who intend to become Brethren. Interspersed with a variety of Notes and Remarks, necessary to explain and render the whole clear to the meanest capacity; also, a New and Accurate List of all the English Regular Lodges in the World, according to their Seniority, with the dates of each Constitution, and Days of Meeting; to which is added, *Masonry Dissected*, by Samuel Prichard, and The Freemason's Winepress, consisting of *Toasts, Sentiments, ana Anecdotes;* and a Catalogue of Books on Freemasonry, and Kindred Subjects. 12mo. pp. 200. $2.50.   New York, 1857.

Gowans, William.

A Catalogue of Books on Freemasonry and Kindred Subjects. Compiled by W. G. 12mo. pp. 59. $1.25. New York, 1858.

" Book Catalogues are to men of letters what the compass and the lighthouse are to the mariner, the railroad to the merchant, the telegraph wires to the editor, the digested index to the lawyer, the pharmacopœia and the dispensatory to the physician, the sign-post to the traveller, the screw, the wedge, and the lever to the mehcanic; in short, they are the labor-saving machines, the concordance of literature."— *Western Memorabilia.*

Ramsay, Allan.   The Gentle Shepherd:

A Pastoral Comedy, in Five Acts. To which is added the Life of the Author, an authentic Portrait, Criticisms on the Play by various eminent writers, a new and carefully compiled Glossary. and a Catalogue of all the Scottish Poets. 12mo. $1.00. 1852.

The Same Work.

Large paper, with Portrait on India paper. 8vo. Only 100 copies printed. $3.50.   1852.

The Same Work.

Extra large paper, with Portrait on India paper. 4to. Only 50 copies printed. $6.00.   1852.

The Same Work.

Cheap edition, without the introductory Matter, Portrait, and Catalogue. 37½ cents.

Coleridge, S. T.

Biographia Literaria; or, Biographical Sketches of My Literary Life and Opinions. From the Second London Edition. Prepared for publication in part by H. N. Coleridge. 2 vols. thick 12mo. pp. 804. $1.50.   1852.

The Same Work.

Large paper. 8vo. pp. 804. $3.00.   1852.

California.

The Wonder of the Age. A book for every one going to or having an interest in that *Golden Region;* being the Report of THOMAS BUTLER KING, United States' Government Agent in and for California. 8vo. pp. 34. 12¼ cents.   1850.

Rochefoucauld, Duc de la.

Moral Reflections, Sentences, and Maxims. Newly translated from the French; with an Introduction and copious Notes, and a Life of the Author. With an Elegant steel Portrait. To which is added the Moral Sentences and Maxims of the *good* Stanislaus, King of Poland. Also a Catalogue of all the Books written on Proverbs, Maxims, Sayings, Sentences, Apophthegms, Similitudes, etc., etc. 12mo. pp. 237. $1.25.   1851.

The Same Work.

Large paper, with the Portrait on India paper. 8vo. pp. 237. Only 100 copies were printed. $2.50.   1851.

The Same Work.

Extra large paper, with the Portrait on India paper. 4to. pp. 237. Only 25 copies were printed. $6.00.   1851.

Taylor, Isaac.

Physical Theory of Another Life. To which is added a Catalogue of all the author's writings, and a Catalogue of all the books published on the Immortality of the Soul. 12mo. pp. 278. $1.00.   1852

Taylor, Isaac.

Elements of Thought; or, Concise Explanations (*alphabetically arranged*); or, The Principal Terms Employed in the Intellectual Philosophy. 12mo. pp. 180. 75 cents. 1851.

Faber, Rev. George Stanley, B. D.

Difficulties of Infidelity. To which is added, Modern Infidelity Considered by ROBERT HALL, and a Catalogue of all the books that have been published on the Evidence of Revealed Religion: also, a list of Mr. FABER's published writings. 12mo. pp. 300. *cloth*. $1.00. 1853.

O'Meara, Barry E., Esq.

Napoleon in Exile; or, a Voice from St. Helena. Being the Reflections and Opinions of Napoleon, on the most Memorable and Important Events of his Life and Government. In his own words. With Engravings. 2 vols. 12mo. pp. 540 and 552. *cloth*. $2.00. 1853.

The Same Work.

Royal 8vo. 2 vols. pp. 540 and 552. $3.00. 1853.
"A work professing to give minute details of the *private life*, and especially the *unreserved conversation* of the MOST REMARKABLE PERSONAGE who has appeared in modern times, must possess the very highest claims to attention. * * * Mr. O'Meara very naturally kept a journal of what passed between himself and his illustrious patient, and the work before us consists of this journal."

Kingsbury, Harmon.

The Great Law Book. The Kingdom and Reign of the Messiah, his Subjects, Precepts, and Government. With Preliminary Remarks on the Bible, its Author, Dispensations, and other Kingdoms. 12mo. pp. 312. 75 cents. 1857.

Gowans, William.

His Book Catalogues, from 1 to 18, both inclusive. Royal 8vo *cloth*. $2.00. New York, 1842–59

REMAINDERS OF EDITIONS

BY OTHER PUBLISHERS.

Gall, John Joseph.

The Phrenological Works of. Translated into English by W Lewis. 6 vols. 12mo. *cloth.* $7.50. Boston, 1835

Blake, W. J.

The History of Putnam County, New York, with an enumeration of its Towns, Villages, Rivers, Creeks, Lakes, Ponds, Mountains, Hills, and Geological Features, Local Traditions, and short Biographical Sketches of Early Settlers. 12mo. *cloth.* pp. 368. $1.50. New York, 1849.

Louisiana.

Historical Collections, embracing translations from many rare and valuable documents relating to the Natural and Local and Political History of that State. Compiled with Historical and Biographical Notices, by B. F. French. 2d vol. Map. 8vo. *cloth.* pp. 301. New York and Philadelphia.

This volume, besides seven other rare tracts, contains Daniel Cox's Description of Carolina.

Bastow, George.

History of New Hampshire, from its Discovery in 1614 to the passage of the Toleration Act in 1819. Second edition. 8vo. *cloth.* pp. 456. $1.00. New York, 1853.

Valentine, David T.

History of the City of New York. Maps, Plans, and Illustrations. 8vo. *cloth.* pp. 404. $1.50. New York, 1853

Rhode Island Repudiation.

Or, The History of the Revolutionary Debt of Rhode Island, by John W. Richmond. 8vo. pp. 224. 75 cents.   Providence, 1855

Stobo, Robert,

Major of the Colonial Army under General Braddock during the French War in the Western Territories of North America With a Plan of Fort Du Quesne. 18mo. pp. 92. Pittsburg, 1854

Stuart, Moses.

A Grammar of the New Testament Dialect. Second edition, correeted and mostly written anew. 8vo. *cloth.* pp. 312. 50 cents.   Andover, 1857.

Fourier, Charles,

The Life of. By Ch. Pellarin, M. D. Second edition, with an Appendix. Translated by Francis Geo. Shaw. 12mo. pp. 236. 50 cents.   New York, 1848.

Thomas, Gabriel.

An Historical and Geographical Account of the Province and Country of Pennsylvania, and of West New Jersey, in America; the Richness of the Soil, the Sweetness of the Situation, the Wholesomeness of the Air, the Navigable Rivers and others, the Prodigious Increase of Corn, the Flourishing Condition of the City of Philadelphia, with the stately buildings and other im provements there; the strange creatures, as Birds, Beasts Fishes, and Fowls; with the several sorts of Minerals, Purging Waters, and Stones lately discovered; the Natives—Aborigines their Language, Religion, Laws, and Customs; the first Planters the Dutch, Swedes, and English; with the number of its inhabit- ants. As also, a touch upon George Keith's New Religion, in his second change since he left the Quakers, with a Map of both countries. 12mo. pp. 100. $1.50. (Reprint, New York, 1848.) London, 1698.

Treasury of Knowledge,

and Library of Reference, containing Gazetteer, Dictionary, Tables, Grammar, American Biography, etc., etc. New and Revised Edition. 3 vols. 12mo. *cloth.* $2.50.

New York, 1855

Toussaint L'Ouverture,

The Life of. The Negro Patriot of Hayti: comprising an Account of the Struggle for Liberty in the Island, and a Sketch of its History to the present period, by Rev. JOHN R. BEARD, D. D., with numerous illustrations. 12mo. *cloth.* pp. 340. 60 cents.
London, 1853.

Newton, Sir Isaac.

Principia. The Mathematical Principles of Natural Philosophy, translated into English by ANDREW MOTTE: to which is added, *Newton System of the World,* with a Portrait taken from the bust in the Royal Observatory at Greenwich. First American edition, carefully revised and corrected, with a Life of the Author, by N. W. Chittenden, M. A. 8vo. *sheep.* pp. 581. $3.25.
New York, 1846.

Gouraud, Francis Faurel.

Practical Cosmophonography: a System of Writing and Printing all the principal Languages, with their exact Pronunciation, by means of an original Universal Phonetic Alphabet, etc., as they occur in different Tongues and Dialects, etc., illustrated by numerous plates, explanatory of the Calligraphic, Steno-Phonographic, and Typo-Phonograpic adaptations of the System; with specimens of the Lord's Prayer, in one hundred Languages: to which is prefixed, a General Introduction, etc., etc. 8vo. *cloth.* $1.80   New York, 1850.

Wise, John.

A System of Aeronautics, comprehending its Earliest Investigations and Modern Practice and Art, designed as a History for the common Reader, and Guide to the Student of the Art. Containing an Account of the various attempts in the Art of Flying, by Artificial Means, from the Earliest Period down to the Aeronautic Machine by the Montgolfiers, in 1782, and to a later period, etc., etc. Portrait and 12 Plates. 8vo. pp. 310. $1.50.
Philadelphia, 1850.

Knapp, Samuel L.

Advice in the Pursuits of Literature, containing Historical, Biographical, and Critical Remarks, 12mo. *cloth.* pp. 306. 56 cents.
New York, 1837

Brodie, Sir Benjamin.

Mind and Matter; or, Physiological Inquiries, in a Series of Essays, intended to illustrate the mutual relations of the Physical Organization and the Mental Faculties; with additional Notes, by an American Editor   12mo   *cloth.*   pp. 286.   56 cents   New York, 1857.

Boston Massacre.

A short Narrative of the Horrid Massacre in Boston, perpetrated in the Evening of the 5th of March, 1770, by Soldiers of the 29th Regiment, which, with the 14th Regiment, were then quartered there; with some Observations on the State of Things prior to that Catastrophe.   With Frontispiece.   8vo.   *cloth.*   pp. 122. $1.00.   New York, 1849.

Andrews, Stephen Pearl.

Discoveries in Chinese, or the Symbolism of the Primitive Characters of the Chinese System of Writing as a Contribution to Philology and Ethnology, and a Practical Aid in the Acquisition of the Chinese Language.   12mo.   *cloth.*   pp. 137.   50 cents.
                                                      New York, 1854.

How, Henry.

Virginia, Historical Collections of: containing a collection of the most interesting Facts, Traditions, Biographical Sketches, Anecdotes, etc., relating to its History and Antiquities, together with Geographical and Statistical Descriptions, to which is added, An Historical and Descriptive Sketch of the District of Columbia, illustrated by over 100 engravings, giving Views of the principal Towns, Seats of Eminent Men, Public Buildings, Relics of Antiquity, Historic Localities, Natural Scenery, etc., etc. Royal 8vo.   *sheep.*   pp. 544. $2.50.   Charleston, S. C., 1856.

Taylor, James B.

Lives of Virginia Baptist Ministers.   Second edition, revised and enlarged.   12mo.   *sheep.*   pp. 492. $1.50.   Richmond, 1838.

The book may be styled the Virginia Baptist Biographical Dictionary : it gives the lives of one hundred and eighteen Baptist Ministers.

Cooke, George Frederick,

Memoirs of the Life of, late of the Theatre Royal, Covent Garden, by WILLIAM DUNLAP, composed principally from Journals and other authentic Documents left by Mr. COOKE, and the personal knowledge of the writer. Portrait of COOKE. 2 vols. 18mo. pp. 403 and 400. $1.25.   New York, 1813.

Glenn, James.

The Venereal Disease: its primary cause explained, and the possibility of its being fully prevented described. Never before published. To which is added, A Few Remarks on the Laws regarding Seduction, Adultery, and Prostitution. 8vo. pp. 12. 20 cents.   New York, 1857.

Poor Richard's Almanac (*Ben Franklin*),

Including all his Wise Sayings, Maxims, and Doggerel Distiches, with a Life of FRANKLIN by himself, Portrait and three plates, a combination of the years 1736, 1737, and 1738, reprint, elegantly got up. 25 cents.

*** A copy of an original edition of the above three years was lately sold in New York for $56.00.

Peterson, Rev. Edward.

History of Rhode Island. Illustrated. 8vo. *cloth.* pp. 370 $1.50.   New York, 1853